# THE COMPLETE IDIOT'S GUIDE® TO

# Investing in Fixer-Uppers

*by Stuart Leland Rider*

## ALPHA

*No one exists completely in a vacuum, and to get things done and to succeed in life, most of us have had some help. I'd like to thank my wife, Christine for her lifelong support and critical eye, without her I would have strayed from my purpose. In addition, many people have given me their time and money to further my career. Without their trust and confidence, I would never have had the chance to try. I especially would like to thank Charlie Branagh who literally handed me $500,000 for my first deal three months before we had a written agreement. My 10 year partnership with Charlie has been one of the real privileges of my lifetime, and even though he has gone on, I carry his trust and wisdom with me always.*

**Publisher:** *Marie Butler-Knight*
**Product Manager:** *Phil Kitchel*
**Senior Managing Editor:** *Jennifer Chisholm*
**Senior Acquisitions Editor:** *Mike Sanders*
**Development Editor:** *Nancy D. Lewis*
**Production Editor:** *Billy Fields*
**Copy Editor:** *Amy Lepore*
**Illustrator:** *Chris Eliopoulos*
**Cover/Book Designer:** *Trina Wurst*
**Indexer:** *Ginny Bess*
**Layout/Proofreading:** *Becky Harmon, Mary Hunt*

# Contents at a Glance

## Appendixes

# Contents

# Appendixes

# Foreword

As faith in the stock market and its infrastructure as optimal investment vehicles is waning, savvy investors of every stripe are considering other means of building wealth and securing their retirement. While most believe that the stock market will be a beneficial investment over the long-term, that belief is cold comfort for those who have watched their portfolios wither over the past three years.

There are essentially two ways to create a spread (gain) between an investment in real estate buying and its economic returns (revenues): (1) hold it for appreciation or (2) change the character or use of the property to add value. Essential to a strategy to change the use of the property is to decide whether to improve and sell the property or improve and operate it as an income-producing property.

One investment vehicle stands alone in allowing the individual investor control over the market: the fixer-upper. A fixer-upper is one in which someone has put off the care of a property, probably because of lack of funds. It also usually indicates a need to sell. If purchased correctly, you can realize instant appreciation when you buy it. Essentially, the investor-buyer is adding value by changing the character of the property.

Fixer-uppers can be anything from a home that needs paint and carpet to major restorations of residential and commercial properties, as well as conversions of obsolete buildings to alternative uses. In virtually all cases, the market and potential gains are knowable. A competent appraisal will establish its value as-is and when fixed up. The investor will need a competent construction advisor to understand what is needed to bring the property to optimum condition—and to what extent that work can be staged to conserve resources while generating income. Presumably it's in an area that is already built up so you're not trying to anticipate the market. It's there. In fact, good returns can be made even in softer markets. Through your analysis you will know what the value is at fix-up, and the cost to bring it to that condition. If you can't sell high, you may have to buy lower to produce the gain.

For the novice investor, single-family homes are an excellent vehicle. The markets are easy to understand and they are extremely liquid for those with decent credit through financing. Even in so-called "soft" markets, market value does not necessarily decline at the same pace as demand, so owners can "cash out" without having to sell—or pay taxes on the funds. Another huge advantage of single-family homes, is that if used as a primary residence, and—under current tax rules—it is owner-occupied for two years, any gain up to $250,000 for an individual and $500,000 for a couple, filing jointly is avoided.

I have worked with Stuart for nearly 10 years as an analyst and investor. You'll find his advice clear and to the point. The novice and intermediate investor will learn all they need to know to begin investing in fixer-uppers. Stuart is an engineer by background and the systems, sample agreements, and checklists provided in this book will keep the investor on track from the purchase through the sale of the property.

—David W. Kipnis, CEO Marketing Solutions and past vice president of U.S. Homes

# Introduction

Everyone lives somewhere, and not all homes are in great shape. For whatever reason, people sell beat-up houses every day. Each house of this type is an opportunity with your name on it.

Every house is part of a larger market, and when you begin to understand your market, you can see how you can take that old worn-out property and turn it into a profitable, modern house.

The same is true of commercial property. Bad management or lack of imagination on someone else's part can spell real profits for you.

It's not rocket science; it's mostly common sense. When you're standing in the right place at the right time, it's good to know what to do. This book will help you know when you're standing in the right place, and it can help you see exactly what to do.

In this book, you will learn the following:

- ◆ What a fixer-upper looks like
- ◆ How to evaluate and select a good project
- ◆ How to make it better for a good price
- ◆ How to sell it for a good profit and start over

There are no trade secrets. There is no mystery. A great many of the people making money in this business are high school dropouts. If you have a good imagination and are willing to do some research, take a calculated risk, work hard, and keep an eye on the details, this is the business for you.

This book should help you get organized. Once organized, you can be more effective in any endeavor. Someone else's misfortune or bad judgment is an opportunity for you. You might as well be the one capitalizing on it.

The beauty of real estate is that there is something for everyone. Whether you want to move in and fix it up over a 10-year period, fix one up and sell it every two years tax free, or do three projects a year, this book can help you get it done. If you have a dream of commercial projects, there are many opportunities just around the next corner. See how it's done.

# What You Will Learn in This Book

*The Complete Idiot's Guide to Investing in Fixer-Uppers* is divided into six sections:

**Part 1, "Why Fixer-Uppers?"** is designed to make you look at the real estate around you with a critical eye. You will learn to understand the city as a real estate market: what is where, what the individual properties are worth, and why. It will tell you how to buy it right and how to set the goals for the sale before you buy.

**Part 2, "Resources,"** shows you how to find information on what needs to be done. This book is about making money, but you will also need to know how to fix a door or wallpaper a room, and this section will tell you where to look for that information or how to find and hire someone to do it for you. Resources include both people and information; learn when to use either for a profit.

**Part 3, "The Work,"** deals with the details encountered in the fixer-upper process. It spells out the nuts and bolts of what you will encounter in both housing and commercial projects. The work entails both demolition and building. Learn how to decide what to take away so that what is left is more. Knowing what to add is vital when you take a project to a new level.

**Part 4, "Control Your Project,"** is a basic part of the game plan. To be successful, you need to make a plan and stick with it. The profit is made when you buy right, but if you lose control of the project in the doing, you might never collect your money. There are simple methods and contracts that will make the process easier. Take the time to do it right.

**Part 5, "Putting Ideas to Work,"** takes you through various types of renovations from the simple to the complex. In addition to showing you what to do, five specific renovation projects are shown graphically for you to contemplate. Each building is different and each market unique. Learn how to think your way through the deal to a profitable conclusion.

**Part 6, "Wrapping It Up,"** is an eye-opening look at what you can really accomplish if you have the determination and desire. You can become independently wealthy. It's done every year by others who are not content to work for wages. A little good judgment, some hard work, some astute risk taking, and a clear view of the future can land you on easy street for life.

**Appendix A** is a collection of terms common in the real estate industry. Some are in the book and some are not. If you find something you do not understand, e-mail me at slrider@riderland.com. I'll add it to the next edition and send you an explanation.

In **Appendix B,** the first sample document provides you with a prototypical subcontractors agreement, which can be executed between owner and subcontractor. The second sample document, **Appendix C,** an agreement of purchase and sale and joint escrow instructions, gives you a working document for purchasing anything. It is in use today for all my projects. These documents will give you something to start with. You and your attorney can use them to create the perfect contract for your job. Many other documents and spreadsheets can be used effectively for this type of work, and they are on the CD-ROM available at riderland.com.

Also available from the author under separate cover is a CD-ROM containing usable versions of the following documents and spreadsheets. The CD-ROM's contents are divided into two folders: Lotus and Microsoft software. All items listed are available in either format.

### Documents:

General Partnership Agreement

Limited Liability Company and Articles of Organization

Exclusive Sales Agreement

Exclusive Leasing Agreement

Development Services Agreement

General Construction Contract

Subcontract

Leasing Plan

Mortgage Application

Commercial Lease (Three parts: main body, general provisions, exhibits)

Purchase Agreement

### Spreadsheets:

Monthly Requisition

Income & Expense—Quick and Dirty

Costs—Quick and Dirty

Costs—Detailed

Five-Year Cash Flow

Five-Year Income and Expense

Operating Worksheet—Including CAM and Allocations

Tenant Information

Bar Chart Schedule

Disclaimer

All sample documents included on this CD-ROM are intended to be used only as a guide to suggested topics for inclusion in commercial real estate transactions, and no representation is made as to their sufficiency or legality in your state or their appropriateness for your proposed project. All legal documents should be reviewed by your attorney prior to use.

To obtain a copy of the CD-ROM, log on to the website www.riderland.com or contact the author at slrider@riderland.com.

# Extras

In addition to all the preceding goodies, *The Complete Idiot's Guide to Investing in Fixer-Uppers* has sprinkled through each chapter small snippets of information in boxed sidebars. These sidebars provide you with additional tips, definitions of key terms, warnings of potential dangers, and additional information that you may find helpful.

The signposts are up ahead—you are entering the sidebar zone:

### This Works

These sidebars are designed to be a "heads up" for you along the way, adding to and amplifying important points to give you extra illumination.

### Trade Terms

Here's where you will find definitions of key terms introduced in the chapter. The definitions also appear in the glossary, along with a number of other helpful terms.

### Warning, Danger Ahead!

These sidebars contain warnings and caution flags. They are intended to make you aware of issues that may be pivotal to your deal.

### Reality Checks

These items warn that you are at a potentially critical stage of the process, and should pay particular attention to this phase of the project.

## Acknowledgments

Special thanks to Nancy Lewis, my development editor. She had the unenviable task of shepherding me through the process of creating something intelligible. It's nice to do it again.

Heartfelt thanks to my wife and best friend, Christine, the English teacher who kept my prose within acceptable limits.

## Trademarks

All terms mentioned in this book that are known to be or are suspected of being trademarks or service marks have been appropriately capitalized. Alpha Books and Penguin Putnam Inc. cannot attest to the accuracy of this information. Use of a term in this book should not be regarded as affecting the validity of any trademark or service mark.

# Part 1

# Why Fixer-Uppers?

Not every dump is a potential fixer-upper. You need to learn what to look for and where to look for it. The market you will be striving for is as important as the building you want to renovate. Making the decision what to tackle is as important as what you do with it once you have bought it. Should you do the work or hire it out? Do you need all cash, or can you borrow the money? What can you do to make sure you will make money before you commit yourself? The chapters in this part will answer these questions and more.

# What Are You Getting Into?

## In This Chapter

- ◆ Fixer-upper houses and commercial renovation
- ◆ Exploring a variety of projects
- ◆ When it's time to sell
- ◆ How high is the profit?

I have never met anyone who said he or she had enough money. With that as a given, most enterprising people are usually on the lookout for ways to make a little extra cash. Since housing is basic to us all, we eventually end up toying with the idea of home renovation as a potential means to make a few extra bucks. Some people even decide to make a living out of it. If you happen to be in the construction business, the process is relatively simple, but for the rest of us it seems much more complicated than it really is.

Way back in the beginning, everyone built his or her own house. Evolution has made specialists of us all, but somewhere deep down in everyone lies a basic instinct and understanding of the building process that we can all tap into. We live in a world comprised of buildings, and we know more about them than we are aware of. The question of how to better understand the building process, make some sense of it, and come out of the experience with a few extra dollars in your pocket is the subject of this book. Sometimes this is easier said than done. The factors that enter into the picture include how to know where to buy, what to buy, and when to sell. As if that's not enough, we have to consider what level of improvements to make and what the buyer will be willing to pay for it. This coupled with the dilemma of doing the work yourself versus hiring professionals makes the whole idea seem complex and disheartening.

If housing is not too exciting for you, we'll also explore the world of commercial building renovation. Hopefully, something in the process and its potential for gain will spark a creative frenzy in you, and you will have a go at it. Whether it's residential or commercial, the potential for upgrading real property for a profit is all around you.

> **Reality Check**
>
> You may wonder if I know what I'm talking about. Well, at this moment, I'm marooned in my office listening to jackhammers and carpenters redoing my own home. I expect to make over $100,000 in the process from start to finish. Is it worth the noise, dust, and aggravation?

# Housing

When you start looking for something to turn into a project, most people will start with the traditional *single-family* house in a traditional neighborhood *subdivision* or *multifamily* project.

**Trade Terms**

A **single-family** house is a detached dwelling with its own yard, generally located in a subdivision or an area specifically designed to serve other houses of the same type. A **subdivision** is a land-development term referring to the preparation of a large plot of land for the express purpose of building houses. They can be designed for single-family or multifamily dwellings or a mixture of both. **Multifamily** dwellings are structures that house two or more dwelling units. They range in scope from duplexes (two-family homes) to tri- and four-plexes, on up to condominium or co-op buildings that can house hundreds of dwellings.

The common types of single-family housing found in the United States have evolved from randomly scattered rural housing to town and urban dwelling types. The more concentrated the population, the denser the housing complexes. Over 200 years ago, there was little housing in the towns. What there was usually consisted of living quarters above the stores. As the citizens grew more affluent, they started to build detached houses on streets within the township. These homes clustered into neighborhoods but lacked the preplanning necessary for today's large-scale developments.

## The Old Days

As the neighborhoods grew, it became apparent that planning was required to take care of the services or *infrastructure* needed to accommodate a growing population. These basic services include access (roads), sanitation (sewers and waste water treatment plants), electricity, telephone, and now cable TV and networking lines. Early attempts to foresee growth necessitated laying out new streets in or near the town to accommodate the projected growth that the new prosperity was sure to bring.

### Trade Terms

**Infrastructure** refers to all the services needed to support any land use such as housing and commercial. These services include (but are not limited to) roads, water, sewer, gas, electricity, and cable TV. Expanded services provided by the community are infrastructure for the entire community but benefit all users within the community. These services include (but are not limited to) freeways, hospitals, police, firefighters, emergency services, ports, and airports.

Housing today reflects every stage of this process from rural farms to old inner-city neighborhoods and every variation in between. New "neighborhoods," now referred to as subdivisions, are planned for hundreds of dwellings at a time. We have even evolved into planning and building whole new communities. These are referred to as master planned communities." Smaller versions comprising only a few hundred acres are referred to as PUDs or planned unit developments.

## Today's Choices

The opportunity for renovation and redevelopment exists in all forms of housing. Rural properties include farms that are being swallowed by the expanding cities, and large-acre developments offer opportunities for upgrading the neighborhood as the suburbs become increasingly fashionable. Tract housing from four-to-the-acre to today's eight-to-the-acre also offers possibilities for the enterprising renovator. Starter homes can be expanded, second stories added, and floor plans upgraded. Condominiums and flats can be renovated, combined, torn down, and redeveloped, or simply redecorated. Inner-city properties are great examples of renovation. Urban dwellers are constantly changing and rearranging real estate within the confines of their high-rise environments.

## Commercial Possibilities

Multihousing is generally regarded as a commercial approach as apartments are emptied and the buildings converted to condominiums. Warehouses and manufacturing complexes, especially in cities, are converted to new uses. The inner-city loft is a very popular conversion and has been in style since the turn of the century when it was only the purview of the bohemian.

Decommissioned gas stations are being made into boutiques and drive-through dry cleaners, and old banks are being converted into offices and restaurants. In Houston, a 40-story high-rise office building was converted into a mini-warehouse. The collected rents are now higher than when the building was used for offices.

In each and every case, what transpired was that someone with an idea purchased something that was no longer needed by the owner and turned it into something else that produced income and increased value. What was the spark? Why do people do these things? The answer is relatively simple—money and lots of it. Profit was, is, and always will be a great motivator. Americans are always searching for new ways to do things, new places to go to, and new styles of living and working.

**This Works**

When you drive down the street, any street, you are surrounded by real estate investments: good ones, bad ones, and ones that need your special touch. Be on the lookout.

When you start looking for something to improve, do not limit your search to just housing. Be aware of all the possibilities.

Finally, you need to know what you are looking at, how it ties into the overall real estate picture, and whether it's a housing or commercial venture. Therefore, the following is an attempt to categorize some common types of real estate that you may encounter.

# Common Housing Types

Housing consists of two common types: single-family and multifamily. The distinction between the two is the sharing of common lot lines, walls, floors, and roofs. Within these types, we have many variations.

Single-family housing includes the following:

- ◆ Rural—Ultra-low density, 10 acres and up
- ◆ Low density, large acreage—5 to 10 acres per dwelling
- ◆ Medium density—½ to 1 acre per dwelling

- ◆ Normal subdivision—Four homes to the acre

- ◆ High density—8 to 12 units to the acre

- ◆ Cluster development—Custom designed, including zero lot line, surrounded by common areas

Multifamily includes the following:

- ◆ Zero-lot-line cluster housing without common areas

- ◆ Common-wall subdivisions

- ◆ Condominium and town houses

- ◆ High-rise condominium and *co-op*

The interesting difference between multifamily and single-family housing lies in the property descriptions. One- and two-story buildings generally share lot lines, walls, floors, and roofs, while multistory buildings require the added description of elevation. This elevation difference delineates the fifth floor apartment from those on other floors. This three-dimensional description is called the horizontal regime and further defines the elevation of the two-dimensional description, thus identifying the unit on a particular floor at a particular elevation above sea level. In cases other than two-story buildings, the land is generally owned in common by the condominium association or co-op. Sometimes these buildings, including the one- and two-story variety, are built on leased land. The land lease becomes a common area expense.

**Trade Terms**

A **co-op** is an eastern phenomenon that's similar in effect to the condominium. Its primary difference lies in the fact that you must be approved by the other owners to live there.

# Alternatives

Each type of housing presents us with opportunities and challenges as well as rewards. The old inner-city neighborhoods have in most cases been torn down and replaced by medium-rise buildings constructed at the turn of the twentieth century. These buildings are now referred to as "tenements" and are generally found in blighted areas of the old inner cities. Some cities have seen the refurbishing of entire neighborhoods from slums back to fashionable neighborhoods. These dwellings are known as "brownstones," so called for the brick from which they were built. These dwellings have been converted into modern one-floor flats as well as multistory attached homes. Most of these conversions have been very profitable for the builders and the cities.

Many of these projects fall into "historic preservation districts" promulgated by the cities and underwritten by public funds. Generally these types of renovations can command city, state, and/or federal dollars for historic preservation. In many cases, there are low-interest loans, tax credits, and other incentives attached to this type of project. Frequently the appreciation of value is much more dramatic than that ascribed to the renovation alone. The resurgence of the neighborhood can result in some spectacular new values far in excess of that ascribed to a single renovation project.

Commercial renovations are broken out into three basic types: retail, office, and industrial. Each type of potential building project is further broken down into its own subsections.

> **Warning, Danger Ahead!**
>
> The historic preservation of individual houses is much like the restoration of vintage automobiles. The costs tend to be far greater, the materials more difficult to find, and the rewards slim to none. So unless personal satisfaction is your game, shy away from these projects. Leave them for the artisans and the lifestylers.

Retail projects include the following:

- Freestanding single-user buildings
- Strip centers
- Community centers
- Regional centers

Office buildings include the following:

- Single-tenant buildings
- Garden offices
- Mid-rise buildings
- High-rise buildings

Industrial buildings include the following:

- Single-user buildings and factories
- Multitenant buildings
- Inner-city buildings
- Miscellaneous structures

As we go through this book, housing will be discussed in each of these categories. We will examine what currently exists in these categories with renovation potential and what can be done with each type of housing.

Similarly, in the case of commercial renovation, older, sometimes obsolete structures like abandoned gas stations and "corner markets" can be transformed into dramatic new uses. Old regional shopping centers have been transformed into stadiums and office complexes. I know of one urban high-rise office building that has been converted into a 40-plus-story mini-storage building.

# The Real Estate Market

As in all endeavors, the market for your product is governed by supply and demand. The real estate market is no exception to this rule. There are some hard-and-fast rules to live by—ignore them at your own peril. These rules apply, in general, to all forms of housing. With that said, remember that the exception proves the rule.

Remember the following pointers:

♦ You make your money when you buy.

♦ Never buy or own the most expensive house on the street.

♦ Do not over improve the house.

♦ Forget your own tastes; concentrate on the marketability of the improvements.

♦ Be mindful of the trends in the market; do not buy into a declining market.

♦ Buy at the bottom and sell at the top.

Sounds easy, doesn't it? You'd be surprised how many people violate these simple rules. There are many more do's and don'ts, but most of all, you will be the best judge of what to do. Look at what you have seen and why it works. Apply this knowledge to everything you look at.

**⚠ CAUTION  Warning, Danger Ahead!** _____

Common sense is the best filter of ideas. With that said, look around you and find the disasters of entrepreneurs who ignored the lessons learned by others. The classic example is the two-story strip center. They are all over the country, and the second floor is almost always vacant (except in Hawaii, where building up is a necessity). The fact of American retail business is that women do most of the shopping, and American women will not walk up stairs to shop, except in Hawaii where they have no choice. I see a new one every year, and I wonder, "What are they thinking?" The answer is, "They aren't."

# What Can You Expect to Make

Since the subject of this exercise is to make some money, we need to keep focused on the potential for profit as we evaluate the possibilities. Profit can be derived simply from buying a tract home every two years and moving onward and upward. Couples who do this find themselves with substantial equity after 10 years and are easily able to afford the home of their dreams.

The most common approach to the fixer-upper is the "lipstick approach," so called because it is strictly cosmetic in nature, discussed more fully in Chapter 8. This approach is a good one for newcomers to the field, but it results in relatively modest gains.

The most common house renovation is a general reconfiguration and modernization. This involves removing and replacing walls, modernizing baths and kitchens, as well as painting and recarpeting. It is a middle-of-the-road approach and lends itself to older homes in the 20- to 50-year-old category as well as urban flats, town houses or row houses.

The big step is to tear down a substantial part of a dwelling and expand or start over. This is exciting and not for the faint of heart. It is the "big daddy" of residential renovations and can be the path to wealth if you have a flair for it. In one neighborhood in my area, people look at $600,000 homes as potential teardowns, while in others a $60,000 house can be a quick lipstick job.

Commercial renovations vary all over the map, from converting single-use properties such as banks and gas stations to renovating regional malls. The former requires some capital that would exceed most residential renovations, and the latter takes hundreds of millions of dollars. Commercial renovations require a more expanded knowledge of the real estate market and tend to be more profitable than residential renovations. Most people in commercial renovation tend do it for a living, and it can be a big business. The trend from big city to suburbs and back again has created opportunity enough for all. Size and budget need not be a deterrent.

## The Least You Need to Know

- The basic requisite in the real estate fixer-upper business is common sense.
- Don't overbuild the market because you cannot realize a good return on over-investment.
- Opportunities are everywhere, look at all possibilities, do not dismiss the obvious or the improbable opportunity.
- You don't need to go it alone, try taking on partners, or hiring some help.
- Do not over improve the project because it will dilute your rate of return; build only what's necessary to attract a profitable buyer.

# Chapter 2

# Where to Buy—Look Ahead to the Sale

## In This Chapter

- ◆ What's in your town?
- ◆ Pick your spot
- ◆ What sells?
- ◆ Is downtown dead?
- ◆ Use your crystal ball

Are you going to purchase something near where you live? If so, why? Have you given any thought to the economic and financial environment of your town, your standard metropolitan statistical area (SMSA), or your region? In my opinion, you should not just jump in where you live; you should invest in an area that will produce the best returns. If you were going to invest in a piece of investment property, I would advise you to locate the healthiest economic climate you could find within a practical distance of where you live and work. Fixer-uppers are no different than any other investment except you will have to participate in the process, so you cannot afford to go too far afield. Therefore, you are practically forced to work within your immediate area.

How then can you maximize your investment by understanding your area? The process is really nothing but applying your common sense and taking advantage of some of the available resources at your command.

# Take Your Town Apart and Understand It

Across America, cities and towns are pretty much divided in the same manner. The only exceptions occur where there is some physical impediment to the layout such as a mountain, a lake, an ocean, or a river. Cities in the United States seem to fall naturally into four quadrants.

*The economic profile of a city.*

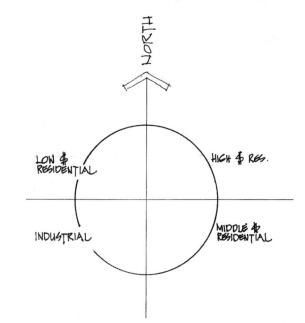

In most cities, the most expensive residential real estate lies in the northeast quadrant, the middle-dollar real estate lies in the southeast quadrant, the lower-end housing is found in the northwest side of town, and the industrial section is relegated to the southwest quadrant. For years I studied this phenomenon, seeking to understand the reason for this natural selection because the town planner does not decide the real direction of growth; cities merely evolve along the general lines of the general plan. The conclusion I came to makes sense to me, and I have not yet come up with a better one:

Rich people will not commute to and from work with the sun shining in their eyes.

If you can come up with a better reason, please e-mail me and I'll include it in the next revision. On the face of it, it seems such a simple idea, but in truth it's most likely the real reason. Every town or city is governed by a *general plan*, which dictates where new growth will take place and what form it will take. It delineates areas designated as commercial, residential, industrial, recreational, and public (such as schools, hospitals, fire stations, and police stations). These general plans are not considered a final blueprint for growth, but a dynamic plan that is modified and adapted as the city grows.

Areas within the general plan are governed by municipal and county codes, called zoning codes, that restrict their uses. These zoning codes carry various designations such as residential, commercial, public, agricultural, and recreational zones.

**Trade Terms**

A **general plan** is a document written by the city's planning department, adopted by the city council, and ratified by the voters. By law, it is generally updated at regular intervals. The writing of the general plan is accomplished along with public hearings and discussions as to its component parts. The results are therefore an amalgam of professional urban planning and citizen input.

Each general code has further designations, as follows.

Commercial areas are broken down something like this:

- ◆ M1 = Manufacturing
- ◆ I = General industrial
- ◆ C-o = Commercial office
- ◆ C-1 = General commercial with use restrictions
- ◆ C-2 = General commercial with fewer restrictions

In residential areas, zoning is broken down something like this:

- ◆ R143 = Equals one residence to the acre
- ◆ R5 = 5,000 square feet of land per unit
- ◆ M1 = Multiple dwelling units, up to 12 units to the acre

These are just some of the breakdowns; each municipality defines its own codes and labels them differently. A copy of the building code is available at your local planning office.

# Your Chosen Area and What's In It

Once you have found out about your general area, you can then take a look at it in a different light. Most likely, you have been driving around it all your life without giving it any thought. Draw a simple line diagram of your city on a large piece of paper, draw in the major freeways and feeder roads, and label the areas so that you can accurately visualize what's where and how people get around. Today, most cities are girdled by "ring roads" laid out in concentric patterns.

Where can you find information, and what exactly do you need to know? You need to know what the zoning is and what changes are occurring in the general plan. What revisions are staff going to propose at the revision hearings in a few years? It's a good idea to know where and when new roads will be built and where exactly the access points will be.

Property, whether existing or to be built, is valued and traded based on its use and location.

Commercial properties are located along the major traffic corridors, and residential properties fan out from there. You will find multifamily homes such as apartments and condos bordering the commercial, with lower and lower-density housing as you get further from the commercial core.

Many sources are available, and most, if not all, are free for the asking. Starting with the city planning office, the chamber of commerce, the highway department, the transportation department (trains and buses), individual suburban town planning departments, and real estate professionals.

Once you have drawn your map, it is a good time to start your search. Since this is probably your first time, it is unlikely that you have a real estate license; therefore, you need some professional help to purchase your fixer-upper. Go to your targeted area and find a Realtor® who specializes in that area. Explain in detail what you are looking for. Most likely, the Realtor® can point out someone working in that area who already does what you seek to do.

**This Works**

"Location, location, location." The old definition of value is now interpreted as visibility and accessibility by automotive standards. We are a nation on wheels, and people need to see the location and be able to get to it.

Many Realtors® are fixer-uppers on the side because of their intimate knowledge of their area of specialty. I doubt they will mind earning a commission on your purchase and eventual resale. Later, once you have become experienced, you might want to get your real estate sales license to further enhance your profitability on each project.

# Current Trends

Is your city dying? Is it expanding? These are important questions. Some towns and cities in the east and middle of the country are shrinking as the farm population moves away. Some cities are filled with obsolete industries and are referred to as being in the *rust belt*.

These cities stagnated and shrunk for many years until the city councils became proactive and started promoting new, more modern industries to replace their defunct ones. Today, many of these so-called rust belt cities are undergoing a transformation. Old factory areas are being replaced by new developments. Many of these cities had industry in key waterfront locations to take advantage of shipping. When the industry left, the waterfront property remained. Many developers rushed to fill the vacuum with waterfront housing and commercial developments.

**Trade Terms**

The **rust belt** generally takes in the eastern cities and the old industrial cities of the Midwest. Its name derives from the rusting machinery contained in old abandoned factories.

If you are in a growing area, the direction of growth will become an important factor. Many outlying areas will be absorbed into the new growth, creating opportunities for renovation and redevelopment of the old outlying properties, both commercial and residential.

When cities grow, they leave behind areas that become blighted, trending toward what we used to call slums. There are instances in growth areas where the growth is so swift that it leaps over building sites and leaves them behind. These properties are considered ripe for exploitation. These sites are potential infill deals. Old houses can be converted to office buildings, vacant lots may become corner gas stations, and so on.

**This Works**

Trends in areas are also a good indicator of what's needed. As cities expand, people tend to move to the suburbs, and then they spend hours behind the wheel of their car going to and from work. This creates an opportunity to redevelop the closer residential areas to help the city regenerate. It also creates opportunities to move some of the jobs to the suburbs. In reality, growth is a catalyst for constant change.

# What's Happening Downtown?

One of the most interesting opportunities lies in the downtown areas and what's going on there. Cities today are fighting the suburban growth by revitalizing their core areas. My town, Phoenix, Arizona, has built stadiums and ballparks, hotels, and convention centers, and the result is a reemergence of the downtown dweller. This has sparked a wave of renovation and redevelopment as well as new restaurants and service. There is ample room for all kinds entrepreneurs. They range from people who convert houses to people who tear down skyscrapers and build ballparks. You should fit nicely somewhere in the mix.

## Dying Cities

These are a real problem. If you live in an area that is shrinking, you need to take a much more careful look at the situation to find opportunity. When cities shrink, they leave behind neighborhoods that are declining in value rather than appreciating. A good place to look for opportunity is in an older area that was once considered elegant but was replaced in the past by the then-newer and trendy suburbs. When cities shrink, people tend to move back to the core if they can find viable neighborhoods to move back into. People want to cluster together, so renovating the run-down, once-fashionable district becomes a great ploy. The more people who return to the inner city the better. It will start a trend back to the core.

**Warning, Danger Ahead!** _____

Static cities with no growth and no discernable growth trend make me nervous. There is no real way to tell what's going to happen. They might explode and grow like mad, or they might start to wither away. Since I do not have a crystal ball, I tend to give these cities a pass. I have no advice to offer you in this instance. Your best guess about what to do is most likely better than mine if you know the area well.

## Redevelopment Areas

Urban redevelopment is a function of the old and mature city. Towns and cities that have embarked on an organized plan of urban redevelopment are good bets to look over for renovatable property. Likely bets are found on the periphery of areas that have been condemned and are in the process of redevelopment. These new areas will require services such as restaurants and service industries, at least during the transition period. Most urban renewal is a long-term proposition that takes 20 years or more. These areas are definitely worth a good look.

# Where Is Your Town Going to Be in Five to Ten Years?

This is the question you will have to answer to tap into a changing market. To invest in areas where the trend is away is to invite disaster, whereas investing in the path of growth is a sure formula for success. Commercial opportunities lurk along the transportation corridors and in the core areas of newly discovered suburban communities. Chances are, if a peripheral suburb is enjoying a new spurt of growth, there are old buildings that can benefit from a facelift and perhaps a change of use. A dentist that I scuba dive with recently purchased an old core-area house and converted it to a dental office in the front and living quarters in the rear. He is part of a revitalized core area of an expanding older town.

## Overlooked Opportunities

Infill sites are very interesting. In the west, infill sites are created when people speculate on land and run the price up too high for normal development. Developers simply skip over them and move on with the trends. Often these sites have older buildings on them. They stand out from their surroundings like missing teeth. What can be done with them? Empty sites are development opportunities, but sites with buildings on them are all potential renovation projects. The contiguous areas will dictate what can be done. If the area is residential, a refurbished house could be feasible. If it is an older, large dwelling, perhaps it could be converted into apartments, commercial space, or even a care facility.

> **This Works**
>
> In my book *From Dirt to Dollars*, I discuss the opportunity to develop existing structures as being equivalent to and comparable with, a development project done from the bare dirt up. For example, a well-known mini warehouse company successfully redeveloped a largely vacant high-rise office building in Houston Texas as a document storage facility.

## The Path of Growth

Old buildings that sit along the path of growth can be interesting opportunities as well as potential disasters. Just because something is there does not necessarily mean it is still useful. Buildings can be functionally obsolete, but in areas of stringent growth restrictions such as California and the state of Washington, almost all old buildings are recycled into new uses. Functional obsolescence occurs when a building cannot be physically modified to meet a useful purpose. Sometimes it is as simple as ceilings that are too low; other times it is related to building codes that come into effect when you attempt to change uses. In 1978, I converted an old stage stop into a bar. The intervening uses had fortunately been quite unsavory and colorful, and it was the building's colorful past that provided the impetus for conversion. The biggest problem was how to convert what was basically an old shed on very minimal foundation, mostly piled rocks, into a building that met seismic standards for the state of California.

The solution was somewhat straightforward but radical. We removed the old floor, preserved the boards for future use, and built a temporary frame for the structure. We then removed the old foundation and poured a new one to accommodate the exterior cosmetically as well as the new structure, which met seismic standards. This structure was then erected inside the old building and attached to it. It was now the sole support of the building. The old building structure was reassigned as the skin of the rejuvenated building. We then built walls inside to conceal the new frame and relaid the old floor on new supports. After that, it was just a matter of converting the interior with new tenant improvements built in the authentic style of the old West.

Was it worth it? Absolutely! The costs of this renovation proved to be about twice the cost of demolition and construction of a new building, but there was no choice. A new building would not have been permitted on that site because it was in a designated historical district. Fortunately, the project was successful enough to show a good return on investment.

## The Least You Need to Know

♦ You must get a handle on the area you decide to work in because your take on the market situation must be right on for your project to succeed.

♦ Pay attention to growth trends and get out in front; let the market come to you.

♦ Find an area that is being rejuvenated and get into a project before all the really good opportunities are picked over.

♦ The more fixer-upper activity the better because each project reinforces the other.

# What to Look For—
# Residential and Commercial

## In This Chapter

- ◆ Finding the right house
- ◆ What's hot?
- ◆ Size matters and so does style
- ◆ The commercial property
- ◆ Your game plan

Before you attempt to launch a fixer-upper project, you should take a long look at the real estate market. The housing market is divided into two categories: new homes and resale homes. The commercial market is a little more complicated. We will explore both in this chapter.

## Understanding Housing

New housing, while not a direct competitor to your fixer-upper, is still a good place to get ideas. All the latest innovations and trends will be found in the new-home market. Homebuilders spend a lot of money and time on market research, and their ideas are worth looking at. What we accept as a standard feature in a home today was once a new idea that debuted in a new model home. Things like walk-in closets, plant shelves, tile floors, Jacuzzi tubs, clamshell showers, recessed lighting, built-in appliances, computer wiring, and computerized power monitoring all came out as innovations in new homes.

Most old houses lack the modern touches. If you are going to attempt to renovate anything, you need to establish what your target market will be. Your most pressing competition will be the houses in the immediate area of your project. The trick is to find out what these homes have in the way of amenities and then improve on them without spending too much money. Improving the house too far beyond the norm in the neighborhood will result in over improving the house. In the case of modernizing a house that lacks even the basics, such as wiring and modern baths and kitchens, you are looking at a serious upgrade, and the neighborhood must measure up to the market.

# The Latest Trends

What has transpired in the housing market lately? It varies around the country, but in general, people are placing more importance on the home and are creating retreats where they can spend longer periods of time. The family home has become much more of an entertainment center as well as a refuge. We now have media rooms, larger bedrooms, and more space in general. The faster the environment outside, the more the house becomes the only place in which people can have peace and quiet. New homes, even starter homes, are bigger. Many starter homes are designed to be expandable at a later date. Other than luxury homes, the general trend is to create large amounts of living space with the recreational amenities built into the house and grounds. Some commentator has even suggested that Americans are "cocooning."

How then does that relate to the potential fixer-upper project? You must look for potential projects that have expansion capabilities. Logically enough, this is found most often in older homes. Newer houses are built on increasingly smaller lots. An older home will likely have room to add the third car garage, the media room, and a swimming pool.

| Reality Check |
| --- |
| New homes are getting bigger and more expensive, and the easiest way to cut costs of development upfront is to decrease the lot size. Whereas a normal subdivision lot used to be around 10,000 square feet in size (4 homes per acre), now they are as small as 6,000 square feet (6 to 7 homes per acre). |

# Size and Amenities

Size matters. Starter homes range from 1,400 to 1,700 square feet in size, and the average single-family house has grown to 2,400 square feet. Very much in demand today are home offices, media centers, and room to play in the back yard. The master bedroom has also come into its own with spacious walk-in closets, his and her sinks, separate baths and showers, as well as a separate toilet room. Family rooms are getting bigger, dine-in kitchens are very popular, and workrooms are definitely in. Sometimes it makes you wonder if there will be any room left for the kids. All this suggests that likely candidates for renovation are the large, older homes that were fashionable in the 1920s. Most of these can be found in a downtown location in the smaller towns and in the close-in suburban locations of larger cities, usually within a trolley ride of Central and Main. With the advent of urban sprawl, these areas are now in demand as commute-weary people seek to regain some of their time. A great selling point with these houses is the amount of time that can be saved in a workday when the commute is eliminated or considerably shortened.

In addition to size considerations, new houses are full of details that you will not find in older homes. Most older homes have few closets, no built-ins, single-car garages (if any), small windows, wood floors, and antiquated baths and kitchens. What they do usually have—and what you need to look for—is large rooms, pantries, washrooms, dumb waiters, breezeways, mud rooms, porches, foyers, interesting architecture, and good millwork. Sometimes you will find a house with a metal ceiling. This can be an important design feature when remodeling if you chose to go with the period architecture rather than modernizing it.

**This Works**

The holy grail of fixer-uppers is to keep the great features of the older houses and incorporate the modern features that people have come to expect. If you can do this successfully, you should be able to make a good profit. If you can also dramatically shorten the commute, you have hit a home run!

The difficult houses to refit are the early 1950s and 1960s tract houses. They were constructed in haste with minimal or no design considerations, and they were mostly identical within the neighborhood. These properties are a true challenge. The bulk of these renovations are simply cosmetic, but where you can find a house with expandable potential, there is a chance to add rooms and amenities. There is also the possibility of adding a second story. These homes are scattered throughout the country in areas that have little or no topographic interest. The challenge then is to differentiate your project from the rest of the neighborhood without overspending or creating something that is too one-of-a-kind in the process. Values in tract homes are derived in part from the tract's homogeneity. The fact that these houses are so similar allows the market to establish average prices for each model, with market variations that center around extras such as pools, expensive decor, and larger than normal lots or views. Unless you have had some experience and have an active imagination, I would recommend that you give these properties a pass on your first try. The only exception I can think of is a simple "lipstick job" (see Chapter 8).

The upshot of all this is that you need to determine what sells in the housing market in your chosen area. This is not brain surgery. There are houses on the market that have been remodeled, so go and look at them. Take notes, talk to Realtors®. Find out what seems to sell fast and what slows down a sale. You will find out things about your area such as above 2,500 square feet, a house without a three-car garage is a slow seller. It might be that a full stand-up basement is a must. In more upscale development areas, an au pair setup is customary, and at the top end of the market, a servants' quarters above the garage is expected.

---

**Reality Check**

My grandfather purchased an old estate in Middletown, Connecticut, in the late 1940s. It was an old mansion with a carriage house and 25 acres. He remodeled the mansion into a two-story home for himself and two sizeable apartments for lease. He then converted the carriage house into a large, three-story, single-family house. Subsequently, he subdivided the land into six parcels and sold off five of them, retaining the main house and 10 acres for himself. The net result was that he acquired a large modern home for himself on 10 beautiful acres with two rental properties, but the net cost to him was zero. He called it "Yankee ingenuity," but I say he had a flair for the business. Unfortunately for the industry, he was a librarian, so we will never know whether it was beginners' luck or whether he could have been one of the great ones.

---

# Commercial Projects

An important part of the potential market lies in the commercial field. The goal is the same, but the marketing is a little different. The most significant difference between commercial and residential fixer-uppers is that you will need to consider tenants as well as buyers in the process. Commercial property is normally leased to, or occupied by, one or more tenants. Therefore, you must locate a property that can be acquired, renovated, re-leased, and/or sold at a profit.

By way of introduction to the commercial aspects of this book, I'd like to mention that, in addition to my residential fixer-uppers, I have completed seven sizeable commercial renovations. I will use them as specific examples of various ideas as we go through this book.

Commercial renovations include the following types of projects:

- Apartments

- Condominium conversions

- Single-user buildings

- Special-use buildings

- Office buildings

- Retail projects from strip centers to regional malls

- Industrial projects

- Mine conversions and reclamation

- Recreational projects such as marinas and sports facilities

- Land reclamation and expansion

**This Works**

The premier reason for considering a commercial fixer-upper is that the profit potential far exceeds that of housing renovation. Each $1.00 increase in the net cash flow of an investment project is saleable in today's market for $12.50. You'll learn more about this in the discussion of cap rates in Chapter 15 when we examine the dollars and cents.

It seems that there is something for everyone, and you need to hear about and consider all the possibilities. With that said, as soon as you finish reading this section, you will think of at least two potential deals I have not mentioned. Opportunity abounds, so embrace it.

## Apartments

Multifamily rental properties are fairly straightforward, and the opportunities lie in two directions: upgrading and conversion. Upgrading an apartment complex involves a two-stage approach. First you need to upgrade the exterior and common areas (perhaps by adding amenities such as recreation or new services) and then the units themselves. The common areas of a project could involve a facelift or modernization of the building exterior and landscaping or the addition of services such as laundry and/or daycare facilities, perhaps even a new swimming pool and exercise facility. You could also arrange for some of the local service industries (such as dry cleaners) to pick up and deliver at the complex. The list is endless, but you must value engineer each improvement against the potential rental increases. Your yardstick should be as close as possible to a 12 percent net return on total investment before debt service.

## Condos

Condominium conversions have proven to be fairly popular as well as successful in certain circumstances. To be able to convert apartments to condominiums, it is necessary to set the project up legally as a condominium. An apartment complex, unless planned initially as a condominium conversion, is one legal piece of property. To convert the property from apartments to condominiums, condominium documents, as well as subdivision documents, must be prepared and approved by the local government, either city or county. In most cases, subdivision and condominium documents are also scrutinized by the state. This process can be lengthy, and in some states it might take up to two years. Is it worth it? You bet. A condominium is worth on the market at least twice as much as an apartment.

> **Warning, Danger Ahead!**
>
> There is also the matter of the apartment tenants that still reside in your future condos. They must be phased out and the property renovated so that it can be prepared for sale. Some states have very stringent laws regarding the ability to force the renters out. Check on the legal issues before attempting this type of renovation.

## Single-User Buildings

This category of commercial building encompasses many different types of structures, the most visible of which is the old gas station or store. These buildings have limited uses, but if you can find a tenant who can live with the general configuration, you have a viable conversion. Gas stations have become a bit of a hot item since the advent of the drive-through dry cleaner. These old buildings have the advantage of great location and a covered driveway adjacent to the building. Most of the time, fast-food restaurants like the locations of these old facilities, but the building must be torn down to accommodate the new use. This goes beyond the normal fixer-upper but is also profitable.

## One-Of-A-Kind Buildings

Special-use buildings (such as schoolhouses, lighthouses, small suburban hospitals, churches, and the like) also present some creative challenges. I have seen successful houses created from all of these. When I moved to California in 1973, I put in a bid on an old schoolhouse on 10 acres with the express purpose of converting it into a home. I was unsuccessful in my bid, but the winner did the conversion, kept one acre, and subdivided the balance into nine more lots, making a small fortune in the process. Old hospitals, especially small ones, can be converted into assisted-care facilities and retirement residences. All of these require a little imagination and the required cash, and obviously, the larger the project, the more money is required.

**Trade Terms**

A **100 percent location** is the best location in town. Today that would equate to the most vehicle traffic, and the best access, such as a major freeway exit.

# Office Buildings

Office buildings vary from the single-tenant building to high-rise, multitenant buildings and office parks. Fixer-upper opportunities lie in the older buildings that border on functional obsolescence. These would be characterized as third-tier properties, generally suffering from benign neglect but still viable. You can find ample candidates in decent locations, just off the *100 percent locations*. These buildings are generally well occupied by second- and third-tier tenants. These tenants are smaller service organizations that do not require glamour locations and great exposure, and government and government-related tenants.

Since the government is considered a good risk, there are many landlords that seek to specialize in this type of tenancy. Properly managed, these buildings are very creditworthy securities.

**Reality Check**

Government tenants are tough because they exert a greater than normal strain on a building. The employees, being civil servants, generally are harder on building maintenance than their civilian counterparts, and the employee-per-1,000-square-foot ratio is 6 plus rather than the 4 per thousand found in civilian offices. This puts added demands on the parking as well as the building services.

# Retail Buildings

Again, single-user buildings are the simplest form of this genre of investment property. The value of the building is directly related to the creditworthiness of the tenant and the remaining length of the lease. These buildings are everywhere, and they tend to come on the market during the final five years of the lease term. Usually some absentee, coupon-clipping landlord has gotten cold feet about the tenant's desire to renew the lease or knows for sure that it will not renew. This is both a problem and an opportunity. For the seller, the value is severely discounted; for the buyer, there is a gamble on filling the potentially empty single-tenant building. If you have some knowledge of the town and what's going on, you might find this to be a deal too good to pass up. Often these buildings are owned by passive investors or are held in some trust's portfolio, and these types of owners often are ill equipped to deal with the process of refurbishment and re-leasing. They just want to sit back and collect the rent. I have seen this type of building sold, refurbished, re-leased, and resold to the original seller at a very tidy profit. Both sides benefit from the transaction. The original seller just goes back to coupon clipping, and the entrepreneur moves on with the profit.

## Strips

Strip shopping centers come in two varieties: *anchored* and unanchored.

**Trade Terms**

**Anchored** is a term applied to a center that has a credit or "national chain" tenant as the major occupant. The term refers to the concept that this draw or "credit tenant" gives greater creditability to the center, allowing the other tenants to feed off the anchor's draw. It also helps greatly with financing, wherein the better terms go to the centers with the better credit tenants.

Unlike the larger neighborhood centers, strip-center tenants tend to be smaller tenants who feed off the public's need for convenience. These centers cater to quick-impulse items for passing motorists. Tenants like 7-11, Stop 'N' Go, and convenience stores group with coffee shops, dry cleaners, and video-rental stores to allow the public to transact needed business to and from work. A popular small version of this center is now personified by the C-store (convenience store) attached to most modern gas stations. The trend in C-stores is to get bigger and more diversified to compete with the strip centers. A great coup is to marry a gas station/car wash to a strip center for a convenient one-stop shopping experience.

## Neighborhood Centers

A big step up from the strip center is the traditional neighborhood center that consists of a supermarket, a drug store, a bank, and a series of mom-and-pop local stores. These centers become possible fixer-upper projects when the anchor tenant, either the supermarket or the drug store, moves on. Again, many of these investments are owned by passive, absentee landlords who are unable or unwilling to do the hands-on management required to revitalize the center. Again, it is a two-edged opportunity but can be well worth the effort.

## The Upsized Neighborhood or Community Center

Likewise, the community center, a hybrid of the neighborhood center, normally contains all the same stores as the neighborhood center with a "junior" department store or discount retailer attached. The same scenario applies here—problem and opportunity. For the local investor with good contacts in the commercial leasing field, this is a definite fixer-upper opportunity.

Obviously, all these commercial fixer-uppers require more money, time, and expertise than just buying a neglected residential property and turning it over. They do, however, represent a significant part of the fixer-upper spectrum and can be dealt with by people with some experience and available capital. At the top of the heap of the fixer-upper market is the regional mall fixer-upper. There are fewer than a dozen companies in the country with the money and expertise to tackle this type of project, but they are fun to watch. The results are sometimes very exciting because regional malls are undergoing somewhat of a renaissance as they convert from pure shopping to a combination of shopping and recreation. I hope the trend continues.

## Industrial Projects

Industrial properties do not generally lend themselves to redevelopment unless the surrounding community grows outward to swallow them up. The most visible of these opportunities is the conversion of old sweatshop factory buildings into residential loft properties. Others like Ghirdelli Square or Cannery Row in San Francisco and Monterey, California, respectively, are factory-to-retail conversions. Again, this type of project is out of the reach of the beginner, but if you have commercial leanings, you can work up to fixer-uppers like these.

Recreational properties like marinas, bait-and-tackle shops, boat-rental facilities, tour operators, theme parks, and private airports all represent a different and more challenging potential project. Retired military bases are turned into commercial and residential property. More and more bases are being phased out, and something will be done with the decommissioned property. Even mines have been redeveloped. Retired and played-out salt mines have been converted into document storage and now even storage facilities for nuclear waste.

# Making Your Plan—Getting Ahead of the Curve

Am I suggesting that you tackle anything like these larger projects? Not really. I am merely suggesting that you not look at economic possibilities with only one mindset.

If you think fixer-uppers are only refurbished houses, you might stumble over and ignore the deal of a lifetime. Most people who are interested in entering the fixer-upper marketplace will tackle a house or two, if only to improve their own living standard, but if it calls to you and you have a fertile imagination—and if you understand that reward follows risk—then one of these seemingly off-the-wall projects might have your name on it.

Where in this mix of opportunities do you fit? Only you can answer that. You and your background, your expertise, and your bankroll are unique. Since the spectrum varies from paint, wallpaper, carpet, and landscaping ("the lipstick approach") to a capital investment of hundreds of millions for a regional center, there must be something here that speaks to you and your circumstances. The major goal of this book is to make you aware of opportunity as you pass through your town and to help you organize your thinking to see what, when, and where you might like to give fixing up a piece of property for profit a try. The major aspect of taking the plunge is observing what is going on in your target community and taking advantage of things that others are unaware of. It is done every day by enterprising people looking to better their financial situation without making a lifelong commitment or taking a flyer in the stock market. I believe that most investors today wish they had tried something besides the stock market over the last two years.

> **Reality Check**
>
> The single best thing about real estate is that if you buy it right, you will not lose any money. You might fail to make a killing, but you should almost never lose any money.

## The Least You Need to Know

- Not all fixer-uppers are equal—size and risk are directly related to reward. Innovation is risky but incredibly profitable if you're right.

- Residential projects are a good place to start because housing is the most familiar type of building to most of us.

- Commercial projects can be much more risky because they tend to be larger projects and involve third-party leases—they can also be more profitable if handled correctly, because there is less competition.

- The term "fixer-upper" can be applied to almost any form of real property; let your imagination soar.

# Chapter 4

# Leverage and How It Works

## In This Chapter

- Using other people's money
- All about borrowing
- Where to find the dough
- Cash and what it's worth

The average homeowner has used leverage for years, but most people give it little or no thought. Put simply, leverage is the act of increasing the return on your own money by borrowing someone else's. It is used when we buy our homes, and stock traders have been using it for years by buying on "margin."

Borrowing money, or raising equity capital is vital to most real estate ventures, as few people have enough cash to embark on a project without borrowing. The average lender today requires that any borrower have 25 percent of the projected costs of the project invested before the lender's cash goes into the project. This chapter deals with how to borrow and how to raise equity, and what each type of money is worth to you in the context of your project.

# Leverage

We call it financing, but when it is used for profit, it is called leveraging. How it works is quite simple. For the average homeowner who buys a home for $100,000 and sells it at a later date for $120,000, it is easy to see the results of leverage.

If you purchased your house for $100,000 cash and resold it for $120,000, you made a $20,000 profit, but how does that stack up as a return on your investment? Taking the $20,000 and dividing it by the cost of the house, $100,000, you can see that you have a 20 percent gain on your cost. Simple, isn't it? If, however, you are like the rest of the country's homeowners, you most likely have a mortgage, and that completely changes the deal as an investment.

An investment analysis of the same transaction using the same home, purchased with a conventional 80 percent loan, means that you have only $20,000 invested and $80,000 borrowed. So when you sell the house, taking the same $20,000 gain, you then divide the gain by the actual cash investment of $20,000, and you realize that you have had a 100 percent gain on your investment instead of 20 percent of the total cost, as shown with the all-cash purchase. The difference is the result of leveraging your investment with borrowed money. When you take on a fixer-upper, you will be looking at two things for a potential profit: your time and your investment. I will have more to say about your time in Chapter 7. The basic thrust of getting involved with a fixer-upper is to make money on your cash investment; therefore, leverage becomes a major part of the plan.

**This Works**

I recommend that whenever you take on a fixer-upper project, you borrow as much of the cost as possible. Most lenders today will loan you a substantial part of the purchase price and a good portion, if not all, of the costs of improvement.

# Loan Types and Liens

There are different types of loans available for different types of projects:

- **Second-home financing.** This is most likely to be the same as if you acquired a cabin or vacation home. Normally this is a conventional 80 percent loan with perhaps a ¼ to ½ percent premium on the interest rate. This type of loan is used when you keep the fixer-upper as a rental property.

- **A&D loan.** This is more commonly described as an acquisition and development loan. This loan is generally for 100 percent of the purchase price plus the costs of the improvements. The lender will also require you to personally guarantee the repayment. This is known as a *full-recourse* loan.

- **Mini perms.** These are loans that start out as A&D loans but are converted to permanent or *amortizing* loans when the construction is completed. They are commonly granted for rental property.

- **Lines of credit.** These are revolving loans that are advanced and repaid with interest only during the life of the loan. People who do fixer-uppers for a living usually have lines of credit to finance their work. Money is advanced as needed, interest is paid monthly, and the loan is due and payable upon sale of the property.

- **The second or home-equity loan.** This is a loan granted in addition to the original financing for the purpose of fixing up the house. This loan is common for people who live in the house as it is being upgraded.

- **Hard-money loans.** These are the most expensive loans on the market. They are usually for much more money than a conventional lender will give you, generally for 100 percent of costs, and they come at a premium of points and interest. They are referred to as "hard" because of the high rates of interest and points. It is not uncommon to find a hard-money loan with 5 points and 18 percent interest. I have a friend who builds spec houses with hard-money loans. It is risky but profitable.

### Trade Terms

To **amortize** a loan is to pay off part of the principal with each regular payment. The amortization schedule shows all parties which part of each payment over the life of the loan goes to interest and which goes to the principal of the loan.

**Full recourse** means that in the event of the projects failure and subsequent foreclosure and fire sale, the lender can come after you for the full amount of the shortfall. If you and your wife or your partner in the deal have also been required to sign the guarantee (a typical scenario), you are all jointly and severally liable for the shortfall.

"Joint and several" means that you are each liable for 100 percent of the loan shortfall, and the lender's normal procedure is to collect from the one with the most cash and let the partners sort it out later. If you are the one with the most cash and/or liquidity, you have been elected the "deep pocket" and will have to collect your partner's share of the losses yourself.

All of these loans have a purpose and a price. Let's touch on them all so you can understand your choices.

## Loan Basics

The following are some details you need to understand in connection with all loans:

- The principal is the loan amount.

- The note is the loan document.

- The term is the length of the loan (for example, 30 years or so).

- The rate is the interest charged on the principal.

- The annual percentage rate (APR) is the percentage charged annually to accommodate the interest and the principal repayment. For example, for a loan at 7 percent for 30 years, the annual percentage rate necessary to accommodate both principal and interest is 7.99 percent.

- *Points* are fees charged by the lender and the mortgage broker to make the loan. When taken by the mortgage broker, they are fees to the company for arranging the financing. When taken by the lender, they increase the interest rate actually paid for the loan.

 **Trade Terms**

A **point** is 1 percent of the loan amount. For example, one point on $100,000 is $1,000. If you are putting 10 percent down on a $100,000 home, thus paying $10,000 and financing $90,000, any points will be calculated on the $90,000 loan, not the $100,000 original sales price. Thus, one point on the transaction would be $900. **Fees** are considered to be prepaid items like appraisals, documentation preparation, origination fees, and closing costs (taxes, title costs, and so on).

- A discount point is a point paid to the lender to lower the interest rate on the loan, thus enabling a lower monthly payment. Lenders love this because they know that the average loan is repaid in less than 11 years, effectively increasing their annual yield even further.

- *Fees* are a catchall to boost the lender's and broker's profits. They try to lay off all the possible costs of the transaction on you the borrower. This further increases their profits.

- Penalties can also be a part of a loan, but generally you only see them in connection with a commercial project. Lenders like to "lock in" the loan for specific periods of time so that the loan can be resold in the secondary market.

Commercial loans are customarily "bundled" together in large lumps of 100 million dollars or so and are sold on Wall Street to investors. This is the secondary market.

♦ Prepayment penalties are generally ruinous. Their effect is to achieve yield maintenance to the lender as if you kept the loan for the full term. The effect is to make all the future interest due at the time of the early payoff. It is a very strong deterrent to an early payoff.

The companion document to the loan is the lien or mortgage that is recorded against the property to let everyone else know that the lender has a claim against the property. Normally the "first" *mortgage* or *deed of trust* is subordinate only to the taxes. A second loan, today known as a home-equity loan, is recorded as being "junior" (or in second position) to the primary financing. You can even have third and fourth liens and so on.

**Trade Terms**

A **mortgage** is the document recorded to evidence the loan granted by the lender. This is an eastern U.S. term. The **deed of trust** is the western U.S. version of the mortgage. The actual loan is evidenced by a document called a note. The mortgage and deed of trust secure the note on behalf of the lender.

## Primary Dwelling Loans

Most people are familiar with the standard 30-year mortgage, and most of us have had a passing acquaintance with the variable-rate mortgage. These two types of loans are used when you buy a house to live in. What you may or may not know is that you can sell the house you live in every two years and not pay taxes on the profits earned. You can do this every two years for life. If you are getting involved in a fixer-upper project that you do not intend to live in, the standard 30-year fixed or variable-rate loan (up to 97 percent of cost) is not going to be available to you. These loans, known as primary-dwelling loans, come in a variety of sizes and interest rates:

♦ **Conventional loan**—Typically 80 percent of the purchase price is the cheapest loan to get, and it comes at the best interest rate.

♦ **FHA loan**—Normally allows up to 95 percent of the price but can also be had (for a premium) at up to 97 percent of the purchase price. These loans come with heavier upfront *points* and *fees.*

♦ **VA loan**—These are available to veterans of our military. They're typically available for 100 percent of the purchase price. This loan also comes with fees and points.

When you get involved with a fixer-upper that you intend to live in while working on it, these primary-residence loans are available to you; however, if you intend to fix up a home and resell it ASAP, you will be faced with the possibility of having to borrow money at different rates and terms. If you intend to fix it up and keep it as a rental property, you will find that you can probably still get a conventional loan for 80 percent, but this time it might not be 80 percent of the purchase price; it might be 80 percent of its value as a rental property. This may result in a loan amount that is larger or smaller than that of a conventional primary-residence loan, depending on the appraisal. Given a good credit history and a certain amount of liquidity, some local banks might be willing to make you an A&D loan.

The first time you do a fixer-upper, you might be able to persuade the bank that you really intend to live there. This is what most people do. When they fix it up and sell it, they merely tell their lender that they have changed their mind. This only works once.

# Where to Borrow

People borrow money these days from an amazing variety of places. In the past, it was local banks that made the loans, but today most people involved in the real estate industry are also in the loan business:

♦ Real estate companies make loans and resell them in the secondary market.

♦ Finance companies like Di-Tech advertise on TV; they also package and resell their loans. They even advertise loans of up to 125 percent of the purchase price.

**Trade Terms**

The process of **underwriting** a loan is the analysis of the borrower's ability to repay the loan, approving the appraisal of value, and finally approving that the loan meets the lender's criteria for funding and perhaps reselling the loan.

♦ **Mortgage bankers** who represent specific lenders make loans exclusively for their stable of lenders, and they are compensated directly by the lender. These are the least expensive people for the borrower to do business with. They *underwrite* the loans on behalf of the lender.

♦ Sellers also make loans to buyers, often taking a second loan over the mortgage financing, or where permitted by the primary lender, wrapping around existing financing. The wrap loan is also referred to as "an all-inclusive loan." The wrap is generally at a higher rate than the underlying loan, thus increasing the seller's/lender's yield on the amount financed.

- Mortgage brokers are people who arrange for and sell the loans to the best bidder. They collect fees from both lender and borrower. Generally, they are the most expensive to deal with.

- Banks are some of the best lenders, especially for fixer-uppers. They will do things that conventional lenders will not. They do lines of credit, seconds for the fixing up, and generally will then roll it all together for a permanent loan when it's finished.

# Equity and Where to Get It

The equity in any deal is the hard cash you have invested in the transaction. Usually this is the hardest part of any deal for people to come up with. For the last 28 years, I have been in the development business, and I have 100 percent of the time used other people's money for the equity in my projects. I am exclusively a "joint venture" company. The upshot of this is that in exchange for the use of the money, I have had to give away to the investor a share of the profits, generally 50 percent.

This does not make too much sense on small deals, but if you are long on credit and short on cash, you too can raise equity to do your deals. Each deal is unique, and the terms are strictly negotiable between the parties. Some logical sources of cash are as follows:

- Banks and other financial institutions
- Family and friends
- Arm's-length investors
- Second or home-equity loans
- Homeowner/renters
- Prepurchases
- Cross-collateralized loans
- Hard-money loans

Sounds weird, doesn't it? Let's take them one at a time and see what you think of the possibilities.

Banks, life insurance companies, *real estate investment trusts (REITs)*, and trusts are conventional sources for income property or commercial loans. They are generally amenable to looking at increasing their yield by participating in the equity of a project. They can do it in several ways. They can joint venture, in which the equity financing is in the form of a partnership and the bulk of the money comes in as the mortgage, or they can do a "participation" loan in which they loan the money in one loan that, in addition to the basic interest, has a kicker or a participation in the profit. This participation can be in the form of an additional interest premium on part of the loan or a participation in the cash flow and resale profits. These loans are exclusively reserved for commercial and income property, and they tend to be for amounts in excess of $5 million.

**Trade Terms**

Real estate investment trusts (REITs) are publicly traded companies formed to own and operate a variety of commercial real estate projects. In general they tend to specialize in one particular type of real estate such as retail projects, office buildings, or apartments. Taxwise, they are structured to pass through to the stockholders all the benefits of single taxation and depreciation.

Family and friends are the most common source for fixer-upper money for the beginner since the amounts tend to be modest. Passing the hat is very common. The downside is, of course, the fact that dealing with family is fraught with peril. If something goes wrong, it can ruin your family life forever. Divorce and acrimony are rampant, so if possible get your money elsewhere.

First on my list of money people are the arm's-length investors. Most often they are professional investors who use entrepreneurs like us to leverage their money. Since they do this routinely, they are very able to access the potential risks and are well able to shoulder any losses should a disaster occur. Seldom are they investing money that is vital to their well-being. They are generally fair to deal with and are responsive in times of trouble. They want you to succeed and consider themselves on your side. In most cases, you both have a lender who will have foreclosure rights, so the investor must see you through to recoup his or her investment.

The most typical loan for the average homeowner/fixer-upper is the second loan, or home-equity financing. These loans are designed specifically for the purpose of allowing a homeowner to improve the property. These days, however, they are used for everything under the sun from car purchases to vacations and paying off credit cards. If you use them exclusively for improving your property, you will show a profit instead of draining away your capital gains.

Another potential source for equity is the buyer for the improved property. You can find and arrange with the buyer, for a discount in the price, a participation in the fixer-upper project. Often renters can be persuaded to advance sums of money to improve the property in exchange for lesser rent for a period of time. Renters will sometimes agree to improve your property at their expense and time in exchange for forbearance on the rent.

If you are doing a substantial upgrading of the property, it is possible to have it presold by your Realtor®. This is no more difficult than preselling a house built on speculation. Prepurchases have the advantage of allowing you to take the contract to a lender and borrow against it to do the work.

Not very common, except for people who do this for a living, is the concept of cross-collateralized loans. This is a loan that is secured against more than one property. For example, if you are going to buy a fixer-upper, you might ask your lender to make you a 100 percent loan on the fixer-upper and secure it against the property and your own home. The double security is called cross-collateralization. This most often requires substantial equity in your own home. The risk, of course, is that if anything bad happens with your deal, your home may be in peril. This type of loan can sometimes come at a lower than normal rate due to the excess collateral.

Finally, we are back to the hard-money guys. They have their place in the market. When you cannot get money anywhere else, they are always there. They are expensive, so make sure your deal has enough room to pay the extra costs. If you miss the target, they will foreclose you out of the deal in a heartbeat to protect their cash. The documentation normally allows them to take over without the formality of a foreclosure. Most hard-money lenders are individuals or partnerships. Institutional lenders seldom venture into this field.

The most common of all is the partnership between people who have money and people who do the work. Normally this can be an arm's-length investor, but it often is between acquaintances. An ideal partnership occurs when a tradesman and a Realtor® team up to locate and fix up homes as a sideline for both parties. If it goes well, it could become a full-time business. Other new wrinkles are emerging in the single-family market, such as people sharing the profits on a house. If someone wants to purchase a home but lacks the necessary down payment, it is no longer uncommon for him or her to find an investor to put down the cash. The homeowner then moves in, makes the mortgage payments, and then when the property is sold, the investor recovers the down payment and the parties split the profits. This is a good deal for both parties, as the homeowner gets a place to live where he or she can acquire some equity, and the investor gets a good return on a secured investment. If you apply this idea to a fixer-upper project, you will be able to leverage your money even further, thus maximizing your return on investment.

## The Least You Need to Know

- Fixer-uppers require cash as well as loans, as most lenders will require 20 to 25 percent of the costs to be paid by the borrower.

- Find the loan you are comfortable with and borrow as much as possible; leverage will increase your profitability.

- If you are short on cash, there are other sources, such as family, potential partners, or hard-money lenders for additional money or all the equity required for the deal.

- If at all possible, avoid using family money because the personal fallout may be more than you can handle. Even hard-money lenders are less risky than family cash, to them it's only money, and there are no hard feelings when they foreclose on your dream.

- Remember that it's only money, and half a loaf is better than none; borrow carefully.

# Locating Your First Fixer-Upper

## In This Chapter

- ◆ The search
- ◆ The paperwork
- ◆ How to hedge your bets
- ◆ Pick your target
- ◆ Scope out the work

It is time to start looking for your first project. In this chapter, we will explore the approaches to a project in both residential and commercial fields. Your first basic decisions will involve choosing between the two possibilities and choosing the depth of the redo. If you have done your homework, you will have completed your survey of your chosen market. Your diagram should clearly show what's where in your target market. You know what homes are selling for in the area of choice, and if you are interested, you know what the rent levels are for well-located, modern, commercial buildings. What's left is to make your pick and buy it right. You make your money when you buy. Work hard and you'll collect your profits.

# What to Look For

For the purposes of this book, I will explore picking out both a house to be renovated as well as a small strip commercial retail building. The house will be a conservative approach for our first venture, and the retail center will be a modest upgrade.

If I were looking for my first home to buy for a fixer-upper, and I did not intend to move into it but instead just refurbish and resell, I would look for an area with a substantial number of retired persons, although not necessarily an adults-only community. It has been my experience, looking at my friends and family, that as people get older they become less and less interested in their housing. They start to neglect routine maintenance, doing only what is necessary to keep the dwelling functioning. The result is usually a good house in a good neighborhood that has become shabby and full of deferred maintenance.

These houses are all over. You could make a career out of following estate sales around town. Often these homes are not even on the market at first. It takes time to settle things. If you go to estate sales, you might find some bargains, but you might also find out when the house will be put up for sale. A discrete word indicating your interest might even result in a direct sale. Speed seems to be the biggest criterion in settling estates. Seldom does anyone involved want to go through the trouble of fixing up the deceased's property because they are too emotionally involved.

You should not feel that you are being opportunistic; it is really only a part of life. People who divorce are also in a hurry to dispose of property so that they can get on with their new lives. Someone has to buy these properties. These types of opportunities generally are available at less-than-market prices. If you see a good market for the refurbished and modernized version, snap it up. Never offer full price but do not low-ball the offer. We'll discuss the purchase agreement later in this chapter.

If you are looking for a commercial opportunity, you should look along established commuting routes on the edge of the city. What we need is a small strip center that is 15 to 20 years old. By now the original tenants should be running out of their leases, and the center will be looking somewhat dated. If the location is still a good one, the center will be ripe for a refit and re-leasing. Since most commercial property is sold based on a capitalized cash flow, you are going to purchase it based on the existing leases and their remaining terms. You can also deduct some money from the price to take care of obvious deferred maintenance items like parking lots, roofing, and *HVAC* units.

**Trade Terms**

HVAC is an acronym for heating, ventilating, and air conditioning.

Each of these components has a useful life and must be rebuilt periodically. You are going to do it as part of the refit, but why not try to have the seller pay for all or part of it? This will be covered in the purchase agreement later in this chapter.

# How to Buy It

In real estate, all agreements must be in writing to be enforceable. The law pertaining to this is called the "statute of frauds." If you are going to be involved in real estate, you need to know what it requires of you and the people with whom you will be dealing. There are four essential components to a contract to make it legal and enforceable, and they are as follows:

- The intent of the contract must be legal.

- The parties thereto must be competent.

- The agreement must be in writing.

- Consideration (compensation) must have been paid.

**This Works**

Always put contracts in writing. It will save you every time! It is also the mark of a professional.

If these four conditions are present in the contract, you have an enforceable contract. It is true that many parts of real estate transactions and renovation are done with a verbal agreement, but if a problem arises, you are left with no way to enforce your rights under a verbal agreement.

The first contract you will encounter in the fixer-upper process is the purchase agreement, and its contents are different for residential projects than for commercial projects.

# The Purchase Agreement

In most (if not all) cases, when you are purchasing a house, you will be using the local real estate board's version of a real estate purchase contract. This is the case because about 80 percent of the people in the residential real estate business are not highly trained or experienced. The pros account for less than 20 percent of the number but do over 80 percent of the business. By standardizing the contract and setting it up as a fill-in-the-blanks document, the local board attempts to minimize the problems inherent in real property transactions. This document is so full of fine print that, to make sure you get what you want, you simply add an addendum to the contract to spell out your key issues. If you use the following language in the preamble to the addendum, you will eliminate any conflicts with the preprinted form you are dealing with:

> Notwithstanding anything before mentioned in this agreement, if there are any conflicts created herein, the terms and conditions contained in this addendum shall govern.

With this in mind, you can then lay in your terms and conditions.

The basics in both versions of the purchase agreement, other than the contingencies, cover things like price, timing, title, rights of inspection, the representations of both buyer and seller, and the date of closing. Contingencies are a vital part of any purchase agreement because you really don't know the specifics of what you are buying. These contingencies vary with residential and commercial purchases. The considerations in commercial are somewhat the same as residential regarding the physical condition of the property, but there are the added concerns of leases and other operating agreements in a commercial fixer-upper.

**This Works**

The commercial contract is a different matter. Many commercial brokers have a version that they like to use; most buyers use their attorney to draw one up. This can be expensive, and I can help you cut through the fog by outlining what you need. I sell a CD-ROM on my website (www.riderland.com) that contains a dozen contracts needed in the business as well as a variety of spreadsheets. These documents are not intended to be a fill-in-the-blanks opportunity; rather, they provide a starting point for drafting what you need with the help of your attorney, and they can save you thousands of dollars over having your attorney start from scratch. Check it out.

# Contingencies

The basic purpose of the contingency portion of the contract is to do two things: lay the costs of curing any perceived problems on the seller if possible and buy yourself as much free time as possible to allow you to perfect your game plan. Every contract has a "free-look" portion built into it because there are things you need to investigate and approve before pursuing the purchase. Your goal is to stretch out the free-look period as long as possible. The common elements to both contracts generally include, but are not limited to, the following:

- ◆ Condition of title
- ◆ The physical condition of the building

- The availability of financing to facilitate the purchase
- Zoning and building regulations as they relate to your game plan

These elements are vital to the process; use them to your advantage. Do not be pushed into acting in a hurry. Time is on your side, so use it.

Now let's examine each of these elements so that you can fully appreciate its significance.

**Warning, Danger Ahead!**

Remember, there are no "standards," everything is negotiable. Sometimes real estate agents think in standard terms, because it makes their job easier.

## Title

The condition of title is a concern in several ways. First of all, does the seller have the right to sell the property? This seems like a stupid question, doesn't it? However, if it is an estate sale, the will might not have been cleared by probate, the will might be contested, the title might not have automatically passed to the survivor, or there might be fraud going on. Your attorney will help you look into this. You must be assured that you are acquiring clear and marketable title to the property.

A vital part of the title document is the area of restrictions that are recorded against the property. There are public-utility easements (PUE), access *easements*, deed restrictions such as recorded *CC&Rs*, and conditions such as *adverse possession*. All of these items need to be addressed, and you must determine that none of them exist (or at least exist in a place that will not restrict your plans).

**Trade Terms**

**CC&Rs** are deed restrictions recorded against the property by the original developer that govern all houses in the neighborhood. Their purpose is to preserve property values.

An **easement** is a right granted to a third party on your land. You cannot build over public-utility easements, and you cannot block access to someone who has an easement over your property.

**Adverse possession** occurs when a person acquires rights or an easement over your property by open and continual use for a specific period of time. For example, if your neighbor built his fence on your property and you were unaware of it or did nothing about it for a period of years, it would become a permanent easement for his property's benefit in perpetuity. Similarly, if the same neighbor has been driving through your property to go somewhere for years, his or her property has acquired a nonspecific easement of access and cannot be closed off.

## Inspection

The physical condition of the building is a concern to both residential and commercial buyer alike. Specific items to be inspected are as follows:

- The roof—Is it in good condition? If not, what will it cost to fix it?

- The mechanical equipment, specifically the HVAC systems—Same concerns as above.

- In residential properties—The grounds, landscaping, driveways and walks, and irrigation.

- In commercial properties—Same as above, plus the parking lot and site lighting.

- The electrical systems—Can they handle an upgrade, or do they need to be replaced or added to?

- The building itself—Its structure and its ability to handle an upgrade.

**Warning, Danger Ahead!**

Do not fall in love with a piece of real estate; this is a business transaction. Pride goeth before a fall.

You will need help evaluating these items, especially the first time through. There are certified home inspectors and contractors to choose from. I recommend using an experienced contractor because he or she can attach a specific dollar value to the item you are concerned about. In addition, the licensing procedure for contractors requires a greater expertise than that required of a home inspector.

## The Money

The availability of financing to facilitate the purchase is of concern to both residential and commercial buyers. I recommend that you check this out before you go shopping. Most lenders will prequalify you and add the specific building when you find it. This saves a lot of time and embarrassment.

## The Government

Zoning and building regulations, as they relate to your game plan, are very important and will be dealt with in some detail in Chapter 12. Does the zoning allow you to do what you want to do? How long will it take to get the required permits and/or variances? If you want to add some space, will the site allow you to do so? All zoning laws spell out setbacks from streets and property lines that you must comply with, and they also spell out the maximum amount of lot coverage (square feet of building on the lot), roof (the amount of permissible roof on the lot), and the number of stories or the maximum permissible building height. Zoning will also restrict certain uses. In residential, it might say that single-family is the only use, so you could not convert it to a two-family apartment. In commercial, it might permit a liquor store but not a bar or restaurant that sells liquor by the drink.

## HOAs or Homeowners Associations

In housing tracts with common amenities such as recreational facilities, it is normal to have a homeowners association (HOA) that owns and operates these common amenities. They access each house within the association for maintenance and upkeep. The HOA is managed by homeowners elected to a board of directors.

## Commercial

Commercial contingencies specific to commercial transactions include, but are not limited to, the following:

◆ Lease details and condition

◆ Operating agreements

◆ Existing loans

When I mentioned earlier that contingencies are put into the contract for your benefit, I meant it. These items, when placed in your addendum or in the main body of the commercial contract, give you time to examine the existing conditions and to decide whether to approve them and proceed or back out of the transaction. If the deal does not shape up or if the real estate is not as represented, retrieve your earnest money deposit and move on to another deal.

## Leases

The details of your lease are vital to your commercial future; you must know what you are dealing with. Take each lease apart and examine it with your attorney for enforceability.

Make a spreadsheet of the details of each lease so that you can refer to it at a glance. The information you need to know includes, but is not limited to, the following:

**This Works**

The standard lease on my CD-ROM available through my website, riderland.com, has been adversarial tested. It works. Make sure the leases you are going to inherit from current tenants also work and replace them with your new standard lease whenever the opportunity arises.

- Name, address, phone, fax, and e-mail of the tenant
- The date the lease was signed
- The square footage of the *demised premises*
- The suite number and/or location
- The rent
- Rent escalations and the effective dates thereof
- The term of the lease
- The dates and terms of any options granted to the tenant
- The expiration date of the lease and any notice requirements thereto
- Any special agreements binding on the landlord and/or tenant

**Trade Terms**

The term **demised premises** refers to a specific legal description of the tenant's space within a multitenant building. For example, "Suite 415, Building B of 15812 Eastridge Drive, more properly described in Exhibit 'A' attached hereto."

# Other Contracts

Operating agreements related to the property are a routine part of any commercial property. As the purchaser, you have the right, generally, to inherit them or to cancel them and make your own arrangements. These agreements include, but are not limited to, the following:

- Leasing agreements are an ongoing part of a commercial property's economic life. Tenants are continually going out of business, expanding, or contracting, and you need to keep the property full at all times. Your leasing agent should be your trusted friend. If your seller has a good one, keep him or her; if not, find the best one you can and pay well and promptly for good service.

- Property-management agreements are also necessary. Unless you plan to manage the property yourself, you need a good one. I recommend that you manage your first property yourself because you need the hands-on experience. Ask the existing manager to stay on to aid in the transition. When you are comfortable, take over yourself.

The care and feeding of contented tenants is the holy grail of commercial property. Learn how to do it well. A full building speaks for itself and fills your coffers.

Maintenance agreements also are necessary because you need to maintain your building in a condition that is state of the art so that the building remains competitive within your market. They include, but are not limited to, the following:

- HVAC maintenance

- Parking lot sweeping and snow removal

- Landscape maintenance

- Janitorial services

- General maintenance

As I previously mentioned, you can choose to inherit the existing agreements or start over. In either case, I recommend a honeymoon period in which you both get used to working together. It is important to know what to expect and to check up on the contractor's performance.

> **This Works**
>
> A sign is a graphic mode of advertising the occupant of a premises, whereas signage is a coordinated group of signs designed to work closely together. Signage is a capital cost to the tenant at move in. The maintenance of the signage is part of general maintenance.

# Existing Loans

In today's economy, you seldom can choose to inherit an existing loan, but if the property is old enough, it might be covered by a loan that can be assumed with or without qualification. There are also some instances in which a property has been sold and the original seller carried back some of the price in the form of a purchase money loan, perhaps in the form of a wrap loan or all inclusive deed of trust. These can be assumable because the seller may have retired and may be using the loan proceeds for income. In most cases, the original note holder would like to continue the payments rather than be faced with a lump sum payoff. In either case, the existing lender is at least a place to start looking for a new loan. Check it out and see what can be done with it. In the event of seller financing, be sure you approve both the carry back loan and the underlying loan.

# Determine Your Goals for Resale

One of the basic items to determine when you buy is your endgame or exit strategy. By that I mean, what are you going to do with the property? If you are adding it to a permanent investment portfolio, you will have a different plan than if you intend to fix it up and sell it at the right moment. If you make your plan prior to purchasing the property, you will know how to proceed with the fix-up in a more directed manner. It will solidify your budgeting process.

If you intend to keep the property, the refit must be undertaken with a view to long-term ownership. This will affect both the physical upgrade and the leasing and tenant mix. You might be wise to look for better-credit tenants than higher rent and seek to make longer and more enduring leases. If you do a physical refit, you will want to emphasize quality and durability over short-term performance and appearance. These decisions are part of *value engineering* and are properly yours to make.

**Trade Terms**

**Value engineering** is the practice of reviewing the cost benefit ratio on all proposed new improvements or amenities.

**Reality Check**

Your responsibility is not to caution the buyer, only to represent your property honestly. The better it looks and the higher the rents, the faster it sells and the larger your profits.

Should you decide to fix it up and spin it (sell it off at or before completion, or subject to completion), you are looking to get the most sizzle for your dollar spent. Long-term results are not as important to your game plan as marketability. You might therefore accept a tenant with lesser credit who will pay more rent than a "national" tenant. This will raise the bottom line and increase the sales price. Similarly, you should stick to necessary renovations only and spend some money on image and sizzle. This will attract a buyer faster than substantial improvements that are not visible.

# Set Up the Scope of Work

Using this free-look phase of the purchase, you must determine what work you will need to do and formalize your game plan. Part of this is making a financial plan. (This will be dealt with in detail in the next chapter.) Financial plans are done in spreadsheet form. Income and expenses are handled in both spreadsheet and formal accounting format. Know the difference and learn how to do both. The spreadsheet is the entrepreneur's basic tool, and there are some great computer programs available, specifically Microsoft Excel, Lotus 123, and Quattro Pro. The most common computer programs used in business are made by Microsoft, but that does not make them any better than the others, only more universal. Pick one that you are comfortable with and become proficient with it.

The use of spreadsheets is called "doing the numbers." Do your own. The old adage that figures never lie but liars can figure is, sadly, very true. If you research and prepare your own projections, you will have greater confidence in the results.

Finally, during the purchase part of your fixer-upper, it is vital that you keep in mind the mindset of the players. They are not necessarily on your team in the way you might want them to be. If you do not pay attention, your costs can escalate. Some checks and balances can be built in to the process with the following people involved in your fixer-upper:

- The real estate broker will tell you that this is a good opportunity. Make him or her prove it. Make sure you see current comparables on purchases as well as on sales of finished products. Go and look at them to put your project into perspective.

- The seller wants to unload the property at the best price. Stick him or her with fixing any deficiencies not disclosed during the sales process. Residential sellers must sign a disclosure form, but commercial sales representations should also be in writing.

- Your attorney wants to protect you and bill as much time as possible during the process. Negotiate flat fees for all the chores he or she will handle. If the attorney is experienced (and you should only work with an experienced one), a flat fee should not pose any problems for either of you.

- Your contractor wants to make as much as possible on the work. Make the contractor earn the job. Bid it out with reputable contractors and hold them to the letter of the contract and the work specified in the plans.

- Make thorough plans with your architect and planner. They will serve you well when they come to do the work. Again, negotiate and pay a flat fee for the service.

- Make your Realtor® or sales agent work for the resale. Make him or her submit a game plan and stick with it. Cover all the bases.

**Warning, Danger Ahead!**

Make sure you are not overprotected by your attorney. Avoid the meticulous, anal, "deal-killer" attorney. An attorney who makes the documentation too stringent can cause the other party to withdraw from the negotiation, due to excessive legalese and attorney fees that are too high for the deal.

**Reality Check**

Make all your own decisions. It is your money, and you will have to live with the consequences of these decisions. Especially do not let your attorney make business decisions for you. He or she is not a businessperson but a legal expert. Do your own negotiating. It is considerably less expensive than having the attorney do it; it is also less time consuming.

## The Least You Need to Know

- This is your money on the line, so pay attention, and be thorough with your free-look period. Do your due diligence carefully, remember the paperwork is where the value is!

- Get lots of advice but make your own decision. Attorneys are for legal advice, not business advice. Get business advice from experts in the field, but make your own decisions.

- Run your own numbers. Remember the old saw, "figures never lie, but liars can figure." Get your information from the leases, a written agreement is the only enforceable one in real estate.

- Project your costs on the high side and your potential sales proceeds and/or rents on the low side, and you will find that if your deal pencils out with this worst case approach, then reality should be even better.

# Part 2

## Resources

For most people their first fixer-upper will be a house, but for some it might be an office building. It will depend on how you see the marketplace where you live. Everything about the process, from finding a project to doing the work, leads up to the eventual sale or rental. This is governed by the marketplace. You need to understand it and decide where you feel comfortable fitting yourself into it.

Many tools are available to help you with the details. Books can show you how to do the work, and you can find qualified people to help you, but it's up to you to make the decisions on what to do and where to do it. The chapters in this part tell you how to find the answers and the help you will need. People and information are your resources, but you are the decision maker.

# Chapter 6

# The Numbers

## In This Chapter

- ◆ The quick and dirty spreadsheet
- ◆ Bean counters and numbers
- ◆ Limiting your liability
- ◆ The game plan and pricing
- ◆ Dealing with the unknown

Whether doing a fixer-upper or just purchasing real estate, your primary tool is what is known in the business as "the numbers." This includes formal accounting reports, bookkeeping, and spreadsheets. Collectively, these can tell you at a glance what is going on with your investment.

To be meaningful, you must develop these individual tools to answer your own questions. There are so many ways to produce numbers that you will have to develop your own criteria to address your particular concerns.

As a developer, my only measure of a deal has been the cash-on-cash rate-of-return analysis. Most investors are horrified by this simplistic approach. They customarily want to see the internal rate of return, the after-tax yield, or a present worth analysis. My criterion, developed for me, simply tells me if I'm making money and how much I am making as a percentage of cash invested. Since I am accustomed to working with investors (other people's money [OPM]), I am concerned about achieving the yields that I have represented as possible for the particular transaction.

Since this is your first time out of the barrel, I suggest that you keep it simple, look at the simple spreadsheet, and leave the sophistication to others. After you get some experience and get to the point where you want to build a portfolio of investment real estate for yourself, you can add whatever other tools you think you might need. In this chapter, we will review two variations of this tool: the "quick-and-dirty" one-page profit and cost sheet, and the project spreadsheet, which is merely a detailed version of the first spread over the life of the project.

# The Spreadsheets

For the purposes of a fixer-upper project, assuming that the project will be sold upon completion, you need to start with a simple, one-column spreadsheet that clearly sets down the costs involved in the project as well as what you think the completed project will sell for. The following is a typical example of such a document prepared for a simple "lipstick approach."

## The Quick-and-Dirty, One-Page Feasibility Study

| Item | Notes/Who Does What | Budget |
|------|---------------------|--------|
| Purchase price | | $100,000 |
| General cleanup | Myself | $500 |
| Interior Paint | Myself | $800 |
| Carpet | Purchased | $2,500 |
| Wallpaper | Myself | $250 |
| Exterior paint | Contractor | $2,000 |
| Landscape cleanup | Contractor | $1,500 |
| Financing cost | One point on $110,000 | $1,100 |
| Interest | @ 8% 3 months | $2,000 |
| Total project cost | | $110,650 |
| Estimated sales price | Based on Realtor® data | $130,000 |
| Less commission | @ 6% | $(7,800) |
| Gross yield | Sale price minus commission | $122,200 |
| Net profit | Yield minus cost | $11,550 |

Remember the proceeds from this type of deal are taxable as ordinary income, and are added to your gross income at tax time. Consult your accountant for tips on how to minimize the impact of additional earnings. However, the worst that can happen is you have to pay taxes on your profit. This quick-and-dirty approach is a simplistic example of having the pertinent information regarding your proposed project at your fingertips. Do not dwell on the numbers; however, if you look carefully, it's not a bad return on the invested capital. In this example, the only cash invested was $650 (the total cost less the loan amount), and the profit was $11,500; that is a whopping 1,776 percent return on investment. The important part of this spreadsheet is that it contains what you need to know to make a decision regarding whether to tackle the project or not.

**This Works**

The quick-and-dirty spreadsheet is prepared during the free-look portion of the purchase. This document, when carefully prepared, will become your most important decision-making tool.

The actual project version of this document is a little more elaborate and will most likely contain a more detailed breakdown of the work. This expanded document will accurately chronicle your project. If we stick to our mythical lipstick project, we will see that the expanded spreadsheet, with you taking the buyers commission at the beginning, spread over three months, will give a more accurate picture of the deal.

## The Project Spreadsheet

| Item | Notes | Month 1 | Month 2 | Month 3 | Totals |
|------|-------|---------|---------|---------|--------|
| Purchase | With deducts | $97,000 | 0 | 0 | $97,000 |
| Misc. and cleanup | $250 | $125 | $100 | $300 | $775 |
| Interior paint | Myself | 0 | 0 | $375 | $375 |
| Carpet | Low bidder | 0 | 0 | $2,175 | $2,175 |
| Wallpaper | Myself | 0 | $325 | 0 | $325 |
| Exterior paint | Low bidder | $2,250 | 0 | 0 | $2,250 |
| Landscape cleanup | Low bidder | 0 | $1275 | 0 | $1275 |
| Financing | Local bank | $1,100 | 0 | 0 | $1,100 |
| Interest | Outstanding balance | $670 | $681 | $700 | $2,051 |
| Total project costs | Through completion | $101,146 | $2383 | $3,553 | $107,326 |
| Actual sales price | | | | | $127,500 |

*continues*

## The Project Spreadsheet (continued)

| Item | Notes | Month 1 | Month 2 | Month 3 | Totals |
|------|-------|---------|---------|---------|--------|
| Commission | @ 6%, worst case | | | | ($7,650) |
| Net yield | Sale less commission | | | | $125,449 |
| Net profit | If sold in third month | | | | $18,123 |

This spreadsheet assumes that the sale occurs at the completion of the project or at the end of the third month. Since interest is calculated monthly based on the outstanding balance of the loan, every month the sale is delayed it adds another $700 to the cost, eating into the profits.

Obviously, the more elaborate the project, the longer the spreadsheet gets. The information, however, tells the same story each time; it is virtually your deal at a glance. If all you do is fix them up and sell them, you will never really need a formal accounting setup. If you decide to keep them, rent them out, and build a portfolio, you will finally be faced with a true double-entry accounting system.

# Accounting Systems and Bean Counters

There are many accounting systems on the market, and your accountant will select one you can work with. I personally use Quickbooks Pro™ for my business. The other part of your decision will be regarding the management of the property in your portfolio. When you decide to keep some of your projects, you will be faced with renting the properties and dealing with maintenance and tenant relations. By now you have clearly become an entrepreneur, and that is in itself a mindset in which you take calculated risks for potential gain.

**This Works**

A good bean counter can make you a lot of money managing your real estate, by taking your product and manipulating costs and revenues through fine-tuning over the period of your ownership. The beancounter tends to be vigilant where costs are concerned, and the entrepreneur gets sidetracked by pride of ownership.

Handling the cash is a tricky subject. Management of income-producing real estate requires a different mindset than creating it. You will eventually need a manager, one who is not only good with numbers but who can also see how to maximize the return on investment by controlling operating costs. This requires a specific skill and a generally anal attitude. People who are good at this are affectionately known in the trade as "bean counters."

These people understand accounting and cost control. This will be especially important after you start accumulating property. If you do not tackle the fixer-upper as a living but fit one in as you can, and you maintain your primary business or employment, you will need to hire a property manager. Get a good one and check on his or her work. Let the manager do the day-to-day work, but keep in touch with your tenants to make sure they are happy with the manager. The only way to find a good manager is to talk to satisfied absentee owners and tenants. Take recommendations, but keep a close eye on the building and the tenants. Have complaints come directly to you.

Once your accountant has set up your accounting system, your manager should be able to keep it up-to-date. The key point you must remember is that *you* must handle the cash. Have the rents sent to you, and you should approve and sign the checks for the bills. This can be time consuming with a large number of properties, but it is always preferable to having someone else handle your money. If this is not possible timewise, have your accountant pay the bills. The manager should handle incidental expenditures only.

No matter what, pay attention to your tenants. They are the sole source of your investment income.

# Ownership and Liability

I won't dwell on this topic unnecessarily, but you should have some idea what the liabilities and options are when you do business in general, and fixer-uppers in particular. I'm sure you are aware that everyone has a liability problem when owning property. You are no different. If you have a mortgage on your home, you have both fire and liability insurance on your home and automobiles. By purchasing another property for a profit, you will be extending that liability even further and placing all your assets at risk. There are ways to limit your liability and still get the job done.

Corporations and limited liability companies will do the trick. The corporation limits your liability to your investment. If it is administered properly, the liability stops at the corporate level. The great flaw in the use of a corporation as an operating company is that the profits are taxed at the corporate level before they are paid out to the owners. Then they are taxed again at the owner's level.

Until recently, the corporate form of ownership was the only ownership entity that allowed investors to limit their liability. Several years ago, a new legal entity was created expressly to address the problems of the real estate industry. It is known as the limited liability company or LLC for short. This entity is a combination of the partnership and the corporation. It allows the liability to be limited to the amount of your investment, and at the same time, it allows the income and expenses to be passed through to the owners and to be taxed solely at the owner's level. This avoidance of the double taxation problem leaves us with an almost perfect ownership entity. Since it is relatively new, established in most states in the late 1990s, it has had little challenge in the courts. Time will tell if it is truly the best form of ownership.

> **Reality Check**
>
> If you get involved in the fixer-upper business, do yourself a favor and set up an LLC expressly for this purpose. That way, if there is a liability issue in the future, you are covered.

With all this having been said, if you intend to keep the project for your portfolio, make sure that when you are finished with the project, it is transferred or sold to your holding company. This company, too, should be an LLC. Talk to your attorney and your accountant. I'm sure they will back me on this.

# Planning the Renovations

If you approach the fixer-upper in a professional manner and use the purchase contract and contingencies to good effect, you should have ample time to create a viable list of renovations and at least a ballpark budget for each line item. An appropriate place to start is with a checklist for inspection of the proposed building. Items to be investigated should include, but not be limited to, these basics:

- The grounds, planting, irrigation, paving, and slabs
- Swimming pools, garages, and other outbuildings
- The lot size and its ability to accommodate expansion if necessary
- Pests—specifically termites, gophers, and so on
- Exterior:

  Siding, trim, and structural condition

  The roof and drains

  Exterior paint and finishes

- Interior:

  Termites, dry rot, and structural condition

  Flooring and finishes

  Electrical and fixtures

  Plumbing and fixtures

Kitchen and appliances

General decor

Room sizes and closets

Window size and condition

Insulation and HVAC system

While you are inspecting this purchase, you should be assembling your team. Taking time to get to know the various key subcontractors (subs) will be vital to your success. The best way is to get recommendations from people you know who have used some of the various trades and go meet them. If you do not have any sources for this, look them up in the Yellow Pages and go talk to them. If you explain that you are embarking on a series of projects, they will view you as a good source of long-term business, and they will be more inclined to give you competitive prices.

It is a good idea to bid out the work at least on the first few deals, just to weed out the high-priced and/or uncooperative subs. In addition, I suggest that you try to deal with subs that have experience in renovation work rather than those who work on new construction. They are more likely to give you realistic estimates or binding prices because they will have already had experience with the unexpected.

During the free-look period, you must make your plan. If possible, together with your architect or planner, put it on paper. The ability to show on paper what will be done is vital to controlling your budget and will also serve as a good sales tool for your Realtor®. For general renovation work, a house planner is adequate, especially as you gain some experience. However, if you decide to start changing rooms and tearing out walls, you will at the very least want a structural engineer to take a look at the project and put his or her stamp on the proposed renovations. Some walls cannot be removed because they are holding up the house. If you still want to move them, the structural engineer can come up with a plan and a sequence of work that can accomplish the task.

A systematic part of the planning process should start with a checklist. This list will, by necessity, be different for each job, but you should maintain a master list that you always start from. There will be items required to do a job that are not on the list. Every time you encounter one, add it to your master list. A master list should look something like this:

**Warning, Danger Ahead!**

It is foolhardy to start removing walls without some technical advice. You could literally bring the house down on yourself. Reputable subs will insist on it, and the city building department will not issue a permit without proper plans.

- ◆ Purchase contract

- ◆ Subcontract form

- ◆ Plans and specs

- ◆ Permit application documents

- ◆ Permits

- ◆ Exterior lot:

  Paving and grading

  Planting

  Irrigation

- ◆ Exterior building:

  Pest control

  Carpentry and structural

  Trim

  Painting and finishing

- ◆ Interior:

  Carpentry

  Electrical

  HVAC

  Plumbing

  Gas

  Acoustical

  Decor items

  Paint and wallpaper

  Flooring and/or carpet

- ◆ Miscellaneous items

This is just a basic list, and while reading it, you have most likely come up with several things that I've clearly forgotten. Steal any good list you can find and keep adding to it. The better the list, the smaller the number of unknowns you will encounter.

# Bidding Out the Project

The process of pricing your renovation project starts with estimates prepared by you and your subcontractors. Once the plan is solidified and you are confident that the project will make money, it is time to solidify your costs wherever possible before you start the actual work and, preferably, before you actually buy the building. This process will serve to cut down the variables and unknowns to manageable proportions. The business of fixer-uppers requires taking risks, but the odds will slant heavily in your favor if you can whittle down the unknowns to a manageable few.

The bid process is quite simple, but there are rules:

◆ *Never invite someone to bid unless you are willing to let him or her do the job*; otherwise, you'll have trouble finding qualified bidders for your next project. Word gets around.

◆ Award the job to the low bidder promptly.

◆ Have the scope of work clearly defined by both plans and written specifications.

◆ Never allow changes in the work to proceed until you have a specific price in writing from the sub and approve it.

**This Works** ⎯⎯⎯⎯

Make sure the lender commits to the timing on payments. This will avoid both embarrassment and problems with the sequence of work.

◆ Specify the terms of billing and payment and have the language approved and the terms agreed to by your lender.

◆ Have a realistic printed schedule and make your subs agree to it as part of their contract.

◆ Use a good contract for the work. Have your attorney prepare one. Do not use the sub's contract. There is a well-tested one on my CD-ROM if you need it (www.riderland.com).

◆ If you are doing some of the work yourself, make sure it is in the schedule as well because your work might affect the other subs' ability to meet their schedule commitments.

◆ If you are doing some work, charge a fair market rate for your time and keep it separate from your profit. On your cost analysis, carry it as an expense item. Your time as a laborer should be paid as part of the cost, and your time as an entrepreneur should be compensated by the project's profit.

# Murphy's Law

What can possibly go wrong after your exhausting research and painstaking planning? Just about anything. Picture yourself tearing into a wall only to discover termites or dry rot. The extent of this could be minimal, or it could be throughout the house. Before you buy a building, it is mandatory to have it examined for termites, and the report should come with a stated guarantee for the period of time you anticipate owning the building. Long-term guarantees are now available, renewable annually. Dry rot is another matter; you and your inspector have to inspect the building carefully during the free-look period. Be sure to check the inspectors E&O policy and the financial backing of the guarantee. Most often this insurance is purchased from a reputable insurance company, one that honors claims.

**This Works**

Make sure someone on the inspection team is an expert on wiring and plumbing. It's also a great idea the have the HVAC system inspected by an expert.

Another instance might be when you are adding some modern toilet fixtures and the pipe comes apart in your hands. Another scenario can occur when your new light fixtures keep blowing the fuses or the circuit breakers, necessitating new or expanded electrical service.

## The Least You Need to Know

- Do the research yourself, from the information in the documents during the free-look period.

- Limit your liability every time. Use the contingency period to document any latent defects and/or deferred maintenance. Try to get the seller to pay for these items before you buy.

- Make a formal plan containing a schedule and financial projections.

- Create good documentation; this is where you can use a good attorney.

- Make and stick to a realistic schedule.

- Finalize your plan, schedule, and prepare your budget before you buy the building.

# Chapter 7

# How to Use Your Money vs. Your Time

## In This Chapter

- ◆ How much is your time worth?
- ◆ Buying the job
- ◆ Skilled labor or handyman?
- ◆ Polishing up your act

With fixer-uppers or any construction project, there is a lot of work to be done covering a variety of skills and trades. Some of it you can do, and some of it you must hire out. Depending on the economic bracket you are working with as far as the resale is concerned, you may be able to do more than with another bracket. The higher the price of the home, the more professional the work must be.

If you are doing a quick lipstick job on a cheap, starter, tract home, you might be able to do all or most of the work yourself. If you are renovating a 5,000-square-foot luxury home, you might be able to do little or none of the work. By starting with a modest project and working with the tradesmen on the job, you will be able to gradually acquire some additional skills that can be put to use with increasing frequency as you tackle more and more projects.

# Your Time and What It's Worth

Eventually, even if you become an expert in all the trades, you will run up against the law of diminishing returns.

You will have to consider how much of your time can be economically spent working with your hands rather than doing your thing as an entrepreneur. When starting out, it is vital that you take stock of your skills in a realistic fashion; it is not cost effective to pay for someone to redo some shoddy or substandard work. Amateurs often act in haste and create problems that skilled professionals avoid. Most people believe that they can paint and do general repairs, and in the context of your own home, these skills suffice. In the world of resale, however, we all run into the more- or less-discriminating buyer.

> **Reality Check**
>
> When I purchased my current home, it had just been freshly painted. The job was so poorly done that I deducted $2,500 from the offer to have it repainted. The seller, therefore, paid for it twice.

There are obvious places where you can do the work, and then there are others that will take some direction. The obvious places where you can do the labor are as follows:

- Cleanup
- Landscaping
- Removal of carpet and other floor finishes
- Wallpaper removal

With some minimal direction from the trades involved, you can add the following to your list:

- Removal of appliances and bath fixtures
- Removal of electrical appliances and light fixtures
- Removal of doors and counters for refinishing

And, to give the devil his or her due, you can add to the list any trade skills at your command. This results in a fair bit of labor that you can provide and get paid for.

What you cannot hire out is the entrepreneurship. You will have to spend time on the following chores at the very minimum:

- The location and selection of the property

- The purchase agreement

- Inspections

- The fix-up plan

- Running the numbers

- Arranging for the financing

- Setting up the ownership entity to limit your liability

- Finalizing the plan and getting together the final cost

- Preparing a schedule

- Overseeing the work

- Paying the bills

- Arranging for the sale

- Concluding the sale and paying off the loan

When it is all done, you will have to decide what to do with all the money. That's the good part. The preceding list defines entrepreneurship. The rest is just labor, and you can hire any competent person to do it. You cannot hire entrepreneurship. That's your job!

# How to Buy Other People's Time

Hiring labor and/or entering into subcontracts is buying other people's time and expertise. It is in this manner that you can increase your output and accomplish things that you cannot do with only your own resources to call upon. There is an art to getting the best price for a good job. When you have a budget that makes sense and are satisfied that you will make enough on the project to be content with the effort, you must concentrate on getting the best results for your proposed budget, keeping in mind that there is always the unexpected.

This process has already been covered briefly in the planning and bidding section, but I'd like to take it a step further.

The emphasis in this process is clarity and uniformity of bidding. You must make sure that everyone is bidding on the same specifications. If someone has a better idea, you should ask all the bidders to consider the new idea as an alternative to the bid specifications.

Once this is done, the next step is the subcontract, and I have included a usable one in Appendix B of this book. Rather than just accepting it as is, you should understand it and how it is designed to work for you. Each section is explained within the contract by bulleted notes.

◆ The main body of the agreement is on the front page of the contract and is as follows:

**Agreement Between Owner/General Contractor and Subcontractor**

This Agreement is made as of the (*Insert date*) between *contractor's name.* (Contractor) and *contractor's name, address, phone, fax, and e-mail* (Subcontractor).

**The Project:** (*Insert project name*)

**The Owner:** (*Insert owner's name*)

**The Architect:** (*Insert architect's name, address, phone, fax, and e-mail*)

◆ The preamble that follows spells out the parties to the contract:

**The Contractor and Subcontractor hereby agree as set forth herein below:**

The Contract Documents for this Contract consist of this Agreement, Exhibit "A" attached hereto, the Drawings, the Specifications Exhibit "B," and Exhibits "C, D, and E." These form the Contract and are as fully a part of the Contract as if attached to this Agreement or repeated herein.

◆ The first paragraphs show the contract documents and where they are listed:

The Work to be performed under this Contract shall be coordinated with all other subcontractors and shall be performed in a timely manner to prevent delays or conflicts. Time is of the essence of this Contract. The estimated start date is (*Insert date*). The start date will be determined by a Notice To Proceed from the Owner that work may commence. Without a Notice To Proceed from the Owner prior to (*Insert date*), this contract is null and void.

◆ Next, the conduct of the work is addressed, stressing cooperation between subs and the necessity for completing work in a timely manner:

The Contractor shall pay the Subcontractor in current funds for the performance of the Work, subject to additions and deductions authorized in writing by the Owner in advance, the Contract Sum of (*amount spelled out*) and 00/00 Dollars ($XXX,000.00) plus per unit tenant improvements more particularly described in Exhibit "B" attached hereto.

- The fixed price is then stated, or if it is a contract for time and materials, it is so stated with the rate clearly defined:

Applications for monthly progress payments shall be submitted to Contractor's Name, address, phone, fax, and e-mail for approval by the Owner on or before the 20th day of each month. Payments will be made for approved work by the first of the following month. The Contractor shall use the Owners Standard Application For Payment, attached hereto as Exhibit "C," for all monthly progress payments. All applications for payment shall be accompanied by unconditional waivers of lien from all suppliers or subcontractors in full for a cumulative total of all prior progress payments.

- How invoices are to be handled, together with how payments are made, is then clearly outlined:

Final payment, constituting the entire unpaid balance of the Contract Sum, shall be due when the Work described in this Contract is fully completed and performed in accordance with the Contract Documents and is satisfactory to the Owner. Walk-through repair requests shall be completed within two (2) working days upon notice from the Contractor. Subcontractor must submit notarized, final, unconditional lien releases from Subcontractor and all material suppliers for all payments received to date plus the full amount of the final progress payment at the time of final payment.

- Next, lien releases and final payment terms are stated so that there will be no confusion at the end of the job:

Customer punch list work requests shall be completed within five (5) working days upon receipt of notice of repair order. Subcontractor shall further assign an individual qualified in making such repairs to work directly with the Contractor and the Owner. Said individual shall be (*Insert name*), contacted by calling (*Insert number and mobile number*).

- The final check of the work (called the punch list) is then discussed as to how and when it is to be handled and completed:

Contractor:              Subcontractor:

Date:

By _____   By _____
     *(Insert name & title)*          *(Insert name & title)*

Additional sections of the contract will include at a minimum, the following items:

♦ An Exhibit "A" is attached that is the legal description of the property.

♦ A site plan is also inserted if the work is to be confined to one building out of many, such as is the case in a condominium complex.

♦ Exhibit "B" is attached as the narrative description of the work to be covered under this agreement, together with a complete list of the plans and specifications and any other pertinent data.

♦ The contract price is broken down, and details are added if necessary.

The final section of the contract contains the boilerplate or legal jargon that is required to ensure that the job will be administered in a professional manner. These are called the "general conditions" and are typically as follows:

**General Conditions**

**Insurance**    Prior to starting work, the Subcontractor shall obtain the required insurance from a responsible insurer and shall furnish satisfactory evidence to the Contractor that the Subcontractor has complied with the requirements of this Article. The Subcontractor shall provide proof of liability insurance in a minimum amount of $1,000,000.00 and proof of disability coverage for all employees in the form of workman's compensation.

**Assignment**    The Subcontractor shall not assign this Contract without the written consent of the Contractor. The Subcontractor shall not assign any amounts due or to become due under this Contract without written notice to the Contractor.

**Lien Releases**    The Subcontractor shall pay for all materials, equipment, and labor used in, or in connection with, the performance of this Contract through the period covered by previous payments received from the Owner and shall furnish satisfactory evidence, with each subsequent progress payment request, to verify compliance with the above requirement. A final release of lien shall be required of the Subcontractor and any major suppliers for final payment. The Subcontractor shall give all notices and comply with all laws, ordinances, rules, regulations, and orders of any public authority bearing on the performance of the Work under this Contract.

**Compliance**   The Subcontractor shall secure and pay for all permits required and not procured by the Contractor and all governmental fees, licenses, and inspections necessary for the proper execution and completion of the Contractor's Work. The Subcontractor shall comply with federal, state, and local tax laws, social security acts, unemployment compensation acts, and worker's or workmen's compensation acts insofar as applicable to the performance of this Contract. In carrying out his Work, the Contractor shall take necessary precautions to protect properly the finished Work of other contractors from damage caused by his operations.

**Safety**   The Subcontractor shall take reasonable safety precautions with respect to his Work and shall comply with all safety measures initiated by the Contractor and with all applicable laws, ordinances, rules, regulations, and orders of any public authority for the safety of persons or property in accordance with the requirements of the Contract Document. The Contractor shall report within 24 hours to the Owner any injury to any of the Subcontractor's employees at the site. The Subcontractor shall, at all times, keep the premises free from accumulation of waste materials or rubbish arising out of the operations of this Contract. Unless otherwise provided, the Contractor shall not be held responsible for unclean conditions caused by other contractors. The Subcontractor warrants to the Contractor and the Owner that all materials and equipment furnished shall be new unless otherwise specified and that all Work under this Contract shall be of good quality, free from faults and defects, and in conformance with the contract Documents. All Work not conforming to these requirements, including substitutions not properly approved and authorized, may be considered defective. The warranty provided in this paragraph shall be in addition to and not in limitation to any other warranty or remedy required by law or by the Contract Document.

**This Works** _____

Commit the idea of preapproved change orders to memory. It will save you thousands over the years and avoid litigation! If you did not approve it before the work was done and payment was agreed upon, then you do not pay for it.

**Change Orders**   The Subcontractor may be ordered in writing by the Contractor, without invalidating this Contract, to make changes in the Work within the general scope of this Contract consisting of additions, deletions, or other revisions, the Contract Sum and Contract Time being adjusted accordingly. The Subcontractor, prior to the commencement of any changed or revised Work, shall submit promptly to the Owner written copies of any claim for adjustment to the contract Sum and Contract Time for such revised Work in a manner consistent with the Contract Documents. All changes carried out by the Subcontractor shall be supported by a written claim approved and signed by the Contractor. The Owner shall not give instructions or orders directly to employees or workmen of the Subcontractor except to persons designated as authorized representatives of the Contractor.

**Claims** To the fullest extent permitted by law, the Subcontractor shall indemnify and hold harmless the Owner, the Contractor, and all of their agents and employees from, and against, all claims, damages, losses, and expenses, including but not limited to attorney's fees, arising out of or resulting from the performance of the Subcontractor's Work under this Contract, provided that any such claim, damage, loss, or expense is attributable to bodily injury, sickness, disease, or death, or to injury to or destruction of tangible property (other than the Work itself), including the loss of use resulting therefrom, to the extent caused in whole or in part by any negligent act or omission of the Subcontractor, anyone directly or indirectly employed by him, or anyone for whose acts he may be liable, regardless of whether it is caused in part by a party indemnified hereunder. Such obligation shall be construed to negate, or abridge, or otherwise reduce any other right or obligation of indemnity that would otherwise exist as to any party or person described in this paragraph. In any and all claims against the Owner, the Contractor, or any of their agents or employees by any employee of the Subcontractor, anyone directly or indirectly employed by him, or anyone for whose acts he may be liable, the indemnification obligation under this Paragraph shall not be limited in any way by any limitation on the amount or type of damages, compensation, or benefits payable by or for the Subcontractor under Worker's or Workmen's Compensation acts, disability benefit acts, or other employee benefit acts. If the Contractor does not pay the Subcontractor through no fault of the Subcontractor, within seven days from the time payment should be made as provided in this agreement, the Subcontractor may, without prejudice to any other remedy he may have, upon seven additional work days' written notice to the contractor, stop his Work until payment of the amount owing has been received. The Contract Sum shall, by appropriate adjustment, be increased by the amount of the Subcontractor's reasonable costs of shutdown, delay, and startup.

**Schedules** The Subcontractor shall cooperate with the Contractor in scheduling and performing his Work to avoid conflict or interference with the work of others. The Subcontractor shall promptly submit shop drawings and samples required to perform his Work efficiently, expeditiously, and in a manner that will not cause delay in the progress of the Work of the Contractor. As part of this contract, the Contractor has provided the Subcontractor a copy of the estimated progress schedule [attached hereto as Exhibit "D"] of the Contractor's entire Work that the Contractor has prepared, together with such additional scheduling details as will enable the Subcontractor to plan and perform his Work properly. The Subcontractor shall be notified promptly of any subsequent changes in the progress schedule and the additional scheduling details.

The Contractor shall provide suitable areas for storage of the Subcontractor's materials and equipment during the course of the Work. All stored material shall be the responsibility of the Subcontractor until incorporated into the building and accepted by the Owner.

**Layout**   Subcontractor shall be solely responsible for the proper location and/or elevation and placement of Subcontractor's work. Contractor shall survey the offsets for the building corners and shall establish a benchmark elevation for the building project, which will be maintained throughout the duration of the building project. Subcontractor shall establish location and/or elevation for all the Subcontractor's work using those reference points. Subcontractor may elect to have the Contractor establish these locations and/or elevations and in so doing agrees to repay Contractor's costs for the establishment of the location and/or elevation of Subcontractor's work.

**Damages**   The Contractor shall make no demand for liquidated damages for delay in any sum in excess of such amount as may be specifically named in this Contract, and liquidated damages shall be assessed against this Subcontractor only for his negligent acts and his failure to act in accordance with the terms of this Agreement and in no case for delays or causes arising outside the scope of this Contract or for which other contractors or the Owner are responsible. If the Subcontractor defaults or neglects to carry out the Work in accordance with this Agreement and fails within three (3) working days after receipt of written notice from the Contractor to commence and continue correction of such default or neglect with diligence and promptness, the Contractor may, after three (3) days following receipt by the Subcontractor of an additional written notice and without prejudice to any other remedy he may have, make good such deficiencies and deduct the cost thereof from the payments then or thereafter due the Subcontractor.

**Arbitration**   All claims, disputes, and other matters in question arising out of, or relating to, this Contract or the breach thereof shall be decided by arbitration. If the Contract Documents do not provide for arbitration or fail to specify the manner and procedure for arbitration, it shall be conducted in accordance with the Construction Industry Arbitration Rules of the American Arbitration Association then outstanding unless the parties mutually agree otherwise. The award rendered by the arbitrators shall be final, and judgment may be entered upon it in accordance with applicable law in any court having jurisdiction thereof. This Article shall not be deemed a limitation of any rights or remedies that the Contractor may have under any Federal or State Mechanics' Lien laws or under any applicable labor and material payment bonds, unless such rights or remedies are expressly waived by him.

**Work Stoppage**   If Work is stopped for a period of thirty (30) days through no fault of the Subcontractor because the Owner has not made payments thereon as provided in this Agreement, then the Subcontractor may, without prejudice to any other remedy he may have, upon seven (7) additional day's written notice to the Contractor, terminate this Contract and recover from the Contractor payment for all Work executed and for any proven loss resulting from the stoppage of the Work, including reasonable overhead, profit, and damages. If the Subcontractor persistently or repeatedly fails or neglects to carry out the Work in accordance with the Contract Documents or otherwise to perform in accordance with this Agreement and fails within three (3) days after receipt of written notice to commence and continue correction of such default or neglect with diligence and promptness, the Contractor may, after three (3) days following receipt by the Subcontractor of an additional written notice and without prejudice to any other remedy he may have, terminate the Contract and finish the Work by whatever method he may deem expedient. If the unpaid balance of the Contract Sum exceeds the expense of finishing the Work, such excess shall be paid to the Subcontractor, but if such expense exceeds the unpaid balance, the Subcontractor shall pay the difference to the Contractor.

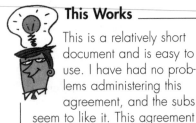

**This Works**

This is a relatively short document and is easy to use. I have had no problems administering this agreement, and the subs seem to like it. This agreement was not drafted by an attorney!

Owner/Contractor:              Subcontractor:

Date:

By _____    By_____

*(Insert name & title)*            *(Insert name & title)*

# The Handyman vs. the Tradesman

People who work in the building trades have served an apprenticeship and are licensed contractors. Everyone else is a glorified handyman. Without a license, the laborer cannot enforce payment from the owner when the job is complete. In addition, if the worker is not licensed, the owner has no evidence that the worker has at least the minimal skills required to do the work.

I believe that there is room in the fixer-upper business for both types of labor. Tradesmen are very good at taking on a big job and getting it done quickly and efficiently, but they tend to be very poor at doing small and unprofitable jobs. This is where the handyman starts to shine. It does not matter which type of labor you are dealing with, the key factor is fair dealing. If you treat both with fairness, you will enjoy a long and profitable association.

The handyman and his or her insurance coverage is an issue you will not have to deal with when using the licensed sub because most subs carry insurance for liability and other hazards. Be sure to require a copy of the insurance certificate before allowing any worker onto the jobsite. You will find that most, if not all, handymen are not insured. You must buy and pay for at the start of your job a "course of construction" policy that is designed to pick up the loose ends. This is part of limiting your liability. These policies are available through companies that deal in commercial liability policies, or all risk coverage. You can find them in the Yellow Pages or through a business insurance broker.

# Learning New Skills

As you go along with your first project, it is smart to work as closely with the subs as you can. This will accomplish two things: You will learn how they do their jobs, and you will soon be more conscious of what defines a good job. Your new skills can be put to good use with smaller jobs in the future, and you will become much more knowledgeable about prices and quality of workmanship.

## The Least You Need to Know

♦ Use your time in a cost-effective manner so that you get paid for your labor on top of your entrepreneurial profits.

♦ Keep focused on making a profit by planning and checking your game plan weekly.

♦ If you do labor, get paid for it separately from your entrepreneurial profits.

♦ Write an enforceable contract so that you can ensure your subcontractors complete the work on time and within budget.

♦ Administer all agreements fairly.

♦ Keep your eyes open and learn all you can, and your next deal will be easier and more profitable.

Chapter **8**

# The "Lipstick Approach"

## In This Chapter

- ◆ Your first deal
- ◆ What to stay away from
- ◆ What is "lipstick"?
- ◆ Deadly pitfalls
- ◆ Commercial cosmetics

Several times in this book so far, I have alluded to the "lipstick approach," so called because it is strictly a cosmetic fixer-upper. A basic project of this type involves mostly paint, wallpaper, and/or carpeting. It seems pretty simple, but the reason why these opportunities exist at all is because some people find even this type of renovation too daunting.

## The Perfect Candidate

Your task is to find the perfect candidate for this type of fixer-upper. As previously outlined, the retirement areas of the city offer a steady supply of homes that fall into this category, but you will be restricted to buyers in the same category with somewhat limited means. To expand on your potential market, you will need to look further afield. This brings us into different types of neighborhoods.

The starter-home neighborhood is evidenced by relatively modest priced homes that are appreciating steadily. These houses, which vary in size from 1,100 to 1,400 square feet in various parts of the country, California excepted, start at $80,000 and top out at $120,000. The newer versions are a little more elaborate and larger, so owners in the more established neighborhoods start upgrading gradually to keep within the envelope of the market. The opportunity for fixer-uppers in this price bracket comes from the very nature of the buyer. Most of the buyers are newlyweds, young parents, or single people. These people have limited income and are chronically short on cash. Most likely, they cannot buy the house and then fix it up. They are forced to pay a little more for the house because they can then roll the extra costs into the financing. For them, the fully refurbished house is a good deal. It costs more, but they only have to pay out 5 percent of the cost for an FHA loan (refer to Chapter 4).

*The starter home.*

As we examine each type of housing, we will find that we are in a different economic portion of the market. Perhaps the next strata is as valid as the starter homes but is 30 to 50 percent more expensive and ranges in size up to 1,700 square feet. The buyers in this bracket are still young families and perhaps some retirees who want to stay in the mainstream. They are still in the category of limited cash but have a greater ability to make the monthly payments. This market is in the $120,000 to $160,000 range. This would be considered the bottom $1/4$ to $1/2$ of the middle-class market.

*The bottom of the middle market.*

Once we go up from that price range, you start to see the upper end of the lipstick approach. You will be looking at houses in the 1,800- to 2,400-square-foot range that are going to sell from $180,000 to $240,000. This puts us squarely into the middle-class market in most of America (or in California and the larger eastern suburbs, in the starter home bracket). These houses are harder to find for this type of approach, but they are available, usually in distressed sale situations involving a death or a divorce. These situations breed the need for a fast sale, and the price is generally good. The sellers seldom want to fix anything and insist on selling as is. Because of this economic bracket, your cosmetic approach will probably include having to upgrade the appliances as well. Make sure you have a large enough margin for this one. Buy it right and you can't miss!

# What Not to Buy

In this category of fixer-upper project, it is vital that you perform a very good inspection during your free-look period. You cannot afford to deal with dry rot, termites, or structural problems. If there are roof problems, you must have the seller fix it prior to closing or reduce the price sufficiently so that you can afford to do the work.

**This Works**

Don't forget to add a little something for yourself in the estimates for your additional time and aggravation. Remember to estimate costs on the generous side. Murphy may be lurking around!

*A top-end middle-market house.*

You can live with any of the previous problems only if you can reduce the purchase price to accommodate these noncosmetic repairs. In this type of situation, you should have no trouble getting the price reduced; the sellers just want to unload and move on. The prospect of having to do some seemingly major repairs just to sell the house will more than likely make them willing to bargain. In effect, you will become their new best friend because you will take these problems off their hands for a modest adjustment in the sales price.

**Trade Terms**

The **multiple listing service** is a real property information-exchange system used by residential Realtors® for the sharing of information on house listings. To be a member of this system—and all residential Realtors® belong—means that all agree to cooperate and split commissions on all cooperative sales. Most MLS systems today are becoming computerized and therefore are increasingly effective in the home sales business across the country.

# What Is Cosmetic?

In this type of fixer-upper, identifying what is and is not cosmetic is vital. The basic beauty of the cosmetic approach is that you should be able to be in and finished within a two-week period. You can start marketing the house as soon as you have purchased it. By the time it gets into the *multiple listing service* (MLS), you should be finished with the work.

The following is obviously cosmetic:

- ◆ Paint
- ◆ Wallpaper

- Carpeting

- Vinyl flooring and linoleum

- Exterior paint

This is a very basic list. The following items might also be considered marginally cosmetic:

- Window coverings (you usually just remove the bad ones and leave the windows bare)

- Replacing baseboards

- Appliances

- Rain gutters

- Landscaping other than a quick cleanup

Items that are clearly a no-no when you are using the lipstick approach include the following:

- Replacing floor tile

- Moving walls

- Upgrading wiring and/or plumbing

- Adding square footage to the house

- Replacing siding

- Roof repairs

- Repair or replacement of driveways and walks

- Upgrading the landscaping other than a minimal amount

- Adding garages or converting garages from carports

- Replacing or adding windows

- Installing new plumbing or electrical fixtures

This final category of upgrade takes you out of the cosmetic category and will require that you purchase a building in one price range and convert it to another price range. You will be shooting for a $50,000 to $150,000 upgrade in the sales price. Most solely cosmetic approaches will fall in the $15,000 to $25,000 upgrade price range.

# Typical Nasty Surprises

When taking on any project, you will be faced with the unexpected, and unless you are born under the right star, you will encounter the occasional nasty surprise. When tackling jobs in this cosmetic category, there is seldom enough room for a large problem; therefore, your inspections become the single most important part of the game plan. The cosmetic approach, by its very nature and markup, requires good pricing in all categories. You must be doubly vigilant when buying out the job (purchasing materials and signing subcontracts). This fixer-upper is the one in which you should count on spending as much of your own time as you have the talent for. Also, don't do an amateur job and have to redo it with a pro later.

Supervise carefully and control the extras and potential overruns. Having a handyman versed in the little things is a great idea. Minor repairs of sheetrock and baseboards, as well as minor electrical or plumbing problems, will fall into the handyman category.

**This Works**

I recommend that of all the skills you can acquire in this business, the jack-of-all-trades would be your best bet.

**Trade Terms**

*NIBDS* is an acronym for net income before debt service. This is defined as effective or actual rents not to exceed 95 percent of all possible rents, less any and all operating expenses. From this figure, you will make any mortgage payments. This figure is used to capitalize the project and determine a market value.

Becoming the general, all-around, fix-it man on these projects will enable you to do some work and supervise at the same time. Seldom can you do a job better or faster than an experienced tradesman. As you work with these people, a little of each trade will rub off on you. Put it to good use. Acquiring enough skill to rival the tradesman is counterproductive. Becoming a painter or an electrician defeats the business of the fixer-upper-for-profit project.

# The Commercial Cosmetic Fixer-Upper

These projects can be relatively easy to find, but there is no opportunity to just paint them over and resell them. There is always the added component of the tenants. Since the value is determined by the rent roll (a list of tenants and their rental details) and the bottom line, the profit will be a function of how much you can improve the *NIBDS*.

When taking on a commercial building (such as a shopping center or office building) as a cosmetic job, your research and inspections must be as meticulous as when tackling a home-remodeling project. There is one added wrinkle, and that pertains to the spaces that are vacant or about to be vacant. These spaces represent your potential higher rents, and they are the very reason you are going to take the project on. The existing tenant improvements—meaning the walls, carpet, and layout—must be reusable without any drastic remodeling.

Most often with this type of project, it is necessary to have a real estate broker with a tenant in tow looking for some new space. Your job is to find a center that needs a tenant and see if it can be purchased at a good price. This requires knowledge of the commercial property in your chosen area.

**Warning, Danger Ahead!**

The longer you work in the area, the easier it will become. Your key to this is a good relationship with a tenant broker. Because tenants constantly need space to expand, this is not as uncommon as you might think. The fly in the ointment is that an astute property owner will also be on the lookout for the tenant. You must beat him or her to the punch.

It is imperative that potentially vacant spaces in your target building be so generic in design that someone else can move in and do business as is, except for the paint and carpet.

## The Least You Need to Know

- There is little margin for error in the "lipstick" fixer-upper; for your first deal, stick with something familiar to you like a house renovation.

- The all cosmetic lipstick approach can and should be a very simple job.

- Be very careful when estimating your costs, so that you do not run out of money before the job is done.

- Control your expenditures carefully by budgeting and sticking to the budget.

- Do the job quickly because time is money. If your project lingers too long, the interest cost will eat into your profits.

- Commercial lipstick jobs are only for the fleet of foot, because you need to know the market intimately, and spend money only where it will raise the rents and therefore the selling price.

# Publications and Resource Material

## In This Chapter

- ◆ Magazines and catalogs
- ◆ The weekly specials
- ◆ Where to buy
- ◆ Books and TV
- ◆ Finding it online
- ◆ What about the parts?

When you get started in the field of fixer-uppers, you will find that the sheer volume of available information can be very daunting. The old problem of what to believe and what is the "best" advice will boil down to you doing your own research and talking to as many experienced people as possible.

As I write, I'm sitting here covered with acoustical ceiling spray. My current remodel necessitated patching a piece of outdated acoustical ceiling. It is one of those jobs that nobody wants. I purchased several types of sprays designed to imitate the original installation. What a joke! Forty dollars and three cleanups later, I had to call in an expert, wait one week for him to come, and then pay him $100 for a $15 job. Become a proficient handyman!

This example is typical of not having the professional piece of equipment necessary for a proper touch-up. It required what the drywall installers call a hopper gun and a compressor—an expensive piece of equipment and a time-consuming setup to patch 2 square feet. The object lesson here is: Do not move the light fixture unless it is unavoidable. If it must be moved, learn how to patch it yourself.

A host of products are sold in handy patch-it kits or aerosol cans for the express purpose of filling the gap between the weekend warrior and the professional. Study them, try them out, and become as proficient as possible. This will save you a small fortune over the long haul. What are the sources of information that can make your life better? They range from trade publications to the Internet. I will touch on some of the most useful in this chapter, but you could devote an entire book to this subject and not get them all. They include, but are not limited to, the following:

♦ Trade publications

♦ Manufacturer brochures

♦ Retailer catalogs

♦ Advertising (local and national)

♦ Online home-improvement-contractor referrals

♦ How-to books and TV shows

Are these useful? It depends on how you approach the research. I have found that taking a general approach is almost impossible. The general references seldom give you any specific direction or helpful products. If you take a directed approach with a specific need, then you can get somewhere. It is as true for a trip to Home Depot as it is for surfing the web.

# Trade Publications

It seems that most building trades used to have an industry publication, but the only regularly printed ones I could find were *American Homebuilder*, *The Earth Movers* magazine, and some road-building-equipment publications. Today, most of this kind of work, outside the large metropolitan areas, is handled by small nonunion contractors. Building work in cities like New York and Chicago remains dominated by union contractors. There seems to be little or no demand for this type of publication anymore. Most of the information required by these professionals is supplied by their material suppliers with manufacturers' product brochures and catalogs. Some suppliers, in conjunction with the manufacturer's reps, run clinics for new product applications.

What do seem to be available are industry publications that feature such things as new products, laws, code changes, and how-to articles. The following is a partial list of what I found:

- *Family Handyman* (www.familyhandyman.com)

- *This Old House* magazine (www.thisoldhousemagazine.com/online.html)

- *Workbench* (www.hallmags.com/title/workbench.shtml)

- *Fine Homebuilding* (www.taunton.com/finehomebuilding/index.asp)

- *Old-House Journal* (www.thisoldhouse.com/toh)

- *Renovation Style* (www.renovationstyle.com)

- *Handy*—Handyman club of America (www.handymanclub.com/home.asp)

If you become busy with the fixer-upper business, you might want to subscribe. I recommend that you drop in to your local library and browse a few issues to see which one(s) will be of use to you in your endeavors.

# Manufacturers' Catalogs

For years, the manufacturers' catalog has been available only to professionals in the industry, primarily architects, engineers, and tradesmen. The mystique was that the average man or woman would be too confused to use the material offered. The information age changed all that. The traditional method of spreading the information was Sweet's catalog. It was distributed and updated free to architects. This is now available to the general public online at www.sweets.com. The contents still tend to be technical, but it will give you a wealth of information about things you never imagined.

Modern products replace hard-to-find and expensive traditional items. Corinthian and gothic columns are available in materials ranging from marble to Styrofoam. They are also available in two sections so that you can hide unsightly pipe columns and wood structural members. They come in fake marble finishes, paint-grade finish, or rough concrete. They can be surfaced in real stone or fake fiberglass stone that is so lightweight that a Styrofoam column can support it.

Moldings that were made from wood over 100 years ago are no longer available because the demand for the woodworker's skill has dwindled, but these are available in paint-ready Styrofoam. When stapled in place and painted, they are indistinguishable from the originals. They come also in a greater variety than the originals at a fraction of the cost.

# Advertising and Specials

In every local Sunday paper's classified section, you will find local retailer flyers advertising their featured product of the week and other specials. These are known as "loss leaders" to get you into the store, and then they "upsell" you with additional features (that, of course, you *must* have). This is not a ready source of materials for the professional fixer-upper, but if you keep an eye on these flyers, you might stumble across good sales on materials you use routinely like paint and floor coverings. Oftentimes, these deals come with coupons that can be redeemed at a later date when you have a specific use for the product.

# Material Suppliers and Pricing

Suppliers of raw materials come in two varieties: wholesale and retail. Wholesalers tend to deal only with the professional tradesman who buys in bulk, but increasingly, the small fixer-upper can get in the door. The magic required to do this is having a legitimate business name and address and good credit. Most of these suppliers like accounts to buy in bulk, and they bill monthly. They will generally take on smaller builders who prefer to deal in cash. You will still have to set up an account. They might offer a slight discount for cash, but do not count on it because their prices are already geared to volume.

Retailers are broken down into several categories:

◆ National discount chains like Home Depot or Lowe's

◆ Local lumberyards

◆ Specialty stores like Standard Brands Paint or carpet and floor-tile outlets

◆ Local neighborhood hardware stores like Ace Hardware and Paul's Hardware

The usefulness of these stores to your business varies. The specialty stores carry a greater variety of items and can get almost anything, but their price is based on the size of the order and the value of your account to them on an annual basis. For medium-size purchases, the discounters seem to have the edge. They carry some of everything in a generally good selection, and their prices are better than local stores and specialty shops. One of their greatest virtues lies in the fact that they will allow you to return all unused materials with no questions asked. This allows you to make sure you do not run out of anything on the job. Periodic runs to return unwanted merchandise become a routine part of your business.

### This Works

The local hardware store comes into its own when you need a small amount of something immediately. Their prices are usually 20 to 40 percent higher than the discounter, but they are closer. I am constantly amazed at what they have in stock. Their back room is usually piled with older, discontinued items that you can find nowhere else. Always ask if they have something. If they do not, most likely they can tell you where to get it. They earn their additional markup.

# Online Resources

The most up-to-date information is, of course, online. This is a function of our marvelous information age. I went to www.yahoo.com, typed in "home improvements," and got more than 30,000 responses. This is a little overwhelming, but it is still going to be the fastest and cheapest way to find out something about a product or a publication. It will not be very effective if you need a hands-on demonstration or some practical instruction, but I would recommend that you start there. The approach I take is to go from the general to the specific. In all the hits, there is a subheading that reads "For more sites like this, click here." This works some of the time, but it is generally no substitute for spending some time refining your search with the advanced search option in your favorite browser.

In my surfing forays, I have come across some generic sites that can give you useful general and specific information for the fixer-upper business, such as the following:

- ◆ Financing options
- ◆ How-to sites, some of which have film clips
- ◆ Wholesalers' and retailers' online stores
- ◆ Technical guides and government publications
- ◆ Contractor-referral sites for different geographical areas

## Financing

Financing is key to most real estate endeavors, so I was especially interested in what the web had to offer. The sites I found were as follows:

- www.eloan.com—A real estate finance center. Search for mortgage rates, qualify for loans, set up a rate watch, and get recommendations.

- www.mortgagebot.com—Internet mortgage-lending service. Apply and get approval online.

- www.homeServices.com—A provider of brokerage and preclosing services, including mortgage origination and title services.

- www.ditech.com—This site is probably the most promoted online lender on the web.

- www.bankrate.com—A source, among other things, for various types of lenders and current rates.

I have never secured financing from any of the online banks, but I did go through the application process with Ditech.com just to see how the procedure works. It was simple and straightforward and seemed to be quite easy to use. I would recommend at least looking at one or two of these sites to see if it might work for you.

> **This Works** _____
>
> Personally, I would rather work with my local bank on a line-of-credit basis. It takes some time and experience for the banks to get comfortable with this idea, but after one or two transactions, you should be able to simplify the process.

Any bank's concern lies in two areas: the value of the real estate and your ability to repay the loan. They do not want to be faced with a foreclosure. If you can satisfy the bank about your credit, the appraisal should cover the bases for the house value after the fix-up. It helps the appraiser if you and your Realtor® furnish some credible houses of comparable value for the appraiser to look at.

## How-To Programs

These programs offer step-by-step advice on home remodeling and repair. I have spent quite a bit of time exploring these, and some are better than others. They all seem easy to use, just click your way through them. The following are a few sites to get you started. These showed up under a search for "home improvement." I suggest you also try searches for "home renovation" and "home building."

- www.hometime.com
- www.oldhouseweb.com
- www.homestore.com
- www.doityourself.com
- www.nettips.com/homepage.html
- www.aasihomeimprovement.com
- www.remodelingonline.hw.net

## The Retailers

Another good source for ideas, instruction, and specific products is the large discount retailers such as Home Depot and Lowe's. These stores provide professional advice and hands-on clinics in conjunction with the manufacturers' reps on a variety of building techniques and services. These programs are geared toward the weekend warrior of the fixer-upper field. If you are interested, I'm sure your local store can give you a schedule of events for the coming year. I recently attended a hands-on floor-tile seminar and found that I could, if necessary, tackle small retiling jobs without having to worry that the results would not be satisfactory. This gave me one more arrow in my quiver as the handyman for my projects. It is not cost effective for me to tackle a large job, but it sure pays off on the little ones.

> **Reality Check**
>
> The most common upgrade that helps sell a house is a small, tiled entry by the front door, usually 4 feet by 6 feet in size. It is too small for a tile setter but perfect for the handyman, and it really dresses up the entry.

## Technical Guides

In the area of technical guides, I favor the how-to books published by many different sources. Amazon.com lists 6,943 books available on the subject of home improvement. Some useful ones are as follows:

- The *Time Life* series
- *Ask the Experts*—Reader's Digest
- *The Home Buyer's Inspection Guide* (out of print but worth looking for)
- *Inspecting a House, A Guide for Buyers and Renovators*
- *New Complete Do-It-Yourself Manual*—Reader's Digest

These books give general step-by-step instructions for individual repair or replacement jobs, but they are not intended for the fixer-upper professional. If you want to be in the business, you should get into the mindset of a general contractor. Look at yourself as the entrepreneur/coordinator. If you focus on that and then do what you have to do with your hands, you will be maximizing your time and income potential.

## Contractor Referrals

These are readily available on the Internet and are most often offered for specific areas of the country. They show up under several sorting criteria. You can find them under the following categories:

- Home improvement
- Home remodeling
- Building contractors
- Construction

**This Works**

Your single best source for good subcontractors is customer referral. There are no stupid questions, only stupid people that do not ask questions. When you are starting out, you will need all the help and advice you can get. Ask for it, grind it through your mill, and then make your own decisions.

If you cannot find a reference for your state, click on the ever-present "Find more sites like this one" link. I caution you about these referrals because I believe these sites to be member sponsored, at least in part. There is nothing sinister in that; it is just business promotion, and it is a place to start.

## The Least You Need to Know

- There is more information out there than you can get through in a lifetime; if you doubt me, go online and search the words "home improvement."
- Ask the experts, retailers, suppliers, and contractors for advice on materials and reliable subcontractors; better yet, ask them if they know a good handyman.
- Look for handy tips to help you do small jobs yourself, like painting and repairing trimwork.
- Spend more time planning than doing so that when the time comes to get the work done, it will go smoothly.

# Chapter 10

# Designers and Other Professionals

## In This Chapter

- ◆ Major building components
- ◆ Architects and engineers
- ◆ Land planners
- ◆ The builders and your money

Almost everyone lives his or her life surrounded by buildings. We are born in them, live in them, work in them, play in them, and die in them. Birth to death, our species needs buildings. Most people have never given any thought to buildings per se; they just accept them. It would be better for you, if you want to make a career or a serious effort at being a profitable fixer-upper, to know exactly what you are dealing with.

A building is not just the sum of its parts. Rather, it converts empty space into something that gives shelter, joy, and value, even though it can, in fact, be reduced to a parts list.

# What Is a Building?

George Carlin would say, "It keeps the weather off your stuff." A house or any other building is composed of several major elements that work together to form a completed building. The major components are as follows:

- The site improvements
- The interior
- The foundation
- The mechanical systems
- The structure
- The decor
- The skin

These seven elements are the major components of any building. If the building is more than one story, you need to add additional mechanical elevation-changing components such as stairs, escalators, and elevators. Let's look at each component and fit them all together.

## The Site Improvements

It all starts with a piece of land (real estate or real property). To construct a building, contractors assemble the components, which, until they are used, are personal property. Once a building is erected, the components used in the process of building cease to be personal property and become part of the real estate. The components of a completed building project usually include some site improvements like utility connections, driveways, parking, and walkways. In addition, it is common to landscape the site for aesthetic appearances. This whole package is referred to as the site work. There even may be some work completed off-site to bring power, water, and so on to the building site. These are referred to as "off-sites."

## The Foundation

Each building sits on a foundation, most of the time constructed of concrete. That's right, concrete—cement that comes in bags. Cement, sand, rock, and water combined in the correct proportions form concrete.

In the distant past, people used piles of rock or packed earth for foundation materials, but since the seventeenth century we have used some form of concrete or another. The purpose of the foundation is to support the structure. Do not confuse the foundation with the floor because the floor is an independent item. It is on and fastened to this foundation that the structure is erected.

## The Structure

Most houses built today use perimeter load-bearing walls and trusses as the basic structural system. Exterior walls carry the load, and the roof and siding provide the lateral support or "shear." The older method of home building (and the method used for most commercial structures) uses the "post-and-beam" method for the load-bearing part of the structure and the siding and roof again for the shear. This results in a structure that resembles a skeleton rather than a box made out of walls. Either method results in the exterior of the building without any decor or skin added.

## The Skin

The skin of the building consists of the roofing material and the siding material, punctuated here and there by *dormers*, *cupolas*, and in the siding, windows, and doors. This part of the building provides the weather protection. It is always exposed to the elements. This is what keeps the weather off your stuff.

**Trade Terms**

A **dormer** or a **cupola** is a section of roof whose peak is at 90 degrees to the roof around it. It is a common feature of Victorian architecture, and usually features a window in the fascia.

## The Interior

The interior is where we live, work, play, and so on. This space is usually divided up into specific areas dedicated to separate functions like living, cooking, bathing, working, sleeping, and playing. These divisions are called rooms, and unless the building is designed by the post-and-beam method, these divisions can be torn out and rebuilt at will. This is defined as remodeling, the basic function of the fixer-upper.

## The Mechanical Systems

The mechanical systems are broken down into the following major components:

♦ The electrical system distributes power to all areas of the building, enabling the mechanical systems, lighting, and appliances to operate.

♦ Mechanical systems include, but are not limited to, plumbing, HVAC and air-handling components, and mechanical distribution systems.

♦ Plumbing, while part of the mechanical system, is really a specialty of its own, especially in houses. It distributes water throughout and enables sanitary, mechanical, and recreational devices. It also provides for the collection and removal of human and animal waste.

- Communications are an ever-increasing part of our daily lives, and where there was once only the telephone line, we now have cable TV and fiber-optic communication lines connected to all sorts of buildings, house included.

- Transportation systems start with the simple stairway and move on to include mechanical systems such as dumb waiters, escalators, elevators, and people movers.

## The Decor

The decor is the last item, and it is the "lipstick" that puts a face on the building, inside and out. It serves to satisfy the aesthetic component required of each structure.

The work of planning and designing the original building and subsequent alterations is undertaken at the top of the professional food chain by architects; civil, mechanical, structural, and electrical engineers; land planners; and interior designers. In the world of the fixer-upper, most of these functions, except structural redesign, will be planned by you with a little help where needed.

# Designers

This category of professional is, at the top of the designer food chain, called an architect or an engineer, but in fact most houses are designed by house planners. These are people with few credentials who have developed a talent or been trained in mechanical drawing and design. Where they need help with particular licensed skills, they employ a structural engineer or a civil engineer. In house design, usually the manufacturer of the roof trusses furnishes the engineering for the structure as part of the cost of the components. All commercial buildings are designed by architects and/or engineers.

To make cosmetic or nonstructural changes in a building, all you need is a plan and a design for the electrical/mechanical changes. You can do most, if not all, of these drawings yourself. All cities and towns allow homeowners to design nonstructural modifications to their own homes.

## Architects and Engineers

Architects and engineers are formally trained and licensed to practice in states where they work. If they want to work in several different states, they must be licensed in each state. They are qualified to stamp the drawings as fit to build. That means they can submit the plans to the city building department for a permit to build.

For most basic renovations, you can draw your own sketches and submit them for a building permit. Often the building department will work out any changes in the details required right over the counter when you submit them. For the all cosmetic lipstick fixer-upper, you need no permit at all. The only exception to the lipstick rule occurs if you are part of a homeowners association that requires review and approval of exterior design and colors (see Chapter 12 for more details).

## Hybrid Civil Engineers

Land planners evolve from architects and civil engineers. You can study and be certified as a land planner today, but I believe it is just a glorified civil engineering degree. These professionals lay out and plan large tracts of land for new neighborhoods, towns, and communities. Savvy developers use them before they turn a site over to the civil engineer. They put an aesthetic spin on land planning and generally improve the dollar value of the end result. Their mantra is quality over quantity. If you live in a subdivision that is laid out like a checkerboard, it was designed by the builder and civil engineer with a view to maximizing the number of houses. If the streets meander and many lots have a view, you can be sure there was a planner in the design mix.

# Contractors and Money

Contractors come in two varieties: general contractors and subcontractors. All contractors are licensed by the state as having met minimum standards of professional competence. The standards are minimal, and you should always get recommendations and referrals when dealing with any contractor. Another important criterion is their financial strength. Make sure they have the wherewithal to finish the job. Make sure they pay their subcontractors and suppliers (see the sections on lien releases and job payment that follow).

In a nutshell, the general contractor takes the overall responsibility for, and is compensated for, the overall coordination of the building project. He or she is presumed not only to be financially responsible, but also to be an expert in building construction and the current building codes.

The contractor is responsible, within the scope of the plans and specifications, for execution of the required work within the code, as well as the quality and timing of all work under the construction contract. Late or shoddy work should be remedied at the contractor's expense.

**Warning, Danger Ahead!**

The general contractor is not presumed to be an architect or a structural, mechanical, or civil engineer. He or she is presumed only to be competent to interpret the drawings and construct the building as drawn, within the Uniform Building Code (UBC) and the local building department's jurisdiction. Errors in design are attributable to the architect and/or engineers.

Timing is always a critical and costly issue in construction. The realistic approach dictates that "force majeure" items such as natural disasters, severe weather, strikes, and so on, that are beyond the contractor's control, are the risk of the owner. Everything else is the responsibility of the general contractor, and the financial consequences attributed to delays should be laid at his or her door. In most fixer-upper projects, you will be the general contractor. You are assuming these risks.

Since the meter is running on the interest clock, this cost can be tied directly to the schedule. To be enforceable, the contract clause must include a reward as well as a penalty. If the work is completed in advance of schedule, a bonus must be paid. If the work is delayed, a penalty can be enforced. The penalty is customarily assessed against the final payment of the traditional 10 percent holdback from the monthly construction draws.

## Progress Payments

Not all jobs are simple and completed in a week. A large renovation job could take months; therefore, payment and liens become an issue. Every month during the life of a commercial construction project, there is a construction draw. The same is true of a large residential project. Customarily, this draw is for a percentage of the total project, is estimated by the contractor, and is approved by the architect, the lender's inspector, and the owner before being paid out by the lender. There are compelling arguments against this method of payment. First, it does not accurately reflect work in place. Second, it never reflects the cash value of the work previously paid for by the general contractor. Third, it allows the contractor to get ahead of the subcontractors, costing the owner too much interest on outstanding construction loan money.

## Alternate Payment Method

A more precise method of payment—that's fair to all: the owner, the lender, the contractor, and the subcontractors—is payment by the invoice method. This method of payment requires that each subcontractor, supplier, or consultant invoice for work completed during the current month.

Be sure to exclude any materials, such as lumber pipes, air conditioning equipment, plumbing fixtures, etc., stored on- or off-site, as these are properly the responsibility of the suppliers or the subcontractors. They become the owner's property only when they are physically incorporated into the project. The owner's insurance will be lower if this distinction is made, and there will be less *shrinkage* of stored materials as a result.

Once the subcontractor costs are tallied, the general contractor adds his or her work, overhead charges, and specific costs incurred, suitably backed by invoices from suppliers or payroll records, and the total cost of construction for the month is tallied. The owner then adds the *soft costs* invoiced for the current month, and the total is forwarded to the lender for payment. Prior to payment, the owner's representative or in most cases the architect and the lender's construction inspector tour the site to verify that the work invoiced for has in fact been completed.

If this method is followed, the owner's expenditure for interest during construction, prior to a sale or the tenants' occupancy, should drop by approximately half. This is a significant savings, and once the sale has closed or the tenants have taken occupancy and the rents are paying the interest, this savings becomes permanent, and money budgeted for this purpose may now be diverted to some other area to good effect.

Another point about payments is tied to the monthly *lien releases.*

**Trade Terms**

**Shrinkage** occurs when building materials sprout legs and walk off in the middle of the night. **Soft costs** are those associated with services such as interest, insurance, architecture, planning, and overhead rather than improvements. The actual building costs are referred to as **hard costs.** A **lien release** is a document stating that a subcontractor or supplier has been paid to date or in full.

This check-and-balance procedure ensures to the owner and lender that suppliers and subcontractors have been paid, thus lessening the possibility of liens resulting from nonpayment by the general contractor. Any supplier or subcontractor not contracted directly by the owner is required by lien law to notify the owner and lender that he or she is doing work on the project. This "preliminary notice" is required by law to protect the lien rights of the supplier and the subcontractor. At the same time, it puts the owner and lender on notice that this person is working on the project, thus enabling the owner and lender to track payments to avoid possible liens.

The invoice method provides an excellent way to track these obligations. If there is any question as to whether suppliers or subcontractors are being paid, payments to the general contractor may be made jointly to include the supplier or subcontractor in question.

One last word on the uses of money is appropriate to avoid the common mistake of being penny wise and dollar foolish. A common mistake made by developers and/or fixer-uppers is trying to save money on the budget. This can become a very short-sighted and ill-advised act. It does, however, depend on the project and the project's concept and goals. Obviously, if one is building or remodeling a project for sale (such as a house), then reduced costs for subcontractors and materials that do not affect quality will have little effect on the project. These savings will, in fact, raise the profits.

In a commercial project in which rentals are the determining factor in establishing value and profit, money saved can be used to improve the project's final value by increased rent payments. If additional money is available from savings in certain areas, these funds may be used to improve the project's quality, to reduce long-term operating costs, or to allow tenants "overstandard" improvements. Typically, the cost of these overstandard improvements is, in reality, loaned to the tenant and repaid with interest, fully amortized, over the base year period of the lease. They are not flagged anywhere as secondary income but customarily are evidenced by an increased rental rate.

### This Works

Each general contractor, subcontractor, and supplier is required to submit with the current invoice a lien release for all prior work paid for by the owner. No further payment should be made until this is submitted.

## The Least You Need to Know

- Make sure you understand the basics of building components, it will save you from costly mistakes like demolishing a bearing wall.

- Do as much of the planning as you can because you will understand the scope of work better.

- Pay for expertise where needed so that you do not have to redo an amateur job.

- Understand the buildings you are working with; each type of building has its own idiosyncrasies.

- Spend the money cautiously because your budget will be limited. Choose renovations that will be cost effective and contribute to the sales appeal of the project.

# Chapter 11

# The Plan, the Team, and the Bricks and Mortar

## In This Chapter

- ◆ Make your plan
- ◆ Buying the work
- ◆ Commercial considerations
- ◆ Who's minding the workers?
- ◆ How and where to buy your materials

Start with the market and start looking for a spread between sales prices of homes in clearly defined markets. What you're looking for is a house in a neighborhood that is selling between 15 and 20 percent below the market. This indicates that there is something wrong with it. It is either a mess, or there is an estate sale, a bankruptcy, or a divorce. Sad to say, but one person's misfortune is another person's opportunity. Keep your eyes open.

If you have found a potential fixer-upper, you must already have a plan of attack in the back of your head. You are looking for either a lipstick deal, a significant teardown and rebuild, or something in the middle. I do not recommend driving around looking at for-sale signs and waiting for something to strike your fancy because you can be seduced by a charming look that may not have any real potential or fit into your game plan.

# The Plan

You need a plan of attack. If it is your first deal and you feel that you want to ease into the business, you might go looking for a lipstick job. For the sake of this example, let's assume that the market is ripe, and you have found a little jewel with the proper spread between acquisition price and eventual sale price. Furthermore, you are going to be a little more ambitious and go for expanding the den, the second bath, and the third bedroom by cannibalizing the forth bedroom. You are going to need some help with this project, so after an agonizing self-appraisal, you have decided that with your modest construction skills you will be able to do the following work:

**This Works**

Permit information takes five minutes over the counter at the building department. The permit itself can take weeks or months, depending on the scope of the work, and the workload of the city building department.

- ◆ A rough plan for a building permit
- ◆ General cleanup
- ◆ Exterior painting
- ◆ Demolition
- ◆ General supervision

This leaves a list of required functions that must be accomplished to complete the task. They include at least, but not necessarily only, the following skills and trades:

- ◆ The building inspection
- ◆ Plumbing
- ◆ Wiring (an electrician)
- ◆ Carpentry
- ◆ Carpeting/Flooring and floor tile
- ◆ Interior paint and decor
- ◆ General handyman items

This is a minimum list of the people and skills you will need to tackle the job. Your first task, to be accomplished during the free-look period, is to inspect the house thoroughly and make a list of the work to be done as well as a plan that shows the completed new layout. Since you want to be frugal with your first endeavor, you have decided to dispense with the services of a general contractor and hire the subcontracts directly yourself.

What you need right off the bat is an efficient and fully qualified home inspector. Together, with your sketch plan in mind, you two will go through the house with a view to what is to be done and what resources the house has to support your effort. The following questions must be asked and answered:

> **Reality Check**
>
> Hiring subcontractors directly means that during the free-look period, you need to get all the subs through the house with a copy of the plan so that they can give you meaningful prices. This is going to create a time crunch.

- ◆ What is the condition of the building exterior and the roof?

- ◆ What is the structural system, and can you tear down walls?

- ◆ Is the wiring and basic electrical service adequate to sustain the proposed changes?

- ◆ As far as plumbing, can you demolish the second bath and expand it without having to disturb the main septic system, or do you have to tear out the floor and reinstall it?

- ◆ What should be added to the decor to emphasize the "new look"?

Once you have the plan firmly in hand, you need to rotate your team through the house so that you can solidify your budget. This is easier said than done because first you need to know what type of work will be expected of each and from whom you can select to make your final choices. In addition, the seller is living there and does not want your horde tramping through the house at all hours of the day and night.

Your best bet is to arrange for two in-depth visits with the sellers absent. This is common, and your Realtor® can arrange it. This will enable you to speak freely about the property without upsetting the sellers. Since you do not want to pick a sub without first knowing your costs, you must select two of each from your research. Group them into two teams so that at each visit there will not be two subs competing for the same business. The results of this approach should yield a good inspection and some constructive and candid feedback from the individual members of the team.

When the prices come in, you will be able to make your final pick for the team to do the work. You might have had a suggestion during the process that results in adding another specialist to the team. No matter what, this will yield some good ideas and competitive prices, and you will have a stronger team as a result of this approach.

# Who Does What?

How do you go about selecting the individuals to do the work? There are as many ways as there are people doing this type of project. I have a routine that serves me well if I am in an area that I am not very familiar with. I ask my friends and acquaintances for referrals, I visit my primary suppliers and solicit recommendations, and I call a few small general contractors to see if they might be willing to make a recommendation. Surprisingly, you will get some great leads.

When you have identified some candidates for each job, ask for some references, both financial and work related. Check on these references and go and look at their work. You are looking for the quality of the work and an ability to keep to a schedule.

In addition, it is crucial that you select people within each trade that have the skills you need. Each trade has specialists within it as well as generalists. Some of the distinctions, outlined as follows, will give you some idea what to look for.

## Carpenters

Carpenters have the following specialties:

◆ Framers are the people who work as a team, and they are responsible for erecting the structure of a new building and putting on the rough roofing and siding. They then move on to a new building. You will only need a framer if you are adding space to an existing building.

◆ Finish carpenters take over from the framers and apply the finished siding and the interior. There are even specialists within this group who deal only with doors and windows. Within this specialty are the people who do hardwood floors and decorative millwork.

◆ Cabinetmakers and millwork specialists install the cabinets and add the fancy trim throughout the house that establishes the basic decor. There are even specialists within this group that make the cabinets and specialty items such as stair railings and trim.

The following trades, considered "specialty trades," are generally licensed and regulated by the states in which they work. They must pass minimal standards of skills and experience and know how to become licensed.

## Plumbers

Plumbers vary from steamfitters to general plumbers. They are most often broken down as follows:

- ◆ Steamfitters are the ones who work in heavy industry and shipping. They handle heavy-pressure piping, boilers, and steam generators as well.

- ◆ Site and underground pipefitters install sewers and water systems up to the buildings.

- ◆ General plumbers do the plumbing for the buildings and hook up and install plumbing fixtures.

## Electricians

Electrical work is also broken down in specialties:

- ◆ High-voltage transmission and power plant work is a specialty that is in the "heavy construction" category.

- ◆ Site electrical work, distributing power within subdivisions, is a further specialty involving underground installation and working with transformers and distribution systems.

- ◆ General electricians deal with installing the basic electrical services in a building as well as the distribution of power throughout the buildings.

- ◆ The final specialty, which is a subspecialty of the general electrician, is the trim man. He installs all the light fixtures and appliances in the finished building.

**This Works**

As you might suspect, within the field of commercial building, everything is bigger and involves larger quantities. Seldom do commercial tradesmen cross over into the homebuilding sector and vice versa. The division of labor effectively mirrors that of the housing industry, with the exception that site electricians seem to install the basic service such as the power panels and the metering stations.

## Painters and Finishers

These guys apply decor to the finished structures. There are several specialties that overlap with other trades but deserve their own mention:

- ◆ Painters and wallpaper hangers

- ◆ Bath accessory installers

- ◆ Glass and mirror suppliers

- Cabinet shops making cultured marble walls and vanity tops

- Kitchen countertop makers working in Formica, Corian, granite, and other stone

- Carpet layers

- Flooring installers using tongue in grove hardwood, vinyl tiles, ceramic tile, and stone

- Hardware specialists and locksmiths furnishing locks and decorative hardware

For more information on building trades, contact your local Registrar of Contractors.

# The Regulators

With all that is going on in the building industry, there are—and should be—people regulating the people doing the work. In most states, this agency is called the "Registrar of Contractors," and it is state operated and regulated by laws passed by the state legislature. The way it works is that individual companies are licensed to do the work. This involves an individual who "qualifies" for the license, having passed the test and posted a bond against faulty work or fraudulent practices. The companies are licensed, not the individuals doing the work. Individuals running their own companies, the one-man band types, are usually licensed as well.

## The Unregulated

Not all people who do construction work are licensed. Most people (over 95 percent) who work in the new building industry are licensed, bonded, and insured, but in the remodeling industry, the overwhelming majority are unlicensed, not bonded, and uninsured. What is the upshot of this disparity in practice? Generally, it boils down to contract law, state regulation, and industry practice. It is industry practice that you seldom or never see unlicensed contractors working on a commercial structure or new housing project. However, the inverse is true in the housing industry. Most work done for homeowners that involves remodeling and repair jobs is done by unlicensed contractors or handymen. The exceptions to this rule seem to be the plumber and the electrician. Consumers are not comfortable with unlicensed plumbers and electricians. Consequently, these two trades are the highest

---

**Reality Check**

The sad truth about hiring unlicensed help is that you have no idea if they are qualified, and nowhere to go for redress in the event of a dispute. On the bright side, unlicensed workers have no lien rights against your property and cannot collect from you easily in the event of a dispute.

paid people in the remodeling industry. Whereas you can hire a carpenter for $15 to $25 per hour, you will pay $50 per hour and up for an electrician and more than $60 per hour for a plumber.

## Legal Consequences

The consequence of using an unlicensed contractor is that you are never sure whether the person doing the work knows the minimum code requirements necessary to pass an inspection for an occupancy permit. On the tradesman's side of the issue, an unlicensed contractor is restricted by law from enforcing payment by lien on the building in the event of nonpayment. All states allow you to check with the registrar about any contractor licensed with the state. They will tell you if there are any complaints against him or her and if there is any pending action like suspending or revoking the contractor's license.

# Where to Buy Your Stuff

Once you have identified the project and put together your team, you will need to buy things to implement your plan. Your subcontractors will supply all the basics, but you might find yourself with some specialty items that will need to be found at prices that are reasonable. Sometimes you will make a deal with a tradesman in which you will supply the raw materials and the tradesman will supply labor only. This is often a time-and-materials deal.

Flat prices for labor are not hard to get. If you ask the tradesman who is supposed to be experienced, he or she can hardly be reluctant to state a fixed price.

> **CAUTION**
> **Warning, Danger Ahead!**
>
> Time-and-materials deals are dangerous because there are no limits on the amounts to be spent. If possible, get a specific price or a unit price for the work, or if all else fails, get a "not to exceed price." Open-ended deals will kill your budget. Put all agreements in writing. Remember the statute of frauds. It is a professional way to do business.

# Retail Stores and Wholesale Suppliers

With time-and-materials contracts, you can then buy your supplies from one major supplier like Home Depot or a wholesale supplier. They will, if the job is sizable enough, offer a substantial discount and delivery. The advantage of this is that you will most likely save some money on supplies. The disadvantage is that, when the supplies are stored on the jobsite, any losses are yours to bear.

Not all items can be purchased from conventional suppliers. If you are working with period architecture such as early colonial or Victorian, some trim items and fixtures will not be available from conventional stores. Many suppliers have a line of decor items that mimic the older styles, but these, while fitting the period, are not authentic. If your project requires that you restore the building to its former authenticity but with a modern code overlay, you will have to get creative.

# Used Building Materials and Specialty Shops

There is a whole industry dealing with used building materials and furnishings. We are all familiar with antique dealers, so why not antique or used building supplies? The most common primary sources for these materials in bulk are demolition and salvage firms.

For a long time, demolition companies used to tear down buildings, load the mess into trucks, and take it all to the dump. With the advent of people looking to move back to the cities, the fixer-upper movement got into the restoration business. This has always been a good business in New England, where they worship the old colonials, but it is now a trend sweeping across America.

**Trade Terms**

A **belfry** is a part of the building that is built up above the main roof, housing church bells, usually with a roof and a steeple above it. It is generally accessed only by a staircase directly from the ground floor.

Most things salvaged by demolition firms are now resold to companies that sell these items to the remodeling industry. These stores can provide old bathtubs and plumbing hardware, metal ceilings, old wainscoting and paneling, as well as a variety of trim and millwork. They can usually locate old *belfries* and windows and doors from original houses.

## The Least You Need to Know

◆ Have your plan in mind from the beginning of the inspection because you will have to determine the extent of the work and the materials and subcontractors needed.

◆ Carefully screen the people doing the work so that it will be done correctly the first time.

◆ Get competitive prices to limit your expenditures to the absolute minimum to get the job done.

◆ Check on references and past work so that you can be sure the people you select are up to the tasks at hand.

◆ Buy your supplies at the right store, and if you can't find it, have it made.

# The Government and You

## In This Chapter

- ◆ Zoning and approvals
- ◆ Zoning constraints
- ◆ Residential zoning
- ◆ Commercial zoning
- ◆ Building codes and their influence

No matter what your field of endeavor, the government will have a hand in it. In the case of the fixer-upper, it can be a light touch as with the lipstick approach, or it can be a two-year-long marathon costing tens or hundreds of thousands of dollars. You and your project will inevitably fall somewhere in the middle.

Taking on a fixer-upper can involve you in the same process as that of a developer starting with an empty parcel of land. This would be true if you purchased a farm, renovated the house, subdivided the rest of the land, and sold it off to builders. Granted, it would be stretching a bit to call this a fixer-upper, but once you get involved in the process, you need to know what it is and how it works. A brief overview of land zoning is in order.

# Understanding Zoning

Every community is governed by a master plan that is updated periodically, usually every 10 years or so. This master plan is a work-in-progress guide to show how the community should grow, a method of organizing land with the purpose of making sure there are adequate services and public facilities to serve all the community needs. Each parcel within the master plan has a specific *zoning* classification.

**Trade Terms**

**Zoning** is a legal description that covers each parcel of land within a given master plan, outlining the legal uses permissible on each individual parcel of land. For example, single-family housing, multifamily housing, retail or industrial uses. Each category is broken down into sub categories such as in commercial, C-O, C-1, C-2, and C-3. Each category has specific permitted uses and building constraints.

For the purposes of this chapter, the word "land" is used synonymously with the word "building" because the zoning and entitlements run with the land rather than with the building.

The following may be more than you ever wanted to know about land and rights, and if all you want to do is lipstick some homes, you can skip over this section. However, the very nature of zoning and its built-in property rights make it potentially the most important part of a deal for a clever entrepreneur. You will encounter it every time you want to change the use of a property, whether you're converting a house to professional offices or converting some extra land into building lots. It's worth it to have a basic understanding of the processes.

# Zoning Requirements

Typically, a parcel of land will be zoned for the intended use. There are, however, opportunities to acquire land with no zoning, usually designated in the master plan as agricultural or with incompatible zoning (i.e., if you have land designated for residential use and you want to put a retail building on it), and to then upgrade or alter it for any proposed project. Regardless of the state of the zoning on a given piece of land, a process of approval by the governing body is required before the land can be built upon or the building converted to another nonconforming use.

The minimum requirement will be to secure a building permit, which can take any-where from two weeks for a fixer-upper to six months, depending on the complexity of the project, the work load, and the attitude of the building department involved. The following are some other potential requirements:

◆ Master-plan changes

◆ Zoning changes

◆ Special-use permits

◆ Site plan and architectural design review and approval

These processes will most often require a series of public hearings before the local planning department, planning commission, and city council and will probably involve little more than making the project conform to local standards and architec-tural tastes. Sometimes, however, in the case of rezoning or special-use permit requirements, it can involve heated public debate, intense opposition, and consider-able increased time and expense. It may also result in frustration and potential aban-donment of the project. Recently, around the country, residents of small communities have banded together to oppose, sometimes successfully, the building of the new superstores.

Experience shows, however, that the process most often results in compromise and in a better project. A community whose needs have been met and whose citizens' input has been incorporated into a project tends to enthusiastically support that project. After all, the community needs the services and revenues that a successful project will bring. While the process should be straightforward, it can become complex, expen-sive, and time consuming. Tracking a project through a typical master-plan change and rezoning, we will find the procedure to be extensive.

First there is the application, together with the fees, executed by the fixer-upper, developer, or applicant and the current landowners. Accompanying this there will be the required 20 sets of drawings, elevations, renderings, models, and so on. Notice will be given to the abutting landowners, and their input will be solicited as well as that of the various departments of the building department: transportation, fire and safety, public works (utilities), sewer and water districts, and perhaps regional plan-ning, transportation, and environmental agencies.

The submittal will then be subjected to a planning-department review, and additional data such as a traffic study, preliminary grading and drainage plans, and sign criteria can be requested. Eventually, the planning staff makes a formal recommendation for approval or denial of the request to the planning commission, and dates for public hearings are assigned. The hearings are conducted first by the planning commission and then the city council or county board of supervisors. The merits of the request for approval or denial of the application are opened for public debate at these hearings: first for the master-plan change and then, if that is approved, the rezoning. Streamlined, this process takes approximately six months. If, as in the state of California, a complicated *EIR* is required, the process may take several years.

### Trade Terms

An **EIR** is an environmental impact report, also known as an environmental impact study. It is a lengthy and expensive document, dealing with all the potential physical impacts of the specific project.

### This Works

The process of entitlement and/or rezoning, when completed successfully for a specific parcel of land, may be the single most profitable action undertaken in real estate.

If and when the master-plan change is adopted and the rezoning enacted, working drawings must be submitted to the building department for approval for a building permit. Preparation of these plans varies from several days for a simple fixer-upper, to 90 days for a modest new-building project, to several years for a complex one. The review process may take two weeks to nine months before a building permit can be issued. Most developers use this processing time to obtain the necessary leases to qualify for conventional financing. The time may seem rather long, but it is a busy and necessary time for preparation to build out a large project. If the front-end work is successfully done, complete with detailed costing and preconstruction planning, the project should enjoy a relatively smooth construction and lease up. In most of my projects, I take two months of planning and preparation for every month of construction.

The old adage, "You make your money when you buy," is very true. Land purchased or controlled with substandard or nonexistent zoning can have its value greatly increased by proper planning and zoning. This process then "entitles" the land. The approvals and entitlements run with the land and can be transferred along with the ownership. The primary attraction for any potential buyer is the fact that he or she saves a considerable amount of front-end time on the project.

There is a whole segment of the real estate industry that makes its money acquiring, rezoning, and reselling land to other developers/investors. The land value can be further enriched by approval of development plans and execution of leases for the proposed project. These, too, can be transferred with the land upon sale. Experience has shown that almost 70 percent of the initial profit projected at completion of construction can be achieved prior to the start of the building process. Building out the project merely places the investment in play.

# Zoning Classifications

Most areas of any county break down zoning into categories:

◆ Parks and wilderness areas

◆ Public lands

◆ Agricultural preserves

◆ Industrial

◆ Commercial

◆ Residential

Each of these designations has many variations and serves different political agendas. Every state is broken down into counties, and this is generally where the planning and zoning process starts. Land that lies outside of municipal boundaries is referred to as "in the county" and is controlled, planned, and zoned by the county. Within counties, there are designations for federal, state, and tribal lands as well as wilderness areas, parks, and wetlands. The rest of the land within the county, outside any municipality, is private land and is broken down into the following basic designations:

◆ Agricultural

◆ Residential

◆ Industrial

◆ Commercial

◆ Public

There can also be other special zoning designations such as railroad rights of way and canal and power transmission designations. Cities, townships, and incorporated municipalities break down their zoning classifications in much the same way. Some states, primarily in the western part of the country, reserve tracts of land for future development, placing them up for public auction when the time is right. This land on hold in Arizona is called "state trust" land. Other western states have similar lands reserved for future development.

## Agricultural Land

Agricultural land, worldwide, is dwindling at an alarming rate. Here in the United States, most states treat agricultural land as a reserve for future expansion. In

California, one of the most fertile agricultural areas on Earth, agricultural land is routinely rezoned for residential expansion, and the rocky and infertile hills and mountains are preserved for their aesthetic value.

The population in the United States has accepted that housing uses are sacred, and everything must make way for urban sprawl. The disparity in the value of land zoned for agricultural uses and land zoned for any type of development is dramatic. Land for farming is worth an average of $4,000 to $10,000 per acre, and land zoned for housing sells in the West, where it is plentiful, for an average of $1 per square foot, or $43,560 per acre. It is easy to understand the temptation of buying land and rezoning it for residential uses. Once the land is rezoned and the houses are built, adjacent commercial land becomes worth between $3 and $30 per square foot, depending on the economics of the surrounding housing. These facts provide the genesis of the rezoning industry. One of my first projects involved buying a housing tract for $40,000 an acre and after rezoning it and doing the preleasing, I was able to sell it for $250,000 per acre. The increase in value was due to both the change in zoning, and the preleasing accomplished because of the change in zoning.

> ### Reality Check
>
> It is not too big a stretch to visualize a future, if and when the population bomb explodes, in which it is financially or morally viable to tear down houses to plant food.

## Residential Zoning

Residential land comes in an endless variety: single-family with variations, multifamily with variations, high-rise, and cluster housing. There is also a commercial variation of housing known as the retirement or assisted-living community (housing with a business component).

Single-family housing zoning varies from single-family units on multiple acres to between six and eight units per acre. It varies from custom-built housing to mobile homes and prefabricated communities. Custom home communities are located on the larger lots, varying from ¼ acre per home to many acres per home. This is the least efficient form of housing and therefore the most expensive—and, by extrapolation, the most desirable. Next come the tract-housing projects that vary from four to six units per acre. This product provides the bulk of middle-class housing throughout the country, selling from a low of $70,000 per unit in "start-up" communities to $600,000 and up per unit in the more exclusive, or expensive, areas.

Multifamily housing makes up the bulk of affordable housing, ranging from New York City's projects (housing for the poor) to apartment complexes in suburbia. It even encompasses luxury housing in urban settings where expensive co-ops house the wealthy. Multifamily housing is generally attached, at least zero-lot line, often multistoried, and benefits from the production-line techniques derived from the tract-housing approach, maximizing the number of units per acre. Zero-lot line "patio homes," where one wall of the dwelling (generally the garage wall), is placed on one of the property boundaries or lot lines, can be as dense as 8 to 12 units per acre, and the density of high-rise buildings is limited only by their height. All of these approaches to the housing market capitalize on increased density and proximity of repetitive building techniques to create a better value for the consumer.

Likewise, the manner of ownership varies all over the lot. Multifamily rentals (apartments) are usually owned by one entity, but other types of multifamily ownership also exist. They are the condominium or town house, the co-op, and the horizontal regime, a form of condominium used in multistory buildings. The condominium generally includes the land under the unit, with the common areas such as parking, recreation, and so on owned by the condominium association. Individual owners pay a monthly fee for the upkeep and taxes on the common areas. The co-op is an eastern, urban, high-rise version of a condominium in which the tenants' association usually has a say in who can be an owner. The horizontal regime is the legal basis of ownership that separates land from building and is used to define individual units in a high-rise building. The homeowners association owns the land and the shell structure, and the occupants own from the wallpaper in.

> ### Reality Check
>
> A recent arrival, typified by an experiment in Prescott, Arizona, is the "condhomium." This innovative approach entails many smaller units built around community food preparation and recreation facilities. The individual units have limited cooking facilities, and the main building houses extensive food preparation and eating facilities as well as community recreation amenities. This is perhaps the well-heeled commune or "co-housing" of the future.

# Industrial Land

Industrial land falls into two general categories: heavy and light industrial uses. The heavy industrial designations are reserved for manufacturing uses in which large quantities of raw materials are transported and processed. These uses are sometimes referred to as "dirty" uses. They are strictly confined to specific areas within the general plan area and are usually port, rail, and freeway served.

Light industrial zoning, the "clean" type, is reserved for light manufacturing such as electronics or assembly type work, typically nonpolluting, and it also extends to business parks that mingle light manufacturing, warehousing, and office uses in a park-like setting. California's Silicon Valley is a typical example of this genre of development, now repeated in Arizona's Silicon Desert.

## Free-Trade Zones

Industrial areas can sometimes be designated as "free-trade zones." Free-trade zones are areas set aside by states and municipalities, with the approval of the federal government, as international manufacturing areas, intended to take advantage of tax regulations regarding the importation, exportation, and manufacture of goods. In areas along the Mexican-American border, these zones are the site of the "maquilladora" manufacturing plants that capitalize on combining mass-produced, American-made, or imported parts and less expensive labor from south of the border. These zones can be located anywhere in the country and are duty-free ports for importing components for assembled goods. The finished product, when exported from the free-trade zone, is taxed at better rates than those imported from another country. This has changed somewhat with the advent and implementation of *NAFTA*.

> **Trade Terms**
>
> NAFTA is an acronym for the North American Free Trade Agreement, which permits tariff-free trade between its members.

## Commercial Land

Commercially zoned property includes office, retail, recreational, and mixed-use facilities. Office uses vary from one-story suburban buildings to high-rise urban properties. Retail property varies from strip commercial centers to regional shopping malls. Recreational facilities vary from small "pitch-and-put" golf courses to sprawling theme parks. Mixed-use facilities include endless combinations of any or all of these.

Today's urban landscape, in ever-increasing numbers, includes high-rise buildings that involve mixed uses. The older approach of the multistoried department store is giving way, due to more expensive land, to buildings that have retail uses on the lower floors and office space on the upper floors. Sometimes, like the Sears Tower in Chicago, the building has retail on the lower floors, offices on the middle floors, and residential uses on the upper floors. This building even has complete recreation and health facilities for residents and office users on the upper floors.

The suburban variation of this theme is regional mall area zoning, which includes a ring road approach to zoning. It is comprised of concentric circles of zoning surrounding the regional mall core. The first ring around the core is generally the discount or box store malls (also known as power centers), restaurants, hotels, and recreation. The second ring is multifamily housing, buffering the large expanse of commercial real estate from the surrounding single-family neighborhoods. Developers of this type of project are generally large and very well-heeled, with access to immense amounts of capital. A regional mall alone can require many hundreds of millions of dollars.

The bonus for the magnitude of risk and expenditure when dealing with this type of zoning is, of course, that once the regional mall is built, the surrounding land increases in value so dramatically that the profits are obscene. The rewards are at least commensurate with the risk. Who in their right mind would have thought that the Galleria in Houston's suburbs would have been a good gamble? The initial structure was surrounded by a sea of single-family housing. Today, it is a huge complex of urban mixed-use buildings and is a shining example of the rewards of innovative and risky entrepreneurial enterprise. Conversely, the Galleria in Scottsdale, Arizona, was a colossal failure and still stands empty after seven years of debate. It is a very expensive, well-built, and luxuriously appointed white elephant, a victim of a lack of understanding about retail development and a design not suited for the area.

## Entitlements

Since the cost of entitling commercial property is expensive, why then is it so lucrative? To entitle a property, you must apply to the city for a specific use, and have it approved through the public hearing process. Once achieved, the entitlements (zoning and/or specific plans) run with the land when the land is sold. The answer lies in the nature of the risk and the amount of the costs. The costs in relation to the potential increase in value through the *entitlement* process, are small in comparison to the total cost of purchasing a parcel of land (with or without a building) that's already entitled and then building out a project.

First of all, land that is zoned agricultural may be acquired through *long-term options* or an *extended escrow*. The why of this is that farmland can continue to be farmed while the process is going on, and because of the potential upside, the buyer can afford to pay the farmer much more than the land is worth as farmland. This makes for a patient seller and a hopeful buyer. A farmer can continue with business as usual while someone else risks his or her money to provide the farmer with more than the land is worth as a farm. It provides a generous endgame for a farmer who would like to get out of farming and cash in his or her chips for retirement or a change of career.

**Trade Terms**

An **entitlement** is specific zoning or approval of a specific use or a specific design for a piece of property. It can be as small as a ½ acre or as large as a master-planned community.

A **long-term option** is an agreement to purchase a piece of land at a future date (several years or more), at a specific price and under specific terms.

An **extended escrow** is an agreement to purchase subject to the completion of certain contingencies with the right to extend the time to accomplish these objectives.

If farmland can be rezoned to residential, it means that the value of the land can be raised from $5,000 to $10,000 per acre to at least $30,000 to $45,000 per acre. Examine the motivation and the cost of the process. If a farm of 640 acres (a section) is optioned at $10,000 per acre, where is the profit? A typical rezoning budget is as follows:

## Rezoning Budget

| Item | Cost | Notes |
|------|------|-------|
| Land option | $50,000 | Nonrefundable |
| Planning costs | $50,000 | Average |
| Engineering | $25,000 | Exploratory |
| Graphics/models | $25,000 | Average |
| Legal | $15,000 | High |
| Total risk dollars | $165,000 | |

If the land purchase price is $6,400,000 ($10,000 per acre) and the potential value when rezoned, or ultimate sales price, is $27,878,400 ($1 per square foot, or $43,560 per acre), the risk seems paltry at three time the cost when you realize that, until the land is purchased, the investment is limited to the rezoning budget. The resulting rate of return on investment if the land is contracted for resale subject to rezoning is astronomical. This is what fuels the suburban growth market. Typically, an entrepreneur interested in rezoning as a business cultivates a reliable stable of builders as buyers and discounts the land to them in exchange for their loyalty as purchasers/users of the finished product, the rezoned land. Even at half price—say, $23,000 per acre—the profits are handsome, as the following table shows:

## Rezoning Profit Recap

| Item | Cost | Notes |
|---|---|---|
| Land cost | $6,400,000 | $10,000/acre |
| Sale price | $14,720,000 | $23,000/acre |
| Cash cost of rezoning | $330,000 | Budget × 2 |
| Net profit | $7,990,000 | Sale price minus land cost |
| Return on investment | 2,421.21% | Not too bad |

Is there any doubt that this is a profitable enterprise with plenty of profit to spread around to the individual experts involved in the process?

Similarly, commercial opportunities abound in both urban and suburban settings. In cities, there are blighted areas waiting for redevelopment. In suburbia, there is the street corner, zoned residential, that can be turned into a gas station site, or maybe there's a large residential piece of land with outdated and rundown houses on it just waiting to become a neighborhood shopping center site worth between $3 and $8 per square foot. Look around—opportunities are everywhere!

Experienced developers are busy being developers and often cannot "see the forest for the trees." This provides opportunities for new entrepreneurs every day of the week. A burned-out block of buildings in the Bronx can become a fashionable new residential or shopping area, and an abandoned gas station site can become a new McDonald's restaurant.

**This Works**

Being in the right place at the right time is luck. Being smart enough to recognize the opportunity is what separates entrepreneurs from everyone else. Fixer-uppers come in all sizes and with different opportunities. Just because it's not a rundown house, don't ignore the building's potential. Take a second look.

# The Building Code

In the instance of building modification, all changes, even trivial ones, are governed by a written code. The national building standard is called the uniform building code (UBC). Local jurisdictions can adopt this as a minimum standard and add additional requirements to meet local conditions. The most visible example of this is along the West Coast from California to Canada and Alaska. Additional seismic requirements have been added to the UBC to accommodate the earthquake problem in these areas.

You must comply with these regulations in all of your work. The tradesmen hired to work on your project are responsible for compliance of their specific work to the code, and you are responsible for the overall job. As the work progresses, you will be required to have the work inspected and passed so that you can proceed to the next step. The only exception to this is the lipstick approach, and even then you might have to deal with the local homeowner's association. If you ignore this and the building department becomes aware of this breech of rules, they can stop the job and require you to bring it into compliance before you can proceed.

**Warning, Danger Ahead!** _____

If you purchase a house that has been modified without a building permit, and you want to renovate it, the local building department will most likely have you bring the old addition up to code before approving further renovation. If you are demolishing the old nonapproved renovation, then you should have no problems. In some cases, if it has been there long enough, it is practically "grandfathered" and should cause you no trouble.

In your own home, you can do all the work yourself without the benefit of a license. If you choose to do so, you must have the work inspected by the building department as you go along. With fixer-uppers, you might be able to get away with it if you are intending to move in, but you are way ahead of the game if you use licensed contractors for their expertise until you acquire the knowledge necessary to keep everything within code.

## The Least You Need to Know

- Zoning and entitlements run with the land, not the building.

- Changing zoning and land uses can enhance a building's value in a potentially far greater way than physical renovation.

- Look at everything and choose your projects wisely; if your plan is not permitted by the zoning, your project is dead at the outset.

- Build carefully and remember that the building department can shut you down if you do not adhere to their rules and the plans as approved by the building department.

# Part 3

## The Work

The truth of it is this: You make your money when you buy, you maximize profits when you do the work, and you collect your earnings when you sell. The chapters in this part will expose you to all types of real property from farms to urban buildings, from houses to retail centers. Somewhere in this mix is the right property for you. Your first project should be something you are familiar with and something you think you can handle without breaking the piggy bank. Once you find an opportunity and understand the market it is in, you're off and running.

# Chapter 13

# Rural and Low-Density Housing

## In This Chapter

- ◆ Understanding the family farm
- ◆ Subdivision of land
- ◆ The four-parcel split
- ◆ The land—how to use it

Chapters 13 through 15 will discuss housing in its various forms, the underlying land, and unused land available for housing. We will examine the potential for converting residential properties, both land and building, to other uses. For starters, you must permanently alter your concept of land.

As you saw in Chapter 12, unless you are dealing with a single-family lot, land exists as an opportunity independent of the buildings on it. Single-family houses can also be changed into something else, so in a sense, all land represents a different category of fixer-upper. Always check on the land possibilities before making a commitment to a fixer-upper plan.

That having been said, not all land represents a dramatic opportunity. If you are looking at a home in the middle of a subdivision, there is little or no possibility of converting it to anything other than a single-family home. If, however, the subdivision is a small one (under 20 lots) and has passed its prime, there may be a possibility of assembling all the houses into one big parcel and rezoning it to another higher and better use. Conversely, if you have a commercial building that is past its prime, it may be that you could tear it down and convert the land to residential uses. This happened to my first shopping center in California. It was demolished last year, and luxury homes have blossomed in its place. Times change and opportunity abounds. In this chapter, we will discuss rural and low-density suburban property.

# The Family Farm

Rural land, by its very nature, always represents a land opportunity in conjunction with the building's potential fixer-upper possibilities. Each year, thousands of farmers are calling it quits and moving on to other professions. This leaves behind the family farm or some remnant thereof. Many of these farms are in areas with very low population, and there will therefore be little or no demand for any form of land conversion. In areas that are near large population centers, the family farm has definite fixer-upper potential along with the added bonus of a land subdivision spinoff.

## The Building Itself

Most old farmhouses are relatively easy to deal with; they have large eat-in kitchens, pantries, washrooms, big porches, and generous living rooms. Some even have a family room and a parlor or formal living room. The bulk of the renovation for this type of building will be modernization of kitchens and baths. The exterior will be relatively plain and will need an upgrade of trim, siding, and roofline.

**This Works**

Roofline modification can be accomplished by adding dormers and cupolas to the roof itself. You might find, as a bonus, that the attic has now become a viable additional room.

Generally the bedrooms are on the small side, and there is usually only one bath on the second floor. I recommend sacrificing a small bedroom on that level and adding the second bath. Downstairs, there may or may not be a bathroom, and sometimes the washroom will have to be converted to a back-to-back bath and laundry area. Most washrooms are large enough to accommodate this. If not, go with the bath and put the laundry somewhere else. Most rural garages are constructed separate from the home, and where appropriate, the attic can be converted to additional living space. This requires the proper roofline, and the addition of dormers etc., but the additional space is great for kids and guests.

The added bonus when dealing with farms, other than the land, is the outbuildings such as garages, barns, tool sheds, and so on. If there is a livestock barn, it will most likely not be too useful because it is impossible to remove the odor. Old cow barns can be converted to stables, but that's about it.

There is also a demand today for farms in the 300- to 500-acre category with wet-lands and timber stands as part of the terrain. There are federal grants available to maintain wetlands for migratory birds. This effectively converts the farm into a sanc-tuary at the government's expense, at least partially. I have a friend who has spent two years looking for such a farm. This year he finally found one in Iowa. There is a demand for this type of setup, and these converted farms can command a very large premium.

## Surplus Land

The other aspect of the farm is the extra acreage. If you are near enough to a large city, the excess acreage can be subdivided into parcels for mini-farms of 10 to 40 acres each. For land that is immediately in the path of growth, these subdivisions can be the con-ventional suburban four houses per acre. If there is no immediate demand for these mini-farms and you want to hold out for a more dense subdivision, you have another alternative: Lease out the land to the closest working farm. The rent should easily pay the taxes and enable you to inventory the land for a later subdivi-sion. Either way, it is not uncommon to have a double dip on this type of fixer-upper.

> **Reality Check**
>
> Potentially, the renovated farm dwelling, together with its reno-vated outbuildings and 40 acres, could provide enough profit to substantially reduce your invest-ment in the surplus acreage, pro-viding you with a bankable future land subdivision deal.

## Lifestyle Subdivisions

There is a tremendous demand for rural lifestyle subdivisions. In California, a house with 40 acres of grape vineyards sells for an obscene amount of money. Other desir-able alternatives are homes with the same 40 acres planted as orchards. Almost any-thing with standing timber is a great draw. Ponds and creeks are also items that fetch a tremendous premium. I categorize these as mini-farms or lifestyle living. It enables people who have always had a yen to be one with the land to plant truck gardens, raise a few cattle, harvest grapes and make their own wine, or harvest and sell apples, citrus, almonds, or anything indigenous to the area. These subdivisions are immediate sellouts in every part of the country.

# Land Subdivision

Land subdivision is exactly what the words imply: the dividing of a parcel of land into smaller parcels for sale. There are regulations governing this, and they vary from state to state, so you will have to verify the local ordinances relating to your area. In general, land was originally sold or granted in one-mile-by-one-mile sections comprised of 640 acres. Most states allow you to break up these tracts into parcels of 40 acres each without a formal subdivision. A formal subdivision requires that you install, prior to sale, roads and utilities to each lot within the subdivision. Modern subdivisions require city water and sewer to each property line, however rural subdivisions permit the use of dirt roads, wells, and septic systems. You can still do rural subdivisions of 40-acre parcels with dirt roads, wells, and septic systems. This leaves only power and phone to contend with. The local power company and phone company will pay for part of the cost, so these large-parcel subdivisions are still viable land deals for people with a limited amount of capital.

## Forty and Under

Most jurisdictions allow you to break down acreage of five acres and up into four parcels without having to file a formal subdivision map. This process is called filing a *minor subdivision.*

You must ensure, however, that you have utilities to each parcel prior to sale. You can therefore break down parcels of 40 acres into four 10-acre parcels without the formal process of subdivision. These parcels can, in turn, be broken down even further. Someone other than the person who split the original parcel must do the further splitting of these parcels. This is intended to avoid one person circumventing the subdivision regulations. The smallest parcel permitted to file a lot split is a five-acre parcel. For subdivisions of more than five parcels or lots less than one acre, a formal subdivision process must be followed.

If you have a parcel of land that exceeds the minimum requirements of parcel size per dwelling by at least 100 percent, you can split the lot by applying to the planning department.

The subdivision process initially entails a boundary survey and *topo* map. From this document an engineer prepares a preliminary plat showing the parcels to be formed along with proposed roads and utilities, the *off-site* and *on-site* improvements necessary to serve the proposed subdivision.

**Trade Terms**

A **minor subdivision,** in most places is defined as less than five lots. A **topo** map is slang for a topographical map. This map shows the contours of the land parcel in 1- to 5-foot intervals, as well as significant topographical features like rock outcroppings, water, and significant plants and trees. **Off-site** and **on-site** improvements are what the words imply. Off-site improvements consist of work to be done to bring roads, water, power, sewer, telephone, and cable to your property, and on-site improvements distribute these utilities within your proposed subdivision. Additional off-site improvements might include road improvements such as a freeway exchange or the construction of, or enlargement of, a sewer plant to accommodate you new houses.

This plan is then submitted to the planning department, whose staff checks it for sufficiency and compliance with the subdivision regulations. The planning staff, in turn, makes a recommendation to the planning commission for approval or rejection based on the technical merit. The staff does not generally comment on the political aspects of the application. The planning commission holds a public hearing (refer to Chapter 11) to debate the approval or rejection, and the neighbors are notified in advance. If they have objections and/or input, it is accomplished in a public-hearing format.

The plan is then passed on to the city council or county board of supervisors with recommendation for approval or denial for further public hearing and final approval or rejection. Seldom is a subdivision application rejected by this process. It is designed so that the neighbors have a say in how it is designed and integrated into the community. The process often results in a change in density or configuration but seldom an outright rejection.

## The Final Plat

Once the preliminary *plat* is approved with or without modification, the engineer then prepares the final plat for approval by the same process. This is mostly a formality, but it nevertheless goes back through the public-hearing

**Trade Terms**

A **plat** is a drawing of a legally subdivided parcel of land, showing the dimensions of each boundary along with its compass setting.

mill. At the same time, the developer of this subdivision must file papers with the state's real estate commission regarding the subdivision. This requirement must be met before any lots can be sold.

*A typical farm.*

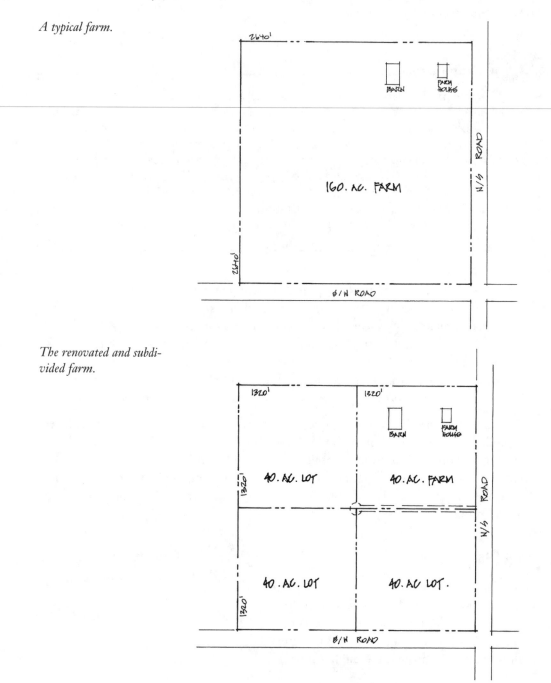

*The renovated and subdivided farm.*

## The Public Report

These papers are known as the subdivision public report. They disclose all the pertinent facts about the subdivision and any documents and/or restrictions to be recorded against the individual lots therein. The most common document is called a deed restriction, or in today's version the *CC&R*.

Typical CC&Rs filed contain restrictions like the following:

- No houses of less than 2,000 square feet on any lot.

- No on-street parking.

- No RV storage or trailer storage in the front yard.

- No auto repair or derelict vehicles to be visible from the street.

- No farm animals to be permitted, and no more than three cats or dogs per lot.

- All houses must be painted according to the subdivision's approved color pallet.

- All landscaping must contain planting on the approved subdivision plant schedule.

**Trade Terms**

CC&R is an acronym for covenants, conditions, and restrictions. These restrictions are recorded with the land parcel map and are designed to restrict uses and practices on the individual lots within the subdivision.

These restrictions are designed to maintain and enhance the value of the houses within the subdivision, and they are managed and enforced by the homeowners association. This association is initiated and administered by the developer until at least 50 percent of the lots are sold; then it is passed onto an elected board of homeowners.

**Warning, Danger Ahead!**

If you are doing the subdivision, do not pass administration of the homeowners association to the residents until you are completely sold out. You will avoid a lot of grief from the new board. Typically they try to regulate your future project or at least the unfinished part. Draft your homeowners association to pass the reins only after all the subdivisions have been approved and constructed, and the majority of the lots are sold.

The upshot of all this is that when you become involved in a fixer-upper in a rural setting, you must realize that the land will be an important consideration. The options for the land component will vary with the size of the acreage, but they most certainly will prove to be the most profitable part of the fixer-upper venture.

## The Bait

A lifestyle subdivision is one where the residents enjoy the same type of hobbies. Some are built around raising some farm animal, others are centered around truck farming, and most popular of all, vineyards. They are usually comprised of a house on 40 acres.

When attempting to create a lifestyle subdivision, it is a good idea to over improve the original farmhouse, even if it requires extensive remodeling, because you need it to be a showpiece for the lifestyle community. It must show the prospective buyers what can be done with 40 acres of grapes or orchard and a building lot. Inspire them to design the house of their dreams, and they will attempt to outdo you and the neighbors. This will result in dramatically increased value of the remaining lots.

# The Land—What to Do

If you have decided to tackle the family farm, you will have more choices than if you are looking to purchase a house and 10 acres. Some of the choices for a farm generally in excess of 300 acres will be, but are not limited to, the following:

 ◆ Lease the land back to a farmer and put it into inventory for future development.

**This Works**

My favorite option is to look for orchard or vineyard property and create a lifestyle farm subdivision with 40-acre parcels. I believe this to be the most profitable move of all if the ingredients are all there. In addition, I favor rolling land over flat land. It is much more picturesque and therefore easier to sell.

 ◆ Use the farm's original purpose, such as orchards, to create a subdivision of lifestyle mini-farms.

 ◆ Break it into 40-acre parcels and just spin them off.

 ◆ Create a formal subdivision.

 ◆ Turn it into a wilderness farm.

Any one of these ideas can be profitable completely aside from renovating and reselling the original farmhouse.

# Conversions and Rezoning

Another ploy with a well-located farmhouse could be to convert it into a country store by rezoning the small corner parcel containing the building to commercial. In Dewey, Arizona, the owners of a farm converted their corner building to a country store and planted pumpkins on the remaining acreage. They called it Young's Farm. Every year they advertise "Pick your own pumpkin for Halloween." It has become so big that the store now operates year round, the planted acreage has been doubled and redoubled, and it draws tens of thousands of tourists annually. It is a runaway success.

## The Least You Need to Know

- ◆ Land is the important component of rural fixer-uppers because it increases the yield on the renovation of the building itself by providing another profit center; lots for sale.

- ◆ Examine the land for subdivision potential to see if you can spin enough of them off to leave you with the house free and clear.

- ◆ Pick the highest and best use for each building you look at. Remember a house is not necessarily a home.

- ◆ At the very least, when dealing with a building renovation on a large parcel of land, after you sell the house, you can inventory the land for a future project.

# Chapter 14

# Medium-Density Housing

## In This Chapter

- ◆ Where do fixer-uppers come from?
- ◆ Old estates
- ◆ Subdivisions
- ◆ Urban neighborhoods
- ◆ Blighted areas
- ◆ Urban renewal

The bulk of the housing you will encounter is in either suburbia or cities. In suburbia, you will be dealing with homes that are between one and four to the acre; the houses on very large lots fall between the rural housing types discussed in Chapter 13, and the typical suburban home. Housing that is denser than four units per acre starts to border on multifamily housing, which will be covered in Chapter 15. In cities, the typical urban neighborhoods range from two to seven stories. These neighborhoods will be the most common venue for fixer-uppers.

What you need to do is be able to identify a potential fixer-upper when you see it. Each type of house will have different characteristics that will spell neglect and opportunity. The general rule of thumb will be that the smaller the house, the smaller the economic opportunity. This is not to say that smaller houses will be less profitable but that they will have a smaller margin. We will work our way from large to small in this chapter.

# Neglect and Obsolescence

Let's face it. What you are going to feed off of in the fixer-upper business is someone else's neglect or inability to keep up the standards of the surrounding community. You must therefore start to be tuned in to neglect and/or obsolescence.

You will find that age has very little to do with neglect. In New England, where houses date back to the 1700s, you can find entire neighborhoods of homes that are 200 years old but in pristine condition. Conversely, you can drive through five-year-old tracts and see the rampant effects of neglect. The disadvantaged house is a function of finance or lack of it. Seldom do people deliberately neglect their house because it represents their largest single investment and future nest egg. Obsolescence is a factor that is not necessarily apparent. You can see houses that are nicely painted and well landscaped but that lack modern conveniences in the baths and kitchens. These houses are referred to as *dated*.

As new people purchase these houses, the neighborhood slowly starts to change, and the "fixed-up" houses start to stand out against the ones that need to be renovated.

**Trade Terms**

A **dated** home can be identified by characteristics designed into the house during certain periods of time. Items such as sunken living rooms occurred in the 1950s, vinyl or linoleum flooring in the 1960s, popcorn ceilings in the 1970s, and houses with seven- and eight-foot ceilings are all built pre-1980. There is nothing wrong with these characteristics; they merely place the house in an era that has passed.

Most of this process is gradual as each new owner makes one or two changes. If you find a house that is as-yet untouched, you have an opportunity to leap out in front and do everything at once. This then becomes a fully renovated house and can command the top of the market for that neighborhood. It is best if you are not the first one to elevate a house to that state in the neighborhood because you want to avoid having the most expensive home on the street. It should be your goal, however, to take the least expensive home on the street and make it the equal of the most expensive one. Offer it for sale at a little less than the value of the most expensive house on the street, and it should move rapidly.

Let's look at different housing types and explore what to look for and what to do with these houses so that you can move them up in the market.

# Large Homes and Acreage

Houses on very large lots are generally thought of as being in the estate category. This term is a holdover from the 1920 to 1930 era, when the robber barons of Wall Street were said to seclude themselves on their estates. Most of these houses are from that era and have been renovated or left to rot. My grandfather's one attempt at a fixer-upper was one such house, albeit on a larger piece of ground. A sure sign of neglect is the grounds. If you are cruising the neighborhood and see obvious signs of overgrown vegetation, you are on the scent. You will find formal gardens, tennis courts, and stables overgrown with bushes and weeds. This is a property to acquire. Most of these properties have huge houses and several outbuildings like garages and carriage houses. They might even have a guesthouse or two, perhaps a summerhouse and gazebo. The possibilities with this type of property are many and varied. Some of these properties have been converted into sanitariums and treatment centers, some into apartments, and some have been restored to their former grandeur. One approach is to level everything and build a new subdivision. This, however, is most likely not appropriate due to the neighborhood. Somewhere in the middle is a good bet.

The place to start analyzing the property is the grounds. They were originally designed to be grand, and they more than likely still retain the basic ingredients of that approach. To start with, clean up the grounds; remove all the excess growth, leaving only the significant plantings. Unearth the abandoned tennis court, the pool, and summerhouse. This will allow you to see exactly what you have and what can be done with it. An ideal ploy is to see if you can create an additional building lot by splitting the acreage without disturbing the natural harmony of the setting. Most often, a 10-acre parcel will yield at least one great site. File a lot split and set that lot aside for the moment.

You now have the original house on a five-acre parcel, having probably lost one or two of the ancillary buildings in the lot split process. That doesn't matter. What you want to create is an elegant family home with a mother-in-law or elaborate guest apartment, the necessary attachments of a three- to four-car garage, and perhaps a pool or formal garden. Inside the house, you will have to renovate the kitchens and baths and modernize the decor. The outside should remain in the period, with attention to replacing needed trim, roofing, and restoring the architectural detail. When finished, this refurbished house can command a high dollar. It will now be in keeping with all the restored homes in the area.

What to do with the five-acre lot? To maintain the value of the restored house and to maximize the yield on the fixer-upper project, you must record a deed restriction that retains architectural control over what can be built on the lot. The alternative to controlling the design is for you to build a house consistent with the neighborhood. You might prefer to keep the lot for a later project, allowing the value to mature a few years. The more restorations completed in the neighborhood, the higher the prices will become over time. This would be my first pick.

# The Modern Subdivision

We have been building housing in subdivisions since the end of World War II. The first one, built in Long Island, New York, was called Levittown after the builder. He set the idea in concrete as thousands of returning GIs flocked to buy these new and affordable houses. The characteristics of modern subdivisions were established in the late 1940s and persist today. The typical suburban subdivision is characterized by geometrically laid out streets and virtually identical houses, perhaps four models in all. The really good subdivisions are laid out by planners rather than engineers, using curving streets and maximizing elevation changes and views. These subdivisions usually have four to six models but with the added interest of exterior variations on the same models. In addition, the developer does not allow the same model to be built side by side.

---

### Reality Check

If I am looking at subdivisions and see a typical one with matching roofs and the same exterior paint scheme, I realize that the subdivision characteristics pose an added limitation to the fixer-upper idea. Exterior changes will be difficult to get past the architectural committee, and I will have to rely on landscaping alone to set the house apart. This means I will have to use mature trees and shrubs to effect any noticeable change, and that is costly. This complication means that the margin between acquisition price and sales price must be larger than normal. I would look in these subdivisions for a lipstick job or a distressed sale for a very rapid turnaround.

---

Subdivisions with a housing theme, such as a golf course or a waterway, offer more variety in the housing because most of these will be semicustom homes. This type of house has more diversity and therefore more potential. In addition, the exteriors are generally more diverse and easier to upgrade.

This type of subdivision will move you into the upper-middle-income house-cost bracket. This is not a problem; it just ups the ante. Time on the market for homes in this type of subdivision becomes an issue, and you will have to build in some holding cost for the increased interest on your investment.

Using the theme of the subdivision, you should look for a house that has been on the market for a long time. It will be overpriced, but it might also have some design flaws that will allow you to hammer the price down far enough to enable you to alter the house to a more universally acceptable model. Do not be seduced into adding things like a swimming pool because you cannot recoup the investment.

When you add a pool to a house, experience has proven that you only get back one half of the investment in the first two years. Set up the yard to receive the pool, but let the buyer put it in.

The cautionary word about tract housing still applies; unless this is an older home with modernizing potential, be careful not to over improve the project. Your best bet is to look for a model you like with some additional amenity like a view or an over-sized lot. This will, if you buy it right, give you a marketing edge.

# Urban Neighborhoods

Urban neighborhoods are housing a completely different kettle of fish. Gone are the front yards and an ability to maximize curb appeal. The keys to urban housing are all in the interior. If you are lucky, there will be a back yard, but if you are in a high-rise, like a co-op, you will have only from the exterior walls in to work with. There are many single-family houses in cities in one-, two-, and three-story configuration, dating as far back as the age of the city. The really old ones will have to be rebuilt from the plumbing up. Most likely, you will find one that is somewhere in the middle. The plumbing has been updated as well as the basic wiring, but the rest of it is outdated and unlivable by modern standards. Some, like the *shotgun* design popular in San Francisco in the late 1800s, are fixed in design and difficult to deal with.

The drawback of urban design is that the neighborhoods tend to be homogeneous in design. The older interiors are filled with small rooms and lack light and air. The fixer-upper must do substantial interior tearing out and rebuilding to achieve any kind of substantial upgrade. The good news is that this is common, and it is not unusual to buy a house for one price, spend the equivalent on renovation, and sell it for three times the purchase price. These are labor intensive, and I recommend that you find a good general contractor who specializes in renovation, and you should also try to become the handiest handyman on the block.

**Trade Terms**

The term **shotgun** refers to a one-sided design built around a hallway that goes from the front door to the back door. On one side of the hall are bathrooms and the kitchen, and on the other side of the hall are the rest of the rooms. The term "shotgun" derives from the joke that you could fire a shotgun at the front door through the entire house and not hit anyone.

Scattered throughout the city you will find blocks of low-rise, newer houses. These came about through sporadic urban renewal and range from the ridiculous to the sublime. Some of them are built over parking, and some are built as a block. Most of them are very modern in design and stand out in the brownstone city like sore thumbs. I have never contemplated one of these, but I have looked at quite a few. In general, I find that they are too different to be in the mainstream of the market, so I have passed over them. Some of the best fixer-upper opportunities lie in the commercial conversion part of the book, as dealt with in the next section.

# The Commercial Conversion

You must have heard the magic word "loft." This has been a home run from the first time it was tried in the 1960s by bohemians and artists. Scattered throughout all cities are small commercial buildings from two to six stories tall that housed a variety of manufacturing businesses. Most of these were characterized as sweatshops before the advent of air conditioning. The exportation of labor overseas and to the South has left these buildings abandoned. The areas where they are found were considered rough because of the commercial traffic and the throngs of workers going to and fro. Now that these buildings are abandoned, the neighborhoods have quieted down and become livable. These buildings, when gutted and slightly modified, are selling like hotcakes.

If you can find one of these, you will love it because the only modifications required are demolition, the construction of bathrooms and kitchens, and the installation of a good hardwood floor.

The rest of the layout is left open. Just add a new elevator, updated fire-prevention systems (sprinklers), and new wiring, and you are home free. This is known as loft living. They are rented or sold as condominiums; they sell very well in all cities. They are so popular that developers are building them from scratch in new buildings.

# The Not-So-Nice Part of Town

Urban blight—known in the old politically incorrect days as slums—is an unfortunate fact of life in all U.S. cities. Sometimes this is caused by crippling economic and social problems, and only a massive urban campaign including resettlement, education, and commercial investment can cure the problems. But sometimes there are neighborhoods that are in transition. Urban dwellers used to congregate together by race and national origins. There are still today high concentrations of ethnic people and people from the same country.

We are a nation of immigrants, and new immigrants seem to flock together for comfort and help with assimilation. Gradually, all these neighborhoods give way to a new bunch as the established residents expand into other parts of the city more suited to their growing affluence. These neighborhoods represent some interesting opportunities. The dwellings can be upgraded and used to induce the more affluent members of the neighborhood to stay there. Urban dwellers like the city, and not all long for the suburbs and the killer commute. If you can catch the wave of change, you can help keep the more affluent members of the community in place. This will, in turn, spur others into fixing up their homes and remaining in the neighborhood. Before you know it, you will have the same social makeup of the neighborhood existing on a different economic plane. You can line your pockets in the process.

The key to all areas of urban living is services. Each neighborhood needs services to survive. Blight occurs when the neighborhood becomes dangerous for merchants to do business there. If you cannot eat, shop, and find other basic necessities in your neighborhood, you will leave. Before looking at any urban housing for a fixer-upper, make sure the neighborhood services can sustain the people who live there.

> **This Works**
>
> It is most important to spot trends. A neighborhood might look fine, but ask around and find out if it is stable, growing, or shrinking. Look at the services themselves. What price category are the restaurants and shops in? The price ranges will reflect the economic trend of the neighborhood and will be a good indicator of just how far you can push your fixer-upper.

# Urban Renewal

The granddaddy of all fixer-uppers occurs in cities that undertake urban renewal. This is defined by the condemnation and acquisition by the city of all properties within a defined area. The process is relatively simple but costly and time-consuming. It also disrupts the established neighborhoods and changes forever the makeup of that part of the city. Most projects entail the acquisition of the property and resale to developers at a price subsidized by the city. This subsidy is what attracts developers to invest in formerly blighted neighborhoods. It takes years for these new areas to become established, and they are never the same as the neighborhoods they replaced.

Urban renewal tends to take place in the oldest and most run-down parts of cities, most often in areas around port facilities or railroad yards. The renewal process injects new life into these areas, and you can look for viable opportunities on the periphery of the renewal project.

## Opportunities Surrounding Urban Renewal

Peripheral projects come in two categories: temporary and permanent. Temporary projects involve providing services to the people constructing the new projects. Service industries, like restaurants and stores, will make a good living off the rebuilding while it is going on. Most renewal projects take 5 to 10 years to complete, so there is ample time to make a return. People who operate these services will need renovated buildings to work out of, and that is your job. The merchants are going to gamble that the completed project will also create a continued demand for their services as shopping patterns evolve during the redevelopment process.

More permanent opportunities lie in the housing neighborhoods that surround the project. Immediately, people working on the redevelopment project for the duration of the project can be attracted to nearby housing, and as the neighborhood becomes more affluent, fixer-upper projects will abound. Aim to sell your fixer-upper with, or slightly ahead of, the trend.

## The Least You Need to Know

- ◆ The cost and returns on any fixer-upper will vary with the size. In general, in any given area there is more margin in a larger house due to the economies of scale.

- ◆ Bigger, however, does not necessarily mean a better return on dollars invested. Sometimes, a smaller unit in a soon-to-be-fashionable area will pay a better return than a large house in a normal area.

- ◆ Look carefully at urban opportunities because the opportunities are not necessarily as obvious as suburban ones. Buildings in the city tend to look alike from the street, and most often, the opportunities lie on the inside of the building.

- ◆ You should stay in markets that you are familiar with and understand fully. A lack of understanding of the social structure of the neighborhood could cause you to create a finished product that does not fit in.

# Chapter 15

# Multifamily Housing

## In This Chapter

- ◆ Homes in a multifamily environment
- ◆ Apartments: urban and suburban
- ◆ Money and value in commercial deals
- ◆ Converting apartments into condominiums

Multifamily housing is included in the commercial part of this book because, whether new or refit, it requires a commercial-building, management, and leasing-team approach. Even the loans involved are secured from a different class of lender.

Some multifamily homes can be a fixer-upper project as an individual dwelling, and they are handled exactly like any single-family house (as outlined in Chapters 13 and 14), with the added dimension of restrictions imposed by their overall inclusion in the multifamily environment. Types of dwellings included in this category are zero-lot-line and patio homes, duplexes, condominiums, town houses, and co-ops and flats.

The rest of multifamily housing is apartments. These developments start out as commercial land and, unless converted to condominiums, remain a commercial deal. In this chapter, we will cover the differences between each type of dwelling, a refit of an apartment complex, and a conversion of apartments to condominiums.

# The Individual Refit

The reason I have included individual homes in this chapter is that these houses were created as a commercial project. Condos and common-wall dwellings are always constructed in large groups and are funded by commercial lenders. This is similar to a tract housing project, but it's built over a shorter period of time. When seeking to do a fixer-upper on one of these types of homes, you need to know your boundaries and how they pertain to your fixer-upper project within the multifamily environment.

## Zero-Lot-Line or Patio Homes

These types of homes have the following characteristics:

- They share one wall of the dwelling on a property line in common with their neighbor.
- They share the lot line, but the unit walls are not shared in common.
- They are, in reality, freestanding single-family homes.

Typically, these types of homes are constructed on very small lots. Each unit is designed with one ten-foot side yard instead of two five-foot side yards. This allows each unit to have a significant, usable yard.

To repaint your garage, you must go into the neighbor's yard. This is the reason why most of these housing groups are managed like condos. The association will take care of the front yards and the exterior maintenance, with each owner responsible for his or her roof and interior yard. Keep this in mind when you are considering one as a fixer-upper. Your emphasis must be all on the interior like an urban fixer-upper.

## Duplexes

A duplex is two homes in one building sharing a common wall. Normally this wall starts with the garage and proceeds through both homes to the back yard. These units are typically managed by an association, but the individual owners maintain their entire property. If you get involved with a duplex as a fixer-upper, you will have to get permission from your neighbor to make exterior modifications or repaint the home. This might sound easy, but if your neighbor is not inclined to share the expense, you might have to repaint his or her unit at your own expense. Make sure you have the cooperation you need before you buy into one of these units. Get it in writing in the form of an enforceable contract.

# Condominiums

A condominium is more a type of ownership than any particular building style. It is created primarily to manage assets to be owned in common by the homeowners. These assets can take the form of the building itself, such as a high-rise, where the condominium association owns the building, and the residents own "from the wallpaper in." Other assets of common ownership can include grounds, parking, and recreational facilities. Even single-family homes can become condominiums. In the late 1970s, a popular type of development was the cluster development. In this instance, if there were to be four homes to the acre, on 50 acres, the developers clustered all the homes on 35 acres, and left the resulting greenbelt, untouched by development, in common ownership for all the homes.

# Town Houses

Town houses are two-story condominiums, sharing common walls with units on either side. The condominium association generally handles exterior work on these units, including roof repairs. Again, this has much in common with an urban fixer-upper. You will, however, have front and back yards to contend with. Sometimes the association, especially in the more expensive units, will also handle the front yards.

# Flats and Co-ops

These units are designed as urban dwellings and occur only in multistory buildings. Each individual owner owns only from the exterior walls in. One hundred percent of this fixer-upper is internal. This type of dwelling usually undergoes extensive renovation with each change of ownership. It is even possible to buy one unit above another and combine them into one two-story unit. If you decide to tackle one of these, bring plenty of money. This is big-city real estate and is generally in the high six figures as a minimum.

# Apartment Refits

Apartments are truly commercial ventures start to finish. First of all, they are built in fairly significant sizes. The efficiency of management and investment starts at about 80 units and increases dramatically to about 350 units. After that, it levels off and declines a bit. Complexes that are very large are usually in urban settings where very large buildings are the norm. Suburban apartment complexes generally top out at 300 units or so. The low-rise nature of suburban building necessitates a campus design, and large complexes can become very spread out. Refits will vary from suburban to urban, so we will discuss them separately.

# Urban Apartments

These units are generally contained in one large building and are comprised solely of flats. These projects pose a fairly straightforward approach to fixing up. The building exterior, usually brick, is cleaned and *repointed*.

The lobby is refurbished and the elevators updated and redecorated. Services are upgraded such as concierge and delivery services. If there is underground parking, a full-service garage can be added so that the residents can have their autos maintained on-site. This is a very good ploy, but you must have a large complex to entice an operator onto the premises. Inside, you will need to upgrade the corridors as well as the units when the leases come due. Urban apartments are very different than suburban units. The annual tenant turnover tends to be very low. In the suburbs, people rent until they can afford to own, but in the city, due to the high price of owning your own home, many people are lifetime renters.

**Trade Terms**

**Repointing** a brick (or any masonry) wall involves restoring the mortar joints between the bricks to replace the mortar that has eroded over time.

**This Works**

When a tenant vacates an apartment, you are dealing with a new tenant who has no history with the complex and therefore is more amenable to the change in rent. Yes, this is all about the rent. I'll have more about the money later in this chapter.

The old joke that says, "If you need an apartment, check the obituaries and run and talk to the super," is no joke. It is most likely the best way to get a rental in an area you want to live in.

# Suburban Complexes

Suburban complexes require an entirely different approach. The work to be done is much the same, but it also involves an extensive landscaping and parking-lot refit. Because of the turnover in suburban complexes, these refits are much easier than an urban complex to fix up and are easier to make profitable. Urban projects are hampered by the lack of space to store construction materials. Consequently, materials deliveries are scheduled only when the materials to be delivered can be put into place immediately. The scheduler on an urban job is called an expediter, and as most superintendents will tell you, he or she is the most important person on a city construction project site.

Inside the apartments there is most likely very little to do. Each time an apartment tenancy turns over, the carpet is shampooed or replaced, the unit is completely painted, and the appliances are completely serviced. The only approach for a refit is to elevate the quality of the unit by upgrading the decor and appliances. Sometimes, because of demand, units can be reconfigured to larger rooms and less of them. Most likely, however, the interior refit will be simply an upgrade of the amenities and appliances.

Other upgrades will be in the common areas where you can add recreation amenities such as pools, exercise facilities, and better laundry facilities. In complexes with large apartments, you might consider adding washer and dryer units in the apartment units themselves. Most complexes have a washroom for each group of buildings. By adding these inside each apartment, you are making the unit's amenities more like a single-family house.

Large, urban apartments always have a concierge who provides many services such as theater tickets, travel arrangements, babysitters, personal shopping, take-out food, and all the services that urban dwellers take for granted.

# Dollars and Cents

What motivates someone to go through such an extensive fixer-upper? The answer is the same as with the house fixer-upper—the money. The money's impact is different than when you fix up a house and sell it. In that instance, you are taking something below market and elevating it to the market. With income-producing real estate, you are dramatically affecting the cash flow. The cash flow, when capitalized, is what determines the value. In a market where income property changes hands at an 8 percent cap rate, every dollar increase in the net income before debt service results in a corresponding $12.50 increase in value.

How does this work? The following section is an excerpt from Chapter 9 of my book *The Complete Idiot's Guide to Real Estate Investing*.

# Calculating Cap Rates

How do people determine what to pay for a piece of real estate? Most people take the broker's word that the market is at a certain cap rate and let it go at that. For many years, the calculation of capitalization rates has been the purview only of the lender, and most people have gone along with it. You may also be forced to do so because of the market. I believe, however, that you should know how to calculate a cap rate and should do so at least to determine the spread between the asking price and what you think the property is worth. It is also helpful when you are ready to sell the property. A proper cap-rate calculation can help you justify your asking price.

Buildings acquire value by capitalizing the income stream, the net income before debt service (NIBDS, refer to Chapter 8). No one disputes this method, but at the same time, few people understand what a cap rate is and how it operates. Traditionally, a capitalization rate, or "cap rate," is an expression of risk. How is it determined, and who says it is right or reasonable? In financial circles, a cap rate of 10 percent is considered average or optimum. A cap rate over 10 percent denotes a higher than normal risk, while a cap rate under 10 percent indicates less than normal risk. Theoretically, with a cap rate of 10 percent, an income stream of $100,000 per year is worth $1 million. It is calculated as follows:

$100,000 ÷ 0.1 [10%] = $1,000,000

In popular theory, this is considered a reasonable return on capital with a "normal" amount of risk built in to the deal.

But is this, in fact, reasonable?

I say that each individual or entity should determine the relative risk of any deal and its relationship to his or her capital for each deal contemplated. How should this be done? Most people say, if it looks risky, ascribe an 11 to 13 percent cap rate to the deal. If it is really off the wall, go higher. I have never encountered a real estate deal with a 20 percent cap rate, but it might be possible. Several methods are used to come up with a cap rate, but I recommend the following. It's as reliable as any I have seen.

My formula is: C = Y – I; followed by R = Y – (MC)

- ♦ C is a constant or a coefficient

- ♦ Y is your desired yield to equity (cash invested)

- ♦ M is the percentage of loan to value

- ♦ I is the interest rate of the financing

- ♦ R is the resulting cap rate

Let's see how it works. Assume the following:

- ♦ You want to buy a building.

- ♦ There will be a 75 percent new loan in place at closing.

- ♦ The interest rate will be 8.5 percent.

- ♦ You are willing to buy the building *only* if you can yield 13 percent on your capital/equity.

What, then, is the cap rate?

C = Y – I or C = 13 – 8.5

Therefore, C = 4.5

Next: R = Y – (MC) or R = 13 – (.75 × 4.5)

Therefore, R = 13 – 3.38, or 9.62% (cap rate)

The value of the investment to you will be determined by taking the NIBDS and capitalizing it at the rate determined by you to produce the desired yield (the cap rate). This has been calculated to be 9.62 percent.

Over the past 30 years, I have not found a formula that works better, but if you have one, please e-mail it to me for evaluation. No matter how you calculate the risk of buying any specific property, you are always the sole factor in deciding what it is worth to you.

This formula has been discussed at length by the readers of *The Complete Idiot's Guide to Real Estate Investing,* and I must explain that the formula is not intended to be a 100 percent accurate determiner of cap rates. Rather, it's a guide to determine what ballpark you should be in. The dollar difference between an 8 percent cap rate and an 11 percent cap rate can be astounding. If you use this formula, please know that it completely ignores the effect of amortization. You might want to run it with the simple interest rate as well as the *APR*. In the end, you alone will decide what a reasonable cap rate should be based on your assessment of the deal.

Let's take a look at a hypothetical apartment fixer-upper as analyzed by the numbers. To start, we'll take an apartment complex of 100 units with a mix of units and rents as follows:

- ◆ 45 single bedrooms @ $650 per month
- ◆ 50 two-bedroom units @ $800 per month
- ◆ 5 three-bedroom units @ $950 per month

The numbers would look something like the following table.

**Trade Terms**

**APR** is an acronym for the annual percentage rate. The APR is a constant used to calculate your payments at a fixed interest rate so that the payments will be sufficient to pay the interest as well as to amortize 100 percent of the loan principal over the original term of the loan.

## Income Analysis at Acquisition

| Item | Notes | Dollars |
|---|---|---|
| Income | | |
| 45 singles @ $650/mo | ×12 for annual | $351,000.00 |
| 50 doubles @ $800/mo | Same | $480,000.00 |
| 5 triples @ $950/mo | Same | $57,000.00 |
| Gross potential income (GPI) | | $888,000.00 |
| Less vacancy | 5% (normal) | –$44,400.00 |
| Effective gross income (EGI) | GPI – vacancy allowance | $843,600.00 |
| Less operating expenses | Est. @ 43% EGI | –$362,748.00 |
| Net income before debt service (NIBDS) | EGI – operating expenses | $480,852.00 |

The resulting figure of $480,852 is used to determine the value at the time of acquisition. If your assessment of the investment at the time of acquisition is that an appropriate cap rate is 9.25 percent, your acquisition price will be calculated as follows:

$480,852 ÷ .0925 = $5,198,400

Having established the acquisition price, your plan is to elevate these units by a fixer-upper plan to achieve a better rent level for the whole complex. Your plan is to end up with the following rental schedule and income stream:

- 45 singles @ 800 per month

- 50 doubles @ $950 per month

- 5 triples @ $1,100 per month

The financial impact of this is in the following table.

## Income Analysis After Upgrade

| Item | Notes | Dollars |
|---|---|---|
| Income | | |
| 45 singles @ $800/mo | ×12 for annual | $432,000 |
| 50 doubles @ $950/mo | Same | $570,000 |
| 5 triples @ $1,100/mo | Same | $66,000 |

| Item | Notes | Dollars |
|------|-------|---------|
| Gross potential income (GPI) | | $1,068,000 |
| Less vacancy | 5% of GPI | −$53,400 |
| Effective gross income (EGI) | GPI − vacancy | $1,014,600 |
| Less operating expenses | Est. @ 43% EGI | −$436,378 |
| Net income before debt service (NIBDS) | EGI − expenses | $578,222 |

What will be the impact of this rent escalation? The answer is simple. If you have elevated the complex to be a more elegant complex, and it is in a market where it will be readily absorbed, you might also have changed its potential cap rate. Better property commands a better cap rate. If we assume a modest cap rate boost to 8.5 percent, the "fixed-up" value of this apartment refit would be the following:

$$\$578,222 \div .085\% = \$6,802,612$$

Your potential gross sales price increase is then the difference between the two, or $1,604,212. From this analysis, you can determine your budget and game plan to make the conversion. Your budget will be more elaborate than the simple one we had for the house in Chapter 6, but the effect will be the same. Keep in mind that you need to factor in the monthly net income that will be available to you as well. Will this be a good deal? The only person who can answer this question is you. Your budget must be sufficient to make the transition, and your ability to market the complex at the new and improved level will determine the outcome.

It's not as mysterious as you might think. Drive around and look at complexes that are operating at the level you want to reach. If you see what they offer as amenities and look at the apartments, you will be able to make a pretty good judgment. Make your plans, bid it out, and proceed.

# Conversions

Converting apartments into condominiums has been a pretty good deal for many years. Apartments sell for a multiple of earnings or at a capitalized NIBDS, as shown. If you refer to the preceding example, you could buy the apartments for approximately $51,000 per unit, and after refit, you could sell them for approximately $68,000 per unit. If converted, these could potentially sell for up to $100,000 per unit in a good market.

Obviously, these figures are used for the purpose of illustration. You will have to survey your market and find out what flats sell for and if, in fact, there is even a market for this type of unit.

The conversion improvements will be much the same as a serious upgrade, except you will have to make everything like new. Most importantly, the process involves filing a new condominium document with your state's department of real estate as well as a subdivision disclosure document before anything can be sold. There is also the added dimension of easing the tenants out so that you can convert and sell the units.

In the past there have been many successful conversions, so many that people have attempted to convert anything, sometimes unsuccessfully. Today, savvy apartment builders are designing their complexes as condominiums with a view toward selling them off in the future and making more than selling them as apartments. There still exist opportunities for conversion. I believe that the best opportunities lie in the smaller complexes with 50 units or less. These complexes most likely are not doing well as investment properties because they defy the economy of scale. You should be able to purchase them at a better price, and because of the smaller scale, you should be able to sell them for more.

> **Warning, Danger Ahead!**
>
> Prepare yourself ... You will have some holdouts who will not want to move. You might have to buy them out. Check out the law in your state as it relates to your obligations to displaced tenants.

## The Least You Need to Know

- When dealing with single-family units in a multifamily environment, you must know the restrictions.

- Apartments can be real moneymakers because when they are upgraded, the rents can increase dramatically.

- Remember the effect that cap rates have on income. One dollar of net income can be sold for eleven to twelve dollars.

- Condo conversions are another way to fix up apartments. By renovating the apartments to like new status, and filing a condominium form of subdivision on the complex, the apartments can now be sold as condominiums.

# Chapter 16

# Office Buildings

## In This Chapter

◆ Differences with commercial buildings

◆ Building categories

◆ Tenants and floor plates

◆ Pro forma: the financial analysis for a commercial project

Office buildings have been my specialty for over 25 years. The difference between residential and commercial real estate is simply the scale and the tenants. Commercial real estate is primarily designed for tenants, while most households own their dwellings. Also, in general, commercial buildings are much larger than houses. This is just as true when the projects are first developed as it is when you are attempting a fixer-upper.

In this chapter, we will explore the types of buildings, their size, and how this can affect your plans and the types of tenants you attract. In addition, we will touch on the paperwork that differentiates commercial projects from residential ones.

# Commercial Contracts and Agreements

One of the crucial differences that comes into play when dealing with commercial buildings is the contracts and agreements necessary to their creation and ongoing management. For commercial projects, this includes, but is not necessarily limited to, the following documents:

◆ Purchase agreements

◆ Construction contracts

◆ Leases

◆ Loan documents

◆ *Estoppel certificates*

◆ Plans and specifications

◆ Property management agreements

◆ Maintenance agreements

**Trade Terms**

An **estoppel certificate** is a document stating that the tenant is in possession and paying rent, that the lease is in force, and that the landlord is not in default.

Documentation will be discussed in more detail in Chapter 18.

The documentation referred to is necessary for all commercial buildings: office, retail, and industrial. The most important document of all is the commercial lease. The documentation discussed in Chapter 18 can be used for large residential as well as commercial fixer-uppers, depending on the extent of the project. A more in-depth analysis of documentation is contained in *The Complete Idiot's Guide to Real Estate Investing.* The in-depth discussion is due to the fact that if you intend to keep your real property with a view to building a portfolio, documentation becomes a paramount issue when it comes to creating and sustaining value.

**This Works**

At my website, www.riderland.com, you can obtain working copies of the documents discussed in this chapter on a CD-ROM, as well as spreadsheets for all forms of real estate transactions. These documents are not designed to be used as is; rather, they are a place to start for you and your attorney when drafting agreements for a specific transaction. Having a working prototype can save you a lot of attorney time. They are the result of 25 years in the business and serve me well to this day.

# All Types of Buildings

Office buildings come in a variety of shapes and sizes, from high-rises to small, one-tenant buildings. In general, you can break them down into the following categories:

- High-rises and "class A" buildings have more than seven stories. The "class A" refers to high-quality urban buildings. These are most often designed to accommodate large, urban-type tenants.

- Mid-rise buildings are defined as having three to seven stories. The rule for the seven-story maximum is derived from the fire-fighting ability of the local fire department. External access equipment and hook and ladder trucks cannot fight a fire above seven stories. Higher than that, the fire-fighting ability must be engineered into the building, hence the definition of "class A." This causes a considerable cost difference between mid-rise and high-rise, and it justifies the taller building's rent structure.

- Garden offices come in one-, two-, and three-story varieties. From an efficiency and cost-effective standpoint, two-story buildings are the best, with single-story next and three-story last.

- Strip commercial offices occur in converted retail buildings and are not really office buildings. This is the least desirable office space because it has only one window per tenant. The bulk of the office space faces blank interior walls.

- Single-tenant buildings are not good investments unless you have a very credit-worthy tenant on a long-term lease. Too often, these buildings are hard to adapt to another use. If you tackle one as a fixer-upper, I recommend that you have a specific tenant in mind before you start.

> **CAUTION**
>
> **Warning, Danger Ahead!** _____
>
> From a cost-per-square-foot standpoint, one, two, or three stories of office building, constructed over a parking lot or underground parking, is the least cost-effective building in the world. The relative cost for parking doubles when you elevate it and triples when you take the cars underground. If you build over parking the fire prevention code dramatically increases the cost of the building with no commensurate increase in its rental potential.

As a rule of thumb, I feel that the more tenants you have the better, and I do not like any one tenant to occupy more than 10 percent of my building. This is because when buildings are properly leveraged (75–80 percent loan to value), 20 percent of the rent is 100 percent of your cash flow.

When you are dealing with a commercial building at 75 percent loan to value—which is the most common commercial loan—it requires 80 percent of the tenants' net rent to make the mortgage payment. This means that 100 percent of your *cash flow* is tied up in the last 20 percent of your tenants.

**Trade Terms**

**Cash flow** is what is left when you deduct your mortgage payment from the net income before debt service NIBDS. The cash flow determines your return on cash invested. If you take the cash flow and divide it by your cash invested, you will have determined your *cash on cash* return. Further analysis can be done to determine your after-tax yield by factoring in the effect of depreciation as well.

## Floor Plates and Tenancy

Every building is rated for efficiency of design. The gross building area is rendered less efficient by deducting common areas that cannot be leased to anyone. Common areas consist of lobbies, corridors, stairways, elevators, and restrooms. Garden office buildings can be designed to be 98 percent efficient, but most mid- and high-rise buildings are only about 85 percent efficient. Some are even under 80 percent. These common areas have to be amortized or *loaded* onto over the usable tenant spaces and therefore have a dramatic effect on the rent. This makes the low-rise garden office more competitive with the less efficient *loaded* buildings.

**Trade Terms**

**Loading** takes the cost of the common areas and adds it to the square-foot price of the net usable square footage, essentially loading the additional rent onto the base rent. Some buildings require rent plus a load factor as a percentage of the base rent.

The floor area of any building is called the floor plate. The tenant spaces are then designed within the floor plate and, when completed, make up the floor plan for the tenant's demised premises.

**Trade Terms**

**Tenant improvements** are the interior walls, ceilings, lights and electrical systems, floor coverings, doors, and telephone systems that are designed and constructed for the tenant's sole use.

## Tenant Improvements and Salvage

When you tackle an office building fixer-upper, you must survey the existing *tenant improvements* to determine if they are universal enough to refit for incoming tenants.

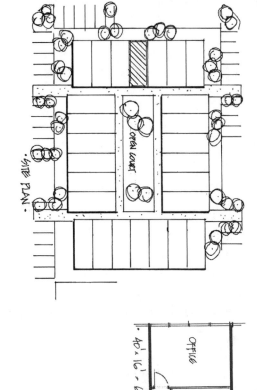

*The building floor plate.*

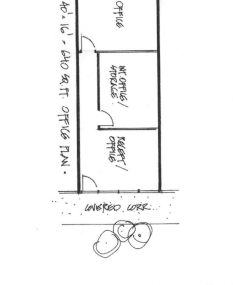

*The tenant floor plan.*

If you determine that a building is full of tiny cubicles, like the office layouts favored by old law firms, you will have to demolish much of this to install a new tenant. You must factor in the cost of both demolition and replacement in your fixer-upper budget. Modern office-tenant improvements range from about $35 per square foot in garden office buildings to about $50 per square foot in mid- and high-rise buildings. Medical buildings can absorb tenant improvements up to $100 per foot.

The list of improvements includes, but is not limited to, the following:

- Demising walls separating one tenant from another
- Entry doors
- Interior walls and finishes
- Interior doors
- Ceiling and lighting
- Power outlets
- Phone and data connections
- Floor coverings
- Wet bars and cabinets

The modern office alternative to intense tenant improvement involves the use of modular partitions that can be moved around. This is called office-scaping, and the costs thereof are born by the tenant because these movable partitions are classed as furniture. If you have a tenant who wants cubicles, tell him he'll have to provide them at his own expense.

Other fixer-upper issues that are common to all types of office buildings are the roof, the mechanical systems, and the parking lot. Make sure you are not purchasing any deferred maintenance in these areas. Examine the site plan to determine the possibility of adding another building by rearranging or double-decking the parking. This might give you a significant boost in profit and annual revenue.

> **Reality Check**
>
> Some years ago, a well-known storage company converted a high-rise building in Houston to a mini-storage building. The company demolished the interior improvements, replaced the passenger elevators with freight elevators, and filled the building overnight. The prime location of this storage building enticed many companies with a need for convenient records storage.

## Old Urban High-Rise Tenants

One of the hardest buildings to deal with is the old urban mid- or high-rise. It is generally rife with functional obsolescence: small lobbies with low ceilings, low ceilings in the corridors and tenant spaces, and run-down mechanical systems. Most likely, the only hope for these buildings in a refit is to determine whether there is the possibility of government tenancy. Most government offices are budget conscious, so an older building with lower rent suits their needs just fine. If you can establish your project as a government building, you should have no trouble keeping it filled. My best advice is to look for this type of building only in areas where you have good access to the centers of government and major transportation corridors. Anywhere else, you need to consider a total change of use.

## The Modern Office Fixer-Upper

Most good fixer-upper opportunities in office buildings will be found in transition areas around cities, on commuter routes to and from the bedroom communities. These buildings will be the ones that have not been modernized to keep competitive with the newer buildings springing up along these transportation corridors. If you find a potential fixer-upper project with no built-in functional obsolescence, you have a commercial lipstick job. Stir in some marketing savvy and you are on your way.

## Tenants, Leases, and Synergy

The key to a good building is a synergistic tenant mix. Medical tenants like to flock together because the building will become known as a medical facility and people will seek it out when they are in need. Other compatible types of mixes are real estate, insurance, title companies, and finance companies. General office uses like to flock together because often employees are interchangeable. Employee turnover is a significant expense for many companies. Often people will job hop within the same building.

## Floor Plates and Tenant Mix

The size of a building's floor plate will determine the size of your tenants. The most critical dimension is the distance from the entry point to the tenant's suite to the outside window wall. Buildings that can accommodate small tenants rarely exceed 40 feet in that dimension. Anything over 60 feet is strictly for very large tenants.

With only one exception, every office building I have developed has confined the floor space to 40 feet, and these buildings today command a waiting list for available space. The smaller the

**This Works**

Companies across the country are downsizing, so I recommend that you confine your fixer-upper efforts to buildings that can handle smaller tenants. At a dimension of 40 feet, you can lease someone a suite 16 feet wide and can take a tenant as small as 640 square feet. This size is perfect for the one- or two-person office.

tenant size, the more tenants you can have in the building. The more tenants you have in your building, the better the security for your investment. If a small tenant moves out, all you have to do is steam clean the carpet, paint the walls, and move another tenant in. Large tenants take too big a bite out of your cash flow when they move out.

If you tackle a building with some sizeable tenants, when they move, replace them with several smaller tenants. This will steer your building to a healthier tenant mix. This is especially vital if you decide to keep the building. From an economic perspective, look over the marketplace and select a rental niche that looks to be relatively vacancy free. Set up your building's economic goals to fall within this niche, and you too should enjoy a full building.

# The Pro Forma: Doing the Numbers

The financial analysis for a commercial project is referred to as the pro forma. It is a two-part document that consists of a cost breakdown and an income-and-expense projection. For the purposes of acquisition, you will run a quick-and-dirty, one-page version as shown briefly in Chapter 15 for an apartment conversion. For a commercial project, it will look something like the following.

The income-and-expense estimate is designed to be a snapshot of the project at completion of the construction and lease-up. The expanded versions that follow are intended to be a much more accurate rendering of the project over the timeframe of its construction and lease-up. You also need to look at the income side over a five-year period.

The following are the full-blown versions, expanded from the one-page, quick-and-dirty versions mentioned previously. The documents included here are for a 35,000-square-foot office building, but they can be adapted for any fixer-upper.

| LAND | Estimated Budget | % Of Total |
|---|---|---|
| Land | $588,060.00 | 16.11% |
| Closing Costs | $10,500 | 0.29% |
| Assessments | $7,500 | 0.21% |
| **TOTAL LAND** | **$606,060** | **16.60%** |

| SOFT COSTS | | |
|---|---|---|
| A&E | $120,000 | 3.29% |
| Engineering | Inc Above | #VALUE! |
| Survey / Staking / Testing | $20,000 | 0.55% |
| Marketing Consultant | $10,000 | 0.27% |
| Leasing Commissions @ $3.00 / SF | $105,000 | 2.88% |
| Insurance / Taxes / Legal / Acctg. | $15,000 | 0.41% |
| Governmental Permits | $15,000 | 0.41% |
| Development Overhead | $105,000 | 2.88% |
| Loan Points  $1,300,000 @ 2 Points Constr. 1 Point Perm. | $78,000 | 2.14% |
| Interest @ 10% (1/2 outstanding for 6 mos) | $70,000 | 1.92% |
| Misc. & Contingencies | $20,000 | 0.55% |
| **TOTAL SOFT COSTS** | **$558,000** | **15.29%** |

| HARD COSTS | | |
|---|---|---|
| Landscape Area 40,000 SF @ $2.00 | $80,000 | 2.19% |
| Paved Areas 64,000 SF @ $2.25 | $144,000 | 3.94% |
| Building Shell @ $32.00 / SF, 40,000 SF | $1,280,000 | 35.06% |
| Tenant Allowance @ $25.00 /SF, 35,000 SF | $875,000 | 23.97% |
| Taxes | $107,471 | 2.94% |
| **TOTAL HARD COSTS** | **$2,486,471** | **68.11%** |

| **TOTAL PROJECT** | **$3,650,531** | **100.00%** |
|---|---|---|

Notes:

| Funding Analysis After lease-up. | During Construction |
|---|---|
| Construction Loan @ 80% of Cost Maximum conserv est. | $2,600,000 |
| Investor's Initial Equity requirement | $1,050,531 |
| Total Available Dollars | $3,650,531 |

*The one-page cost breakdown.*

Leasable space 35,000 SF with rent escalation annual @ 5%

Operating Period

| INCOME | NOTES | Year 1 |
|---|---|---|
| Gross Potential Income [GPI] @ 100% Occupancy @ $14.00 / SF | | $490,000.00 |
| Vacancy Allowance @ 5% | Per Lender's allowance | -$24,500.00 |
| Effective Gross Income [EGI] | Projected net | $465,500.00 |
| | | |
| CAM EXPENSES | All Leases are NNN | |
| Real estate Taxes | Projected until first assessment | $48,000.00 |
| Maintenance/Repair/HVAC | Budgeted | $3,600.00 |
| Insurance fire / liability | Bid | $14,400.00 |
| Elect | Estimated | $7,200.00 |
| Water & Sewer | Estimated | $4,800.00 |
| Refuse | Bid | $1,200.00 |
| Janitorial | Bid | $31,200.00 |
| Windows / sweeping | Bid | $4,800.00 |
| Security | Bid | $8,640.00 |
| Pest Control on demand | Estimated | $1,800.00 |
| Yard Maint & Common Area | Bid | $4,800.00 |
| Subtotal | | $130,440.00 |
| Management Fee @ 10% exp. | Based upon expenses only per lease | $13,044.00 |
| | | |
| Total Common Area | | $143,484.00 |
| | | |
| Tenant reimbursed CAM | Based on 95% occupancy | $136,309.80 |
| | | |
| landlords Expense | For Vacant Space | -$7,174.20 |
| | | |
| Net Income [NIBDS] | Before Debt service | $458,325.80 |
| | | |
| Less Mortgage Payment | Based upon estimated loan | |
| Principal & Interest | 2.8 M @ 8% 30 years | -$229,060.00 |
| CASH FLOW | Return on Investor's Equity | $229,265.80 |
| % Return on Invested capital | Annual ROI | 22.03% |

*The one-page income-and-expense projection.*

| | Estimated Budget | Pre Construction | To Date | Current Month | At Closing | TOTALS |
|---|---|---|---|---|---|---|
| **LAND** | | | | | | |
| Land 1.67 Acres 72745 SF | $364,640 | $14,000 | $14,000 | | $350,640 | $378,640 |
| Closing Costs | $9,500 | | | | $3,500 | $3,500 |
| Assessments | $7,500 | | | | $7,500 | |
| **TOTAL LAND** | **$381,640** | **$14,000** | **$14,000** | **$0** | **$361,640** | **$382,140** |
| | | | | | | |
| **SOFT COSTS** | | | | | | |
| A&E | $60,000 | $44,000 | $571 | | $16,000 | $60,571 |
| Engineering | Inc. Above | | | | | |
| Survey / Staking / Testing | $7,500 | $2,500 | $0 | | $5,000 | $7,500 |
| Leasing Commissions @ $3.00 / SF | $48,000 | $18,072 | $1,197 | | $29,928 | $49,197 |
| Insurance / Taxes / Legal / Acctg. | $7,000 | $2,000 | $0 | | $5,000 | $7,000 |
| Governmental Permits | $10,000 | $3,500 | $85 | | $6,500 | $10,085 |
| Development Overhead | $40,000 | | | | | |
| Loan Points $1,300,000 @ 3 Points | $39,000 | $28,000 | $0 | | $11,000 | $39,000 |
| Interest @ 10% (1/2 outstanding for 6 mos) | $35,000 | $0 | $0 | | $35,000 | $35,000 |
| Misc. & Contingencies | $10,000 | $3,500 | $1,434 | | $6,500 | $11,434 |
| **TOTAL SOFT COSTS** | **$256,500** | **$101,572** | **$3,287** | **$0** | **$114,928** | **$219,787** |
| | | | | | | |
| **HARD COSTS** | | | | | | |
| Landscape Area 19,025 SF @ $2.00 | $38,000 | $0 | $0 | | $38,000 | $38,000 |
| Paved Areas 31,710 SF @ $2.25 | $72,000 | $0 | $0 | | $72,000 | $72,000 |
| Building Shell @ $32.00 / SF, 20,000 SF | $630,000 | $0 | $19,530 | | $630,000 | $649,530 |
| Tenant Allowance @ $25.00 /SF, 16,064 SF | $400,000 | $0 | $0 | | $400,000 | $400,000 |
| Taxes | $33,430 | $0 | $0 | | $33,430 | $33,430 |
| **TOTAL HARD COSTS** | **$1,173,430** | **$0** | **$19,530** | **$0** | **$1,173,430** | **$1,192,960** |
| | | | | | | |
| **TOTAL PROJECT** | **$1,811,570** | **$115,572** | **$36,817** | **$0** | **$1,649,998** | **$1,794,887** |
| Notes: | | A | + | | B | = Cost |

| Funding Analysis After lease up. | During Construction | Pre Construction Cash Requirement | | Maximum Constr. Loan @ 80% of Cost | Maximum Takeout @ 75 % Of Value |
|---|---|---|---|---|---|
| Construction Loan @ 80% of Cost Maximum conserv est. | $1,300,000 | | | $1,449,256 | $1,300,000 |
| Investor's Initial Equity requirement | $511,570 | $115,572 | | $362,314 | $511,570 |
| Total Available Dollars | $1,811,570 | | $152,389 | $1,811,570 | $1,811,570 |

*A detailed cost breakdown.*

| INCOME | NOTES | Operating Period Year 1 | Year 2 | Year 3 | Year 4 |
|---|---|---|---|---|---|
| Leasable space 16,000 sf with rent escalation annual @ 5% | | | | | |
| Gross Potential Income [GPI] | At 100 % Occupancy @ $14.00 / sf | $224,000.00 | $235,200.00 | $246,960.00 | $259,308.00 |
| Vacancy Allowance @ 5% | Per Lender's allowance | -$11,200.00 | -$11,760.00 | -$12,348.00 | -$12,965.40 |
| Effective Gross Income [EGI] | Projected net | $212,800.00 | $223,440.00 | $234,612.00 | $246,342.60 |
| CAM EXPENSES | All neases are NNN | | | | |
| Real estate Taxes | Projected until first assessment | $24,000.00 | $25,200.00 | $26,460.00 | $27,783.00 |
| Maintenance/Repair/HVAC | Budgeted | $1,800.00 | $1,890.00 | $1,984.50 | $2,083.73 |
| Insurance fire / liability | Bid | $6,612.00 | $6,942.60 | $7,289.73 | $7,654.22 |
| Elect | Estimated | $3,600.00 | $3,780.00 | $3,969.00 | $4,167.45 |
| Water & Sewer | Estimated | $2,400.00 | $2,520.00 | $2,646.00 | $2,778.30 |
| Refuse | Bid | $600.00 | $630.00 | $661.50 | $694.58 |
| Janitorial | Bid | $15,600.00 | $16,380.00 | $17,199.00 | $18,058.95 |
| Windows / sweeping | Bid | $2,400.00 | $2,520.00 | $2,646.00 | $2,778.30 |
| Security | Bid | $4,320.00 | $4,536.00 | $4,762.80 | $5,000.94 |
| Pest Control on demand | Estimated | $900.00 | $945.00 | $992.25 | $1,041.86 |
| Yard Maint & Common Shea | Bid | $2,400.00 | $2,520.00 | $2,646.00 | $2,778.30 |
| Subtotal | | $64,632.00 | $67,863.60 | $71,256.78 | $74,819.62 |
| Management Fee @ 10% exp. | Bases upon expenses only per lease | $6,463.20 | $6,786.36 | $7,125.68 | $7,481.96 |
| Total Common Area | | $71,095.20 | $74,649.96 | $78,382.46 | $82,301.58 |
| Tenent reimbursed CAM | Bases on 95% occupancy | $67,540.44 | $70,917.46 | $74,463.34 | $78,186.50 |
| landlords Expense | For Vacant Space | -$3,554.76 | -$3,732.50 | -$3,919.12 | -$4,115.08 |
| Net Income [NIBDS] | Before Debt service | $209,245.24 | $219,707.50 | $230,692.88 | $242,227.52 |
| Less Mortgage | Based upon estimatred loan 1.3 M @ 8% 30 years | -$103,311.00 | -$103,311.00 | -$103,311.00 | -$103,311.00 |
| CASH FLOW | Return on Investor's Equity | $105,934.24 | $116,396.50 | $127,381.88 | $138,916.52 |

*A detailed cost breakdown. A detailed income-and-expense projection.*

## The Least You Need to Know

- Office projects can be a great deal because commercial property has a ready market for good product at recognizable cap rates.

- Choose your project on a major transportation corridor so that the visibility and accessibility will make your remodel stand out to the marketplace.

- Avoid buildings with functional obsolescence; it is almost impossible to correct economically.

- Try to fill your building with small tenants so that no one tenant can control your cash flow. Fully leveraged, 20 percent of the building represents 100 percent of your cash flow.

# Shopping Centers

## In This Chapter

- ◆ The retail business and markets
- ◆ Single-user buildings and strip centers
- ◆ Commercial strip buildings
- ◆ Neighborhood and community centers
- ◆ Regional malls and their impact

Shopping centers come in a variety of shapes and sizes, but whatever the configuration, the most important aspect of this type of commercial real estate is the tenant mix. Each type of center serves a different demographic profile. Retail buildings can be freestanding, single-user buildings, or large mall complexes with hundreds of tenants. For the fixer-upper, the single most important aspect of any project is the tenant (or tenants, as the case may be).

In most instances, the retail building fixer-upper is mostly cosmetic and is often confined to the exterior of the building. Most of us refer to this as a face-lift. Interior spaces are the tenants' responsibility, and when you modernize and refit a center, you will want to encourage your tenants to do the same for their interior decor.

A successful retail fixer-upper will add a demonstrable useful life to the building and at the same time will give the tenants' retail sales a real shot in the arm. Here we will examine the different types of retail center, their tenants, and their role in the marketplace. A retail center is more mercantile entity than real estate. Synergy between tenants will provide the magic to attract the buying public.

# Retail Markets

The most important aspects of a multitenant retail building are the public's reaction to the center and the viability of the tenant mix. The before and after photos that follow are of a strip center. This remodel was cosmetic, but it enabled the landlord to upgrade the tenancy when the leases turned over. The rejuvenated center has an increased economic viability of an additional 10 to 15 years.

*The retail center before renovation.*

Retail centers, from strip centers to regional malls, serve separate needs and market segments.

**Strip centers** feed strictly off the traffic going by the front door. A daily traffic count of 30,000 vehicles is considered sufficient for a good strip center. The types of tenants you can expect in these centers are those who cater to very convenient impulse items. They include, but are not limited to, the following uses:

- Gas stations and car washes

- Convenience stores (such as Circle K or 7-11)

- Dry cleaners

- Coffee shops

- Video rentals

- Auto repair

- Drug stores

*The retail center after renovation.*

**Neighborhood shopping centers** need a resident population of at least 15,000 people within a 3-mile radius to survive. Today's larger megastores will try to stretch even farther to justify the extra square footage. These centers used to be about 120,000 square feet, but now they go up to 160,000 square feet in size. The most common uses are as follows:

- Supermarkets

- Drug stores

- Banks

- Restaurants

- Dry cleaners

- Small electronics stores

- Hardware stores

- Sandwich shops

- Fast-food retailers

- Mail forwarders and postal stores

- Boutiques

**Community centers** are hybrid neighborhood centers that serve a market area up to 10 miles and a population hopefully between 30,000 to 100,000 people. They feature all the uses listed under neighborhood centers plus perhaps a discount store or a junior department store.

**Power centers** are large discount centers that contain the nation's growing list of discount stores and serve a population of 200,000 or more within a 20-mile radius. They can be as large as one million square feet or more. Typical tenants include, but are not limited to, the following:

- Sporting goods (The Sports Authority)

- Home supply (Home Depot or Lowe's)

- Furniture (The Room Store)

- Discount electronics (Best Buy or Circuit City)

- Theatres (AMC Theatres)

- Food courts and freestanding restaurants

- Hobby shops and craft stores (CraftMart)

- Tire stores (Big O Tires)

- Discount department stores (Target, Costco, or Sam's Club)

- Import stores (Cost Plus World Market)

- Shoe stores (Designer Shoe Warehouse)

**Regional malls** are the largest of the shopping complexes and contain top-of-the-line retail merchandise. They are the high-priced end of the shopping experience and cater to variety and service. The newest malls are anchored by six or more major department stores and contain hundreds of other national retail stores. The targeted consumer is getting younger each year and more affluent. In addition, there is an increasing trend toward entertainment in these malls. Even the restaurants are becoming more entertainment oriented. (Have you been to The Rainforest Café lately?)

Any and all of these retail types of complexes can lend themselves to the redeveloper/fixer-upper entrepreneur.

# The Leasing Company

Filling up these centers in the beginning and keeping them full is the job of the commercial leasing agent. There are some major companies that work coast to coast as well as some good regional companies. These companies deal exclusively in commercial space, and they are vital to your success as a fixer-upper of retail centers. You can find them listed in your yellow pages under commercial real estate. Get to know some of the agents well because they will be a permanent part of your team.

# Single-Tenant Buildings

These buildings occur in varying locations around the country. They are as small as the old corner gas station and as large as a decommissioned box store. You will see, with increasing frequency, the empty box store as the discounters jockey for position in the marketplace.

Some of these buildings are simply torn down and replaced by a new building, but there are opportunities to remodel and gain a new tenant. The most significant asset of a retail building is generally its location. Because of the nature of retail buildings, they must be on well-traveled roads and have a high degree of visibility and accessibility. You will find gas stations that have been converted into dry cleaners, liquor stores, and even offices.

---

### Reality Check

Eighteen months ago, one of my tenants, a Canadian discount electronics retailer called Future Shop, decided to pull out of the American market. The decision to close its stores necessitated a new tenant in my center. Working with Future Shop and the brokerage community, we were able to substitute Best Buy as the new tenant. The renovations took four months, and we were back in business without any loss of rent. The center has enjoyed a better acceptance due to the change.

A challenging opportunity for the single-use building is the empty box store. If you can find another discount-type tenant that needs space, all you have to do is alter the entry of the building and change the signs. It is when you cannot find a substitute tenant that you must become innovative. I have seen several of these buildings converted into flea markets and several split between two tenants, and the two-tenant split would be my recommendation. The only renovation needed in this instance is a redo of the storefronts to install the tenants' entry and signage. The major part of this, or any other retail fixer-upper, will be the leasing.

# Strip Centers

These centers are everywhere, and they come in two varieties, anchored and unanchored. An anchored center has a good-credit, national tenant that provides the draw, and the rest of the tenants feed off of this draw. If you decide to tackle one of these centers, the single most important aspect of the center is that it must be well located on a high-traffic street and be easy to get into and out of. If the center you are looking at meets these criteria, you should have no trouble in getting and keeping good tenants. This type of center is not often available unless the area is rundown or there has been a major shift in the traffic pattern. If this has occurred, you must explore the possibility of alternative tenancy.

In a secondary location, retail space can be leased to viable service-office tenants like insurance and real estate offices. Again, most of the refit will be cosmetic on the exterior, with the exception of possible roof and mechanical-system refurbishing. These buildings lend themselves well to a remodel because the canopy and storefront are cosmetic to begin with and, in most cases, are structurally independent of the main building. Again, leasing is the key to commercial refits.

# Neighborhood Centers

This is the bread-and-butter shopping center for retail developers. It most often contains a major supermarket, a drug store, a bank, and several pad buildings, as well as some in-line, local tenants. A well-located neighborhood center is a great long-term investment. The most common fixer-upper versions of this type of center today revolve around expanding the supermarket building and replacing the drug-store tenant. The current trend in drug stores is to be smaller and freestanding. They are candidates for well-located empty commercial buildings in the 20,000-square-foot range. They must be able to install a drive-through prescription window, or they will not take the location. The supermarkets are expanding up to 70,000 square feet and larger as the competition gets keener. If you cannot accommodate your supermarket's expansion needs, you will most likely lose it at renewal time. The project to look for, therefore, is a center with expansion potential where the supermarket has only a short time left on the lease. Have your deal inked with the supermarket before you proceed with the purchase.

As is the case with most things in real estate, you must buy it right. Don't forget that you make your money when you buy. Most owners of this kind of center are people who are in the business of owning and operating commercial real estate, so a center with expansion and fixer-upper potential will not be easy to find. More than likely, the only opportunity for something like this will be an estate sale or a one-of-a-kind situation in a small town. Small towns that are experiencing a spurt of growth will attract new stores and centers. You might find one of the older ones with some expansion capability, owned by someone who is unable or unwilling to expand and redevelop the center. Again, have your major tenant deal made before you roll the dice. Without it, you might find yourself with a large vacancy in the center when the lease runs out.

---

### Reality Check

A challenging opportunity is sometimes encountered in a relatively new center. I know of one where the local residents boycotted a center that was new. The supermarket operator got discouraged and closed the doors. The tenant continues to pay rent, but because of the lack of a major draw, the rest of the tenants are suffering and going out of business. One had an escape clause in its lease relating to the lack of a supermarket tenant and consequently was able to terminate the lease and move out. This left the center with two major tenants dark. This is both a major problem and a major opportunity. Whoever turns this one around will make a lot of money. So far, the current owners have refused all offers to purchase, and after 18 months in this condition, the owners tell me that they have a new supermarket signed, and all will soon be well.

---

# Community Centers

A hybrid of the neighborhood center is the community center. These centers in the past have contained a small department store (or a similar store) as well as the normal neighborhood centers. Today, they are getting much more interesting and seem to be making a change of tenancy to include both normal retail stores as well as discount stores. This changing trend seems to suggest that you could find a neighborhood center with expansion capabilities and, with the right location, create a community center that combines traditional and discount retail. A partial list of potential tenants (by type of store) would look something like this:

- Stationery and office supplies (Staples, Office Depot, OfficeMax)

- Discount pet stores (PetsMart or PetCo)

- Novelty or specialty stores (Marshall's or Michael's)

- Furniture stores (Levitz or Home Place)

- Sporting goods (Popular Outdoor Outfitters)

- Shoe stores (Payless Shoes)

- Specialty dress stores (Ross)

- Import stores (Pier One)

- Linen supplies (Linens & Things)

- Household specialty stores (Crate & Barrel or Restoration Hardware)

- Specialty restaurants and brew pubs (Gordon Biersch)

**This Works**

One of the benefits of the community center fixer-upper is that it is seen as trendy, and there are many buyers around for this type of product. Cap rates seem to vary from 8 to 9.25 percent.

The list goes on and on, and new tenants are being created to meet the demand. I recommend trying to attract established tenants so that their name recognition can work as a draw for your project. If you take a traditional neighborhood center and add a new facade and a couple of jazzy new tenants, you could really create a viable long-term investment out of a stodgy neighborhood center (see the following photo).

*A trendy community center.*

# Box Stores

What we are finding, especially in the western part of the country, is a proliferation of empty box stores. A recent article in the Phoenix, Arizona, paper spoke of two million square feet of this type of vacancy in Arizona. This sounds ominous, but you must realize that this represents approximately 18 to 25 empty stores. The market is one in which three million square feet of retail space is added annually.

As I mentioned earlier in this chapter, these stores are most marketable to new users in the same discount environment. If they are free-standing, you might have a rough time finding a new tenant, but if your building is part of a larger retail facility, like a discount or power center, there are many potential users to talk to. The trick is to find one the right size so that the new tenant can take the whole building. Some innovators are leasing out the front half to a new retailer and converting the back half into office or storage space. You could even create a mini-warehouse in the rear of the building.

> **Reality Check**
>
> In reality, anything larger than a small strip center is the beat of the professional redeveloper. You will not want to get involved in something like a box store or regional mall without some good experience in commercial leasing.

# Regional Malls

At the top of the heap of all real estate investments and potential fixer-uppers are the regional malls. These centers are defined as having at least four department store anchor tenants, a host of national chain-store tenants, as well as a smattering of well-healed local merchants. Lately, I have seen a trend of fixing these up as well as changing the overall tenant mix toward more entertainment uses.

A fixer-upper budget for this type of project could easily top $100 million, so you will not find any amateurs in this field. In fact, there are only a double handful of companies in the country that deal in this type of real estate. They are fun to watch, and the new centers are more fun to shop in and seem to be very well received by the general public. Because of the changing nature of retail shopping today, you will have to find your opportunities in areas that feed off of these centers. In the last 20 years, most regional malls have been located at major freeway intersections or off ramps and have been designed as the center of a complex mix of separate commercial properties connected by concentric ring roads.

# Peripheral Opportunities

Ring roads have spawned a multitude of uses that attempt to feed off the regional mall draw. Many of these buildings are one-of-a-kind, and many are potentially reusable. There is no dearth of potential tenants who would like a chance to try to capitalize on this proven draw. These peripheral uses experience high turnover and provide plenty of opportunity for an entrepreneur with a little vision and cash to spend. Pitch-and-putt miniature golf can be converted into water slides or drive-in theatres. Retail buildings can be converted into offices or mini-storage. The ideas are endless. Exercise your imagination.

## The Least You Need to Know

♦ Retail fixer-uppers are not for amateurs. A retail center of any size is more a mercantile entity than a real estate deal. Make sure you understand the synergy between tenants.

♦ Find a good commercial broker and pay them well. This will help you find and sign the right mix of tenants.

♦ Look for expansion potential so that you can lower your overall costs per square foot of lease space.

♦ Don't overlook conversion potential. There are many buildings that can be converted to retail structures.

♦ Ask yourself, "Is the land worth more empty?" This will tell you whether to remodel or demolish and start over.

# Part 4

# Control Your Project

Profit is defined as what is left over after you have paid the bills. To arrive at a profitable project, you must have a plan. The single most important part of your plan is the budget and the plan to which it pertains. The budget alone is not enough, however. You must control the process to ensure that the budget is followed, not exceeded. Documentation will give you the tools to make sure the budget is doable, realistic, and enforceable.

# Chapter 18

# Documentation

## In This Chapter

- ◆ The purchase agreement and ownership documents
- ◆ Understanding leases
- ◆ Setting up consultants and governmental requirements
- ◆ Permits and loan documents
- ◆ Site improvements, utilities, and the environment
- ◆ Construction and permanent loans
- ◆ Contracts with management

Contracts, more than any other documents involved in entrepreneurial real estate, in all their various forms, determine the cash value of the commercial investment. The process of fixing up a building is almost the same as developing the building in the first place. In essence, you are redeveloping the building. When you purchase and own investment property, it means you are embarking on a process of continuous redevelopment throughout the period of your ownership. All three stages of a building—development, refit, and continuous redevelopment—are intended to be profitable in their own right. One action is as entrepreneurial and financially viable as the other.

As is the case with most documentation, this chapter will be a little windy; however, it is important to your financial well-being, so read it carefully! Remember that although all documents, plans, specs, and contracts are vital in one way or another, the final executed leases will become the primary determination of present and future value.

# Documentation Requirements and Goals

All project documents should be drafted with a view to them being enforceable, inter-related, and self-referencing. Try avoiding conflicts within the overall documentation structure. If this is accomplished, you will have a complete, necessary, and vital set of tools with which to create your final investment objectives.

At a minimum, the set of documents required for the average commercial fixer-upper project will include the following:

◆ The purchase agreement and joint escrow instructions

◆ Ownership documents such as articles of incorporation or organization or partnership agreements

◆ Exclusive leasing agreement

◆ The project lease

◆ All governmental approval documents, including (but not limited to) the entitlement documentation applications as well as approvals

◆ Building permits and occupancy permits

◆ Construction loan documents

◆ Permanent loan documents

◆ General construction contracts and site improvement contracts

◆ Architectural and engineering contracts

◆ The property management agreement

It sounds like a tall order and probably expensive. The truth of the matter is that these documents can vary from a simple 1-page agreement for leasing out an apartment to a 200-page government lease for the Department of Energy (DOE). Depending on the project, the documentation will find its own level of

**Warning, Danger Ahead!**

Be prepared for large tenants to have large legal departments that like long, complex leases. They also will probably have no real appreciation for your deadlines. Sometimes it can seem as if they like to jerk your chain; oftentimes, it is their strategy.

complexity. Generally, the smaller and more rural the project, the more basic the documentation. Large, sophisticated, urban projects require complex and detailed documentation. Common guidelines run through all documents to make them both legal and enforceable.

All real property contracts come into being from the guideline of the statute of frauds. The initiator of these documents is you, and the midwife is your attorney. It is the very proliferation of attorneys that will often dictate the level of documentation. If neither party to an agreement can afford an attorney, it will become a very simple and easily understood document. As more attorneys are introduced into the mix, the document starts to grow. The big trick for the fixer-upper is to have a sufficient level of documentation and no more. Too much or too little can cause real problems.

# The Purchase Agreement

The practical aspects of this document were covered in Chapter 5, but there are basic areas that need to be addressed. In most situations, when dealing with small projects with unsophisticated sellers, it may be prudent to use a local Realtor's® standard, preprinted purchase form with an addendum addressing specific concerns for the site.

In most instances, I recommend that you develop a purchase agreement that can be used in all situations. That way, you know the document well. Understanding a document and its built-in cross-references will enable you to more effectively negotiate the final document. The attorney's favorite trick for creating tools with which to manage a document is to create cross-references and linked conditions. This enables the insertion of conditions that are interlocked and, therefore, less obvious to the seller. This sounds devious, but it is accepted practice for most legal documentation.

**This Works**

I favor a document that tells the seller in plain English what I'm up to and that lays out the schedule, the contingencies, and the price and terms I'm willing to pay for his or her accommodation. Slipping one over on him or her in the document negotiation process will not go over well in the long run.

The following basic information needs to be included in the document:

+ The legal description of the land

+ The size of the land and how it will be determined

+ The price

+ Schedule of payments and close of escrow

- Seller's and buyer's representations
- The designated escrow holder or title company
- Seller's scope of work and the permitted timeframes
- Buyer's scope of work and related timeframes
- Contingencies and how the deposits are treated
- Buyer's and seller's recourse
- Default provisions
- Governing law and miscellaneous provisions

Any attorney worth his or her salt can flesh out an agreement to include many more items, but the preceding provisions will get the job done.

# Ownership Documents

If you have decided to go it alone, this section can be skipped. If, however, there will be two or more people involved in the ownership entity, the decision as to the type of ownership has to be made. The popular choices have already been covered previously in this book, but each form of ownership has a different set of required documents.

## Agreements Between the Parties

The first document is the detailed agreement of the parties, and it is a private document among the parties. These include stockholder agreements, partnership agreements, or operating agreements. These documents amount to the same thing regardless of the form of ownership. They spell out why the venture was formed, its intent, who is involved, how it is capitalized, who is authorized to do what, how control is exercised, who gets what and when, how to resolve disputes, and, finally, how to terminate the agreement. Only the corporation has an indeterminate age. The longevity of both the partnership and the LLC is finite but is extendable at the election of the partners or members.

The second document is a public document, and it must be filed with the state and recorded in the public record so that the public knows who is involved and who is empowered to act on behalf of the ownership entity. This document takes the form of the sections that follow.

## Articles of Incorporation

This is a short form of a corporation's stockholders' agreement, and it simply puts the public on notice that a corporation has been formed. It outlines the basic facts such as the name of the corporation, its date of formation, its principle place of business, its incorporators, their addresses, and in the event of legal notice being required, the name of the agent for service. The document must list the corporate officers so that the public knows who is empowered to act on behalf of the corporation. Other specific information required by individual states will also be included. If the corporation is going to be doing business in other states, it must file "foreign corporation" operating notices in each state where it intends to do business.

## The Partnership Agreement

A partnership must file a statement of partnership for both general and limited partnerships. Like articles of incorporation, this statement outlines who the general partners are, their addresses, the partnership's principle place of business, and all of the same information required of the corporation. It is not necessary to reveal who the limited partners are in the case of a limited partnership.

## Articles of Organization

Articles of organization are filed for limited liability companies, providing the same information required of corporations and partnerships, as well as the method of management elected by the members and the identity of the managing member(s). Legally, they are treated for public liability purposes as corporations, and for tax purposes they are treated like partnerships.

# The Exclusive Leasing Agreement

This document employs the leasing agent (broker) to act on behalf of the owners to represent the property to prospective tenants.

The contract should outline the duration of the agreement, the compensation, and when the compensation is paid, generally half upon execution of the lease and half upon the tenant's commencement of payment of the rent. It should also spell out the duties and obligations of both agent and owner and remedies upon default by either party.

| Reality Check |
| --- |
| Always remember that without tenants, there is no project, and without a good marketing agent, there will be no tenants. |

If incentives are offered, they should be spelled out here; statements regarding how and when they are earned and paid should also be included. As with all contracts, the general provisions, or "boilerplate," regarding governing law, genders, severability, lawful intent, and more must be included. It is the attorney's job to make sure the agreements are sufficient to enforce your intent and spell out the leasing agent's obligations.

# The Project Lease

The executed leases will be the most important single factor in the determination of the cash value of the project, both initially and in the future. This document, above all, must be done properly. It embodies the financial purpose of the project. Get it right!

In the past, most leases fell into three classes:

- Gross leases include the rent and 100 percent of operating expenses and taxes.

- Modified gross or modified net leases include some of the expenses but not all.

- Net (triple net or *NNN*) are leases where, in addition to the rent, the tenant is responsible for 100 percent of the operating expenses and taxes that pertain to the tenant's space.

There were and are so many variations of lease documents that it can be confusing. The true gross lease includes all the operating costs of the building, and the truly net lease includes none of the operating costs. Many of these old, confusing leases are still in force. If you are buying existing real property, the leases need to be carefully examined for their true economic impact on the cash flow.

**Trade Terms**

An **NNN** lease is also known as a triple net lease, which is rent that excludes absolutely all operating expenses. These expenses are billed to the tenant pro rata as additional rent.

For today's leased buildings, the choice should be either a gross or NNN lease. The terms of the lease should be clearly defined so that the gross lease's rent includes all costs of building operation except personal property taxes, for which the tenant may be responsible. The NNN lease, which includes none of the operating costs of the building, requires the tenant to pay as "additional rent" its pro rata share of the building's common area maintenance (CAM) charges, taxes, and insurance.

# Operating Expenses

Typical CAM charges include the following items, pro rated over the number of square feet of leasable space: water, power for the common areas, landscape maintenance, window washing, parking lot sweeping and snow removal where appropriate, janitorial, HVAC maintenance, general repairs except structural, and management costs (typically 10 percent of CAM costs).

The form of lease document chosen depends on your level of experience, the type of building involved, the custom of the industry within the building's market, and the ability of the leasing broker to sell the chosen document. Arguments can be made for and against both types of lease. Personally, I use the NNN lease exclusively. No exceptions!

The reasons for this choice are, rightfully, totally subjective, but I will share them with you. First of all, I feel that the concept is easier to sell and harder for the tenant to take issue with over the life of the lease. The basic difference between the two types of leases lies in cost control. If the landlord is paying all the costs of operation, the tenant is less likely to care about cost control, and subsequently, expense management is a never-ending battle between the tenant who leaves his or her lights on all night and the landlord. Over the years, I have found this to be futile and a complete waste of my time. The NNN lease puts cost management squarely on the shoulders of the tenant, where it belongs. If the tenant wants to leave his or her lights on or run the air conditioning over the weekend, he or she should—and does—pay the bill.

My concept for building maintenance is to set minimum standards for maintenance and let the individual tenants add more service if they find it necessary to their operation and are willing to pay for it. An example of this is daily janitorial service. Office spaces are vacuumed daily, and trash is collected and dumped daily, but dusting is scheduled only once a week and then only if the desks are cleared and ready for dusting. If the tenant wants dusting done more often, the tenant arranges this separately with the janitor and pays for it directly. Similarly, windows are washed a minimum of four times a year and more often at the tenant's request, billed directly to the tenant or tenants as the case may be. In general, utilities (power and phone) are separately metered to the tenant and paid directly by the tenant. Water is part of the CAM charge. Sometimes heating and air conditioning are also part of the common area and are managed for extra service by submetering to the individual tenants.

A good lease document must be easy to negotiate. An overly long or complicated document will tend to generate large legal fees due to the necessity of excessive negotiation. In the case of small, unsophisticated tenants, these cumbersome leases become a deal breaker. In the past, my commercial leases have been as many as 60 pages long, complicated and hard to read. In recent years, I have streamlined the document and have found that, in doing so, it made it easier to negotiate as well as less expensive.

# The Lease Document

The first section, the main body of the lease, contains all the "business points" of the lease. These are all the items within any lease that are generally negotiable between landlord and tenant, and they contain (with the exception of some of the exhibits) the entire business deal.

The second section, the general provisions (a.k.a. the boilerplate), contains all the clauses that are required by the landlord, lender, and the insurer to cover themselves for actions by the tenant that may cause them loss. This portion of the lease, with few exceptions, is totally nonnegotiable. This fact makes this part easy because it becomes a take-it-or-leave-it proposition for the tenant. Should the tenant insist on negotiating the general provisions, I refer him or her to the lender's attorney, with the caveat that I will live with any modifications agreed to by the lender. Lenders do not negotiate boilerplate with tenants.

The final section is the exhibit section. It contains the following:

♦ Property description

♦ Site plan

♦ Floor plan of the tenant's improvements

♦ Construction cost breakdown of who is paying for what as well as how and when it is to be built and by whom

♦ List of rules and regulations

♦ Sample notice of commencement of rent and acceptance of the premises by the tenant

♦ Sample Estoppel Certificate (acknowledgment of lease obligation)

♦ Special provisions exhibit, which spells out exclusives, specific restrictions, and options to renew

Special care should be given to the creation of the project lease because this not only sets the value of the project, but it is also the only tool the manager has to enforce the terms of the agreement. There are traditional areas of dispute between landlord and tenant that should be carefully addressed in the lease, and the inclusion of these clauses is a task you must accomplish or risk long-term management problems and diminished value. Special thought should be given to carefully defining the following items:

♦ Actual operation expenses

♦ Capital costs

♦ Taxes

- A tenant's right of offset

- Late fees

- Default and remedies upon default

- Parking

- Signs (permanent and temporary)

- Exclusives

- Arbitration (binding or nonbinding)

- Hours of operation

- Assignment and subletting

- *Going dark*, a clause almost exclusively for retail projects

- Insurance

- Legal notices

- Permitted timing of—and compulsion to execute—documents such as Estoppel Certificates

**Trade Terms**

**Going dark** occurs when a tenant closes its doors, but remains responsible for the rent. The effect on the center is to remove that tenant from the draw, and the empty store has the effect of depressing the center.

**Reality Check**

Each attorney you encounter will have a pet peeve that has been generated by previous experience. Do not let him or her create a deal-breaker clause to protect you.

There are many other areas of concern in a well-written lease, but if care is given to these basics, the value of the lease—and by extrapolation, the project—should stand firm, and the management headaches should be few and far between.

# Architectural and Engineering Contracts

This is a classic area of contract negotiation. It centers on responsibility and cost. The architectural and engineering professions have created a standard document called the American Institute of Architecture (AIA) contract.

The consultants will tell you that it is the industry standard, and unfortunately, due to its acceptance by many unsophisticated owners, it is. Do not execute it without specific modifications. Most contention between owner and consultant centers around the price of services and the scope of the work. I always take the position that a consultant should be an "expert" in his or her field or should not be hired. An expert should be able to assess the scope of work and quote a fixed price. Only if you make a "substantial" (by definition within the agreement) change in the scope of work should there be an extra charge. Avoid all hourly fees.

Make each consultant financially responsible for all mistakes in design, for both the cost of correcting the design and the cost of any remedial construction work involved.

**Warning, Danger Ahead!**

Get firm costs for all proposed extras before authorizing the work. Make sure the contract states that you will not pay for any changes not authorized in writing and in advance.

If the consultant is inspecting work in progress during construction, make him or her jointly responsible, together with the contractor, for the cost of any remedial work required to correct shoddy, unspecified, or unsafe construction, as well as any losses due to delays in the project's scheduled completion date. Remember, if the tenants are delayed when moving in, so is the rental payment. Interest goes on eternally.

# Governmental-Approval Documents

This is both a tricky and an ever-expanding area of project documentation. It all started with a building permit and now encompasses an entire body of entitlements. Without painting a horror story of possible areas of concern, I need to elaborate only on basic areas of concern common to all parts of the country. They center around three concepts:

- ◆ Zoning controls, which include project limitations of height, setbacks, parking, landscaping, signs, and building coverage

- ◆ City and county requirements, including impact fees and use restrictions

- ◆ Environmental controls

**Trade Terms**

An **Environmental Impact Report (EIR)** is synonymous with an EIS or Environmental Impact Statement. Both are reports on the impact of developing a specific piece of property. They cover, at a minimum, traffic, air pollution, visual impact, economic impact, drainage, social impacts, impact on flora and fauna, and architectural design.

Zoning is controlled by adoption of a general plan for the development and expansion of the town, city, or county. If the existing and/or proposed project's use conforms, usually only the site plan and elevations need to be approved and only when you are making a substantial alteration in the existing structure. California and Washington require the *Environmental Impact Report (EIR)* process enumerated earlier in this book, but only for new projects or projects that intend a radical new use for the property. If there are deviations in uses, shape, and/or encroachments, sometimes use permits or special-use permits are required.

Negotiate the wording of these permits, making sure they work for the project and its specific design requirements. In the event of a new, large, or complicated project or one requiring extensive "off-site" improvements, often a development agreement is executed between you and the municipality. This agreement sets out the off-site improvements required, who will construct them, who will pay for them, and what is required to be completed before the main project can proceed.

A typical example occurs in housing developments where homes cannot be sold before streets and utilities are completed. Sometimes these agreements specify that impact fees be paid at the time of securing building permits so that the municipality can afford to make the improvements to support the project. Examples of impact fees are expansion of the sewer or water treatment facilities or the construction of public schools.

# Building Permits and Occupancy Permits

Building permits involve filling out forms and paying the required fees, which vary from reasonable in a pro-development municipality to confiscatory in a "no-growth" municipality. The issuance of the permit itself occurs after the municipality's building department has examined and approved the project's working drawings.

This is a costly and exhaustive experience, often involving redesign or changing the project's design characteristics to fit the department's interpretation of the governing ordinances. Fighting the building department's interpretations can be disastrous. Serious delays and increased costs will surely follow. Bureaucracy is no joke, and its practitioners have been perfecting the art of frustrating people's desires for many thousands of years. Give them what they want!

Similarly, when construction is completed in accordance with the approved plans and specs, the municipality's building-inspection department issues a certificate of occupancy for each demised premises. This is the same with a house renovation, except that these must be kept in the building on file for verification.

# Loan Documents

The construction loan starts out as a "commitment" to be converted into actual loan documents prior to "funding." The loan commitment and acceptance by you is an agreement by a lending institution to lend money for construction based on some criteria. The criteria usually enumerate a certain percentage of preleasing from acceptable tenants, a receipt of a building permit, and approval by the lender of not only the financial well-being of the borrower, its component parts (the individuals involved), and the proposed tenants, but approval of all the documentation involved in the project. All this must occur within the timeframe specified in the commitment or it will expire, leaving the borrower with a project in default.

When all this has been accomplished at the borrower's sole cost and expense (including legal fees, construction loan administrative costs, and so on), the lender will issue at least two documents for the borrower's execution prior to disbursing the funds. They are the following:

◆ **Note**   This spells out the loan terms, amount, disbursals, interest rate, late fees, events of default, joint and several guarantees, payment schedules and due dates, and anything else the lender can think of.

◆ **Deed of trust**   Sometimes referred to as the mortgage, this is the recordable document that, when recorded, places a lien on the security (the real estate) and anything else (such as additional collateral) agreed upon. This document usually spells out the security, the lender's rights, and the borrower's requirements, as well as the terms of its release, usually the full satisfaction of the note within the prescribed time.

**Trade Terms**

The **permanent loan** is said to take out or retire the construction loan. **Joint and several** is when all parties are liable for the total amount of all unsecured obligations.

Similarly, the *permanent loan* documents start out with a commitment and end in a note and deed of trust. In the case of the permanent or "take-out" loan, the closing costs are higher and the number of inspections and warranties greater.

Usually, however, once the project is complete and fully occupied, personal *joint and several* guarantees are no longer required of the borrower(s).

# Construction Contracts and Site Improvements

This set of contracts will determine the cost, the schedule, and the quality of the improvements. Selection of a reputable general contractor is the key to achieving a quality project. Good general contractors charge a profitable fee for their work and expect to earn that fee. Your role in this process is to find a good one, treat him or her fairly, pay on time, and enforce the terms of the contract, the plans, and the specifications. Key items in the contract to be negotiated are as follows:

◆ Price

◆ Contingencies

◆ Payment terms—monthly progress payments (draws)

- Withholding

- Subcontractors

- Work rules

- Bonding for performance and completion

- Schedules

- Completion date

- Penalties and incentives

- Quality control

- Independent inspection

Here again the ubiquitous AIA document rears its ugly head. Try not to use one, but if you must, modify it to be responsible and performance oriented. Make sure the responsible party pays for the mistakes, including loss of time, interest, and rental income.

---

### Reality Check

To have an enforceable penalty clause, there must be a corresponding incentive clause. It is a good idea. Do not begrudge the payment of incentive fees. Remember that the rent will start early and will compensate you for the additional fees to be paid, and interest will be saved to offset the incentive pay. The penalties, if assessed, should offset the additional interest incurred by the delay.

---

# Don't Forget the Utilities

Utility agreements are customarily executed during the development stage of a project. You might have cause to deal with these if you plan to significantly alter an existing building or add one to the site. They enumerate the source of utilities, how they will be extended to the property line, who will pay for the work, and any easements and preconditions that must be satisfied for the work to be completed on time. These chores and their corresponding timeframes can be costly in both money and time. Start them early and get them completed ASAP.

The time to contact the utility companies is when the architect and engineer are hired. Make them part of the design team. Make sure that the architect and engineer continually interface with the utility companies' engineering staffs to avoid any conflicts between the project's concept and the capability of the existing or proposed infrastructure. Pay attention throughout the process and attend all the meetings.

Do not delegate this chore. Be nice to them! A completed building without power, water, and sewer cannot be occupied. The good news is that the utility companies are reasonable, publicly regulated bodies that are used to doing the work. They do not overpower the situation with legalese. They are one of your natural allies, kindred spirits, interested in progress and more customers.

# Environmental Documentation

The subject of environmental documentation could necessitate a book in itself. There is no way to cover the subject thoroughly without taking it one state and one municipality at a time. Suffice it to say that California is the most regulated geographical region on the planet. Study the situation there, learn to work within it, and you can work anywhere. Most environmental regulation is both necessary and fairly applied.

As with most good things, environmental regulation has been perverted and abused to serve various political agendas. In California, there exist not only the state laws but also the local county overlays, the municipal overlays, the coastal commission, and in certain areas other special jurisdictions like the Bay Area Development Commission (BADC). The net effect of all this regulation is to curtail growth, but it is also making any and all growth hideously expensive while promoting suburban sprawl. It is as if Californians took a look at New York City and said, "Anything but that."

The real effect of environmental concerns has evolved into personal and corporate liability for actions that result in contamination of the environment with hazardous waste and the pollution that results from increasing population, automobiles, and urban sprawl. Many abuses occurred in the past before these laws, resulting in land that is terminally polluted and unfit for use by man or beast.

The worst of these examples is the nuclear test and fabrication sites created and administered by the U.S. Department of Energy (DOE). Many of these abuses are environmental holocausts waiting to happen. The result of all this abuse is now, in most cases, over-regulation.

Contemporary loan documents now require the borrower to indemnify the lender against all past and future contamination of the site. This makes the borrower responsible for prior problems as well as problems caused now and in the future by the tenants of the project. This assumption of liability now runs like a thread throughout all the documentation and chain of ownership, hopefully back to the source of the problem. Here again, a good attorney can be worth his or her weight in gold.

# Management Contracts

This final document, properly drafted, charges the management agent with a fiduciary responsibility to both you the landlord and the tenant. The manager's duty is to maintain the property in a condition that will honor the conditions of the lease documents and produce a profit for the landlord, minimizing potential traumas along the way. The terms of this type of document vary, but a good one should include incentives for the manager to achieve better results and happy tenants and penalties for substandard performance. Because an agent's actions are taken on behalf of the owner, the agent must be carefully selected. Mistakes in representation can have long-reaching consequences. Often owners are tempted to manage, but in general, it is better to have a third party separating owner and tenants. This buffer allows for debate without rancor and gives everyone a chance to think things through without having to make a decision face to face. Important issues in this document are as follows:

- Rent collection
- Maintenance
- Performance fees
- Leasing fees
- Lease-renewal fees
- Trust accounts
- Payment of expenses

The management document spells out in detail the relationship between tenant and manager, and between manager and owner. It provides the framework for the fiduciary relationship between manager and owner.

# The Exclusive Right to Sell Agreement

The culmination of the project is the sale. When it occurs will depend on the project objectives, the quality of its execution, and the desires of the owner(s). If the marketing team has done a credible job and met its performance goals, it might have earned the right to sell the project. Most often, there are firms that specialize in investment sales. These companies will have the best chance to meet the owner's expectations at the time of sale.

A 3 percent commission is fairly common, with decreasing percentages over a $5 million price tag. Make sure the agent's obligations regarding promotion and exposure of the project are clearly enumerated and set a realistic timeframe for the duration of the listing. Somewhere between 90 and 120 days should

**This Works**

There are no standard commissions for this type of contract—negotiate! If you do not ask for a better deal, they will not offer one, so always ask.

show results. Do not permit a catch-all clause, whereby an agent can claim a long list of buyer submittals. Only permit a carryover (after expiration of the agreement) commission obligation if the buyer will substantiate the agent's presentation in writing at the time of registration of the potential buyer. This is a good agreement to have the attorney peruse prior to execution. Don't skimp at the end of the deal.

## The Least You Need to Know

- Documentation is relentlessly necessary. The leases establish the value of the project, and the rest let you control the environment.

- Keep all documents as short as possible and still have them enforceable.

- Write all agreements in plain English; avoid legalese. It is cheaper to negotiate and easier to administer.

- Put yourself on both sides of an agreement and ask yourself, "Is it fair to both sides?" Don't quit until it is, it will be worth the effort.

- A thoroughly one-sided agreement will come back to haunt you with a vengeance, and chances are there will be no repeat business with that tenant.

# Chapter 19

# Cost Control

## In This Chapter

- ◆ Who reports to whom
- ◆ Progress payments: invoice and lien release
- ◆ The testing engineer and construction draw certification agent
- ◆ When building, get the best bang for the buck

A fixer-upper is no different than any other project. Every project goes through distinct stages, and at each stage there is opportunity to plan and control costs. These stages are as follows: acquisition, planning, budgeting, execution and/or construction, and management and/or sale.

By the start of construction of any project, the die is cast. If it is going to succeed, the right moves will already have been made. It can, however, still run afoul if the construction process is not carefully monitored.

This is especially true of commercial projects because they generally entail a large amount of funding in comparison to house remodels. The magnitude of the expense demands a more rigorous control system, especially during the construction phase.

The work prior to the start of construction sets the stage for the construction phase, and for the project to succeed, the following elements—common to all fixer-upper projects, residential or commercial, large or small—must have been successfully completed before you can start:

- ◆ The property has been properly selected for price, location, physical characteristics, and proper condition of title.

- ◆ The market has been clearly established for the intended use, and the numbers show sufficient upside to warrant the investment and potential risks.

- ◆ The consultants, including the general contractor, have been retained with proper accountability and integrated into the design process.

- ◆ Sufficient money has been raised through equity and loans to assure you that the project can be completed without significant problems.

- ◆ The documentation is in place through the completion and the management phase.

- ◆ The construction loan is ready to fund, and the draw system is agreed upon between you and the lender.

- ◆ All utilities are available at the site or are at least scheduled to be available well in advance of the scheduled completion date.

- ◆ The necessary permits have been issued, and the project is 100 percent in compliance with the governing regulations.

- ◆ The preleasing (if any) has progressed to the point of break-even, and the lender has given the go ahead.

If all of these prerequisites have been successfully completed, the project is ready to start the construction phase. At this point, the meter starts ticking on the borrowed funds. Time truly is money. In this chapter, we will examine the players at this point and monitor their responsibilities and backup. Who are they, and exactly what are they being paid to do? Whom do they report to, and in what way are they accountable? Any project, to be successful, must control the costs and timing. At this point, the process of producing the finished goods has come to the final phase—the delivery of the finished project.

# Reporting and Responsibility

How are all of these entities tied together, and how do they function so that you retain control? The answer is contained in the documentation. The key to the enforceability of the documents rests with the expertise, financial strength, and responsibilities spelled out in the contracts.

If the consultants have been properly selected, they will have sufficient credentials, net worth, and liquidity to back up their professional expertise with cash should the need arise. If this is not the case, they should not have been retained in the first place.

# Representation, Expertise, and Accountability

A key factor in drafting the documents should be the spelling out of the consultants' advertised background and their representations regarding their capabilities, experience, financial condition, and expertise. You, as the owner, have the right to rely on these representations. Clearly state the responsibilities and the fiduciary nature of the consultants' relationship to the owner. It is this unifying thread that should link all of the consultants, making them responsible to you and requiring them to look over each other's shoulders on your behalf.

The architect's job assignment is, in reality, the most responsible of all the consultants in the process. He or she is charged with the responsibility of producing a quality building of sound design that meets the requirements of the intended use and that complies with all applicable codes and governmental regulations. He or she is responsible for the compliance of the project's design, up to the time the building permit is issued.

Once the project construction gets underway, the architect then becomes responsible to see that the general contractor does the job properly within the design parameters and the applicable building codes. If new regulations are promulgated after the design has been finalized and the building permit issued, or if new legislation is passed after the date the permit is issued, the cost of compliance with these new requirements becomes the responsibility of the owner. However, implementation of rules or laws passed, but not yet in force, prior to or during the design process, such as the recent Americans with Disabilities Act (ADA) requirements, is the responsibility of the architect.

Construction inspection for compliance with specifications and the quality of workmanship also falls under the architect's responsibility. Lenders require certification monthly that the construction is on time and in accordance with the approved plans and applicable codes. If the design is in error and correction is called for, it should be the responsibility of the architect to pay for the redesign and the remedial work. If the general contractor was part of the design team in a design-build contract, the contractor should share these costs in some prearranged manner with the architect.

| Reality Check |
| --- |
| General contractors are not presumed to be architects or structural, mechanical, or civil engineers. They are not responsible for the mistakes of others, only for errors in execution of the designs. Sufficiency of design is the responsibility of the architect and engineer. |

The general contractor (GC) is presumed not only to be financially responsible, but also to be an expert in building construction and the current building codes.

The contractor is responsible, within the scope of the plans and specifications, for execution of the required work within the code as well as the quality and timing of all work under the construction contract. Late or shoddy work should be remedied at the contractor's expense.

Timing is always a critical and costly issue in construction. The realistic approach dictates that entrepreneurial risks and "force majeure" items such as natural disasters, severe weather, strikes, and so on that are beyond the contractor's control are the risk of the owner. All else is the responsibility of the general contractor, and the financial consequences attributed to this delay should be laid at his or her door.

Since the meter is running on the interest clock, this cost of money can be tied directly to the schedule. To be enforceable, the contract clause must include a reward as well as a penalty. If the work is completed in advance of schedule, a bonus must be paid. If the work is delayed, a penalty can be enforced. The penalty is customarily assessed against the final payment of the traditional 10 percent holdback from the monthly construction draws.

# Progress Payments

Every month during the life of a commercial construction project there is a construction draw. Customarily, this draw is for a percentage of the total project, is estimated by the contractor, and is approved by the architect, the lender's inspector, and you before being paid out by the lender. There are compelling arguments against this method of payment. First, it does not accurately reflect work in place. Second, it never reflects the cash value of the work previously paid for by the general contractor. Third, it allows the contractor to get ahead of the subcontractors, costing you too much interest on outstanding construction loan money.

Similarly, in a housing project, your lender will most likely agree to progress payments, rather than paying only upon completion. The draws for housing are simplified, and are tied directly to specific items being completed. Also their lien program is seldom too sophisticated.

A more precise method of payment that is fair to all—the owner, the lender, the contractor, and the subcontractors—is payment by the invoice method.

## The Invoice Method

This method of payment requires that each subcontractor, supplier, or consultant invoice for work completed during the current month.

Once the subcontractor costs are tallied, the general contractor adds his or her work, overhead charges, and specific costs incurred, suitably backed by invoices from suppliers or payroll records, and the total cost of construction for the month is tallied. You then add the soft costs invoiced for the current month, and the total is forwarded to the lender for payment.

If this method is followed, your expenditure for interest during construction, prior to tenants' occupancy, should drop by approximately half. This is a significant savings. Once the tenants are in and the rents are paying the interest, this savings becomes permanent, and money budgeted for this purpose may now be diverted to some other area to good effect.

**Warning, Danger Ahead!**

Be sure to exclude any materials stored on or off site; these are properly the responsibility of the suppliers or the subcontractors. They become your property only when they are incorporated into the project. Your insurance will be lower if this distinction is made, and there will be less shrinkage of stored materials as a result.

## Lien Releases

Another point about payments is tied to the monthly lien releases. This check-and-balance procedure ensures you and the lender that suppliers and subcontractors have been paid, thus lessening the possibility of liens resulting from nonpayment to subs and suppliers by the general contractor.

Each subcontractor and supplier is required to submit, with the current invoice, a lien release for all prior work paid for by the owner. No further payment should be made until this is submitted.

If any supplier or subcontractor not contracted directly by you wants to be able to enforce payment for his or her work, he or she is required by a statute on *mechanic's lien law* to notify you and the lender that he or she is doing work on the project, prior to starting work on the project.

This puts you and your lender on notice that the person is working on the project, thus enabling you and the lender to track payments to avoid possible liens. The invoice method provides an excellent way to track these obligations. If there is any question as to whether suppliers or subcontractors are being paid, payments to the general contractor may be made jointly to include the supplier or subcontractor in question.

**Trade Terms**

The **mechanic's lien law** states that a subcontractor, or supplier who is contracted with someone other than the owner, like the general contractor, must notify the owner and the lender that he or she is supplying parts and/or labor on the job, in advance of the start of work. This notification, called a preliminary notice or a prelien notice, is required by law to protect the lien rights of the supplier and the subcontractor.

These types of payments involve the issuance of a joint check to both the general contractor and the subcontractor. One cannot cash the check without the other's signature. The net effect is that both parties must endorse the check to be paid.

# Other Resources

Several third-party agents are usually employed to oversee the construction process on behalf of the owner and the lender.

The testing engineer, usually required by both the lender and the building department, is an excellent consultant to check on various aspects of the construction. His or her role is primarily one of quality control, and the timely reporting of compliance or noncompliance can have a profound effect on the schedule and, by extrapolation, the total project cost.

Once a quality control test is taken, it is presumed to be in compliance unless reported otherwise; therefore, timely notice of noncompliance is essential for keeping the work on schedule. Having to backtrack to remove and replace prior work can cause severe delay, not to mention increased cost. The testing engineer should always work for you at the direction of both you and the architect. The building department and the lender will have some minimum requirements for inspection, but the owner and architect's best interests are served when inspections are thorough, random, and timely.

Likewise, the lender's construction draw certification agent, increasingly likely to be an outside consultant, is responsible only to the lender. The owner, however, can make this agent an ally by requiring that he or she be detailed and timely with the reports. Since the owner is paying for this service performed on behalf of the lender, he has the right to insist on having detailed inspections reported promptly. This way, you can more accurately pay for the construction and, if these reports are completed in a timely manner, can make this payment in time to maximize any potential discounts from subcontractors and suppliers.

# How to Fight Murphy's Law

Everyone knows that something always goes wrong, and generally it is something that has fallen through the cracks and is not necessarily attributable to anyone's incompetence or negligence. How do most fixer-uppers and developers plan for this? It is best budgeted for when preparing the quick-and-dirty pro forma (refer to Chapter 16).

When this analysis is made, certain "fat" can be built into the projection for use at a later date. Obvious areas in which to squirrel away money are the contingency and miscellaneous line items as well as insurance and interest budgets. Once complete costs for these line items can be established, lenders will allow the extra money to be moved to another budgeted line item or to be used as part of the miscellaneous budget.

**This Works**

The fatter the tenant improvement budget, the easier the leasing. The less money the prospective tenant has to part with when signing a lease, the easier it is for him or her to make the decision to move in.

Within the construction cost breakdown attached to the construction contract, there should be a line for contingencies. This line item can be a godsend to you and the general contractor. If this line item is incorporated into the contract amount by pre-arrangement, it can be used to correct oversights that are no one's fault. In addition, it can be used to improve the quality of the building or to add to the tenant improvement (TI) allowance. Once the building shell is complete, these unused funds can then be used to add incentive for the leasing process.

This approach gives the broker an edge over the competition and lowers a prospective tenant's cost of occupancy. Tenants really respond to this type of incentive, and it can add real value to the finished product by financing the tenant's over-*standard* improvements above the base term of the lease, adding the payment for the added tenant improvements to the lease's rental rate. This is capitalized as extra value for the building if and when the building is sold.

**Trade Terms**

**Standard** tenant improvements are evidenced by a flat dollar amount but are also accompanied by a laundry list of standard items already prebid.

# Best Building for the Buck

A common mistake made by fixer-uppers and developers alike is to try to save money on the budget. This can become a very short-sighted and ill-advised act. It does, however, depend on the project and the project's concept and goals. Obviously, if one is building a project for sale, such as a house, then reduced costs for subcontractors and materials that do not affect quality will have little effect on the project. These savings will, in fact, raise the profits.

For a project in which rentals are the determining factor in establishing value and profit, however, money saved can be used to improve the project's final value by increased rent payments. If additional money is available from savings in certain areas, these funds may be used to improve the project's quality, to reduce long-term operating costs, or to allow tenants over-standard improvements. Typically, these over-standard improvements are, in reality, loaned to the tenant and repaid with interest, fully amortized, over the base term of the lease. They are not flagged anywhere as secondary income but customarily are evidenced by an increased rental rate.

How does this improve value? Take, for example, over-standard tenant improvements of $20,000 installed for a tenant with a five-year lease. If the tenant agrees to pay for this at 12 percent, which is not unreasonable, the result is an additional annual rental payment of $5,340. This amount of money, capitalized at 9 percent, will yield a value that can be sold with the building of $59,330. This is a good deal by anyone's standard, and the increase in cash flow, by extrapolation, is real. It is not hard to visualize how you can turn some significant fat into gold by an astute bit of negotiating.

## The Least You Need to Know

- Make sure you are ready to launch because once you start the clock, interest can eat you up if there are major delays.

- Get the consultants nailed down tight so that their roles are clear, the reporting relationships are spelled out, and the responsibilities clearly defined.

- Stay ahead of everyone by forward planning and checking everything over and over. Follow through.

- Double-check everything because Murphy is alive and well.

- Make the most of your dollar by value engineering all decisions. Are these additional costs going to result in better rents, or better tenants?

# 20

# The Site and Landscaping

## In This Chapter

- ◆ Easements and setbacks
- ◆ Lot size and amenities
- ◆ Planting, irrigation, and street appeal
- ◆ Creating an oasis and some privacy

If you ever saw the movie *Giant*, you will remember the ranch house was an elegant building in the middle of an open Texas prairie; not a bush or tree in sight. By the end of the movie, the ranch house area had become transformed into an oasis in the middle of the otherwise bleak landscape. This was accomplished by design elements, walls, and landscaping. In effect the naked building had become dressed up.

The design and placement of the landscaping and ancillary structures is the work of landscape designers and architects. Unless the building is in an urban area where there is only asphalt and sidewalks, every building needs some dressing to set it off, and put it in context. The theme of the landscape design should complement the building design e.g., formal, casual, or oasis-like.

# The Survey and Topographic Map

In the beginning, all is raw land. When developers subdivide property, their first step is to gather information about the land itself. This is done by a surveyor, and the two basic types of information provided are a boundary survey and a topographic map. Any residential subdivision or commercial project starts with this basic picture. From there, the planners are able to lay out the lots and start the project design.

Residential subdivisions consist of street improvements, utility-distribution networks, and individual house lots. Each house lot has setbacks and utility easements in addition to the house and outbuildings. The final component of each lot is the landscaping. To pull this all together, a designer must situate the building to comply with the setback and easement requirements and must orient the house properly for the view potential and exposure.

## Easements

An easement entitles someone else to use your property in a specific way. The most typical is the PUE or public utility easement, provided across the front of most properties to allow the utility companies to bring their services to the individual parcel of land.

Easements are granted for many reasons, not the least of which is to provide utilities to each house. Normally, these easements run along the front of the lots in and alongside the streets. In projects with varied terrain, it is quite common to have some situations in which there are easements cutting across the sides and rear of some lots to transition from one grade to another. Most lots will have the public utility easement (PUE) in the front, but when you buy any real estate, you must review the title report to see where your lot's easements occur.

If you look at the following, a typical plat map of a residential lot, you will see the easements shown as part of the overall picture of the lot.

The restrictions imposed by easements are simple. You cannot build over an easement because the utility company must be able to access the utility lines for service. It is never a good idea to plant a tree or a large shrub in the PUE because the maintenance crew might have to remove it to maintain service to the neighborhood. Other types of easements may exist for other purposes. It is quite common for one person to have an access easement over another person's property. Sometimes these easements are very specific, and they are treated the same way as the PUEs. You cannot build on them or restrict access to them. Other easements are nonspecific and allow general passage through the property. This means you must allow passage however it is accomplished.

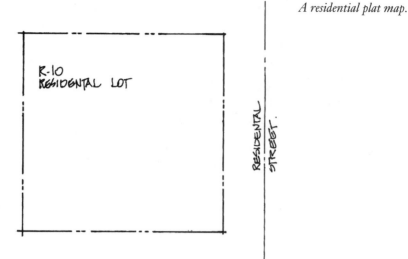

*A residential plat map.*

## Setbacks

Setbacks are another matter because their purpose is different. Setbacks are designed to provide uniformity to a development and are used to control encroachment of one dwelling or building on another. Typical setbacks required in a residential subdivision are 20 feet from the street lot line, 10 feet at the side yards, and 5 or 10 feet from the back lot line. The net effect of this regulation is to confine your improvements to your lot. No building can come closer to any of these lot lines than the setback allows. What is allowed in these areas is landscaping.

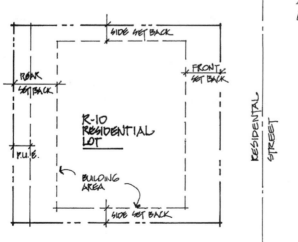
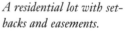

*A residential lot with setbacks and easements.*

When you look at the net effect of both easements and setbacks, you will find that your ability to improve your lot is quite restricted, especially on a small lot. What's left is for building your house, garage, outbuildings, and amenities such as a swimming pool or tennis court. How this relates to fixer-uppers is simple: You will have to work around these restrictions as well as the existing improvements, buildings, and amenities when you make your plan.

Topographic maps will also give you the information you need to maintain proper drainage when doing building modifications and site changes. It is not permitted to alter the natural drainage of your lot to cause your neighbor any hardship. If you flood out your neighbor, you will have to pay the damages, and the town will make you change the yard to negate the drainage problem.

# Commercial Projects

All the information on easements and setbacks holds true for commercial properties as well, with the added dimension in commercial building design of having to accommodate the parking. Each type of development has its own parking requirement. Office buildings require 4 cars per 1,000 square feet of building, and retail buildings require 5 cars per 1,000 square feet of building. The net effect can be that for every car required, you will need up to 400 square feet of lot space for the parking and driveways. This uses up a lot of dirt on the plan and restricts the use of landscaping to confined areas around the building and the periphery of the lot.

**This Works**

Landscaping is an important amenity on any property because it provides the dressing for the building as well as privacy, wind breaks, curb appeal, and a sense of comfort.

As you can see, the space on any lot, whether residential or commercial, starts to be used up in a hurry. What is left is for landscaping and other amenities.

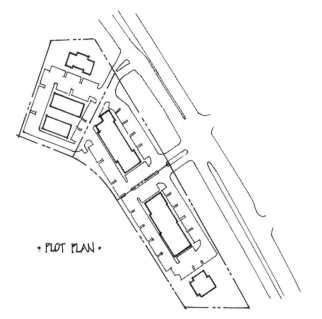

*A commercial building plot plan.*

· PLOT PLAN ·

# Lot Size and Amenities

What you can accomplish with a building lot depends largely on the size of the lot. Multifamily lots are so small that you are lucky to have a private patio and a bush out front, but your average residential lot of ¼ acre will provide ample opportunity for the buildings as well as recreational amenities and extensive landscaping. When you take on a fixer-upper, it is important to realize that a little well-placed landscaping can really make an impression. In general, planting is less expensive than building modification. Hiding less-than-desirable features, such as utility poles, water manholes, electrical transformers, and air conditioners, on any building with plantings is very cost effective.

## Small Lots

When you have very little to work with, it is necessary to use the space carefully. In small lots, the front yard usually is regulated and maintained by the condominium association, but the backyard is all yours. If you are working with a small patio or a balcony space, the use of potted plants on the floor and hanging plants can give the impression of a pleasantly cool and shaded space.

## Normal ¼-Acre Lot

The average lot is about 10,000 square feet, or approximately 100 feet wide and 100 feet deep. Most subdivisions will have the street frontage dimension a bit smaller and the depth a little larger. For the sake of illustration, let's use a lot with the dimensions of 80 feet wide by 125 feet deep. With 10-foot side-yard setbacks, a 20-foot front setback, and a 20-foot-wide driveway, you have left a patch of land that's 40 feet wide for large landscaping in the front.

The depth will be a minimum of 20 feet and possibly more if the house is pushed back on the lot. Most homebuilders keep the house as close to the street as possible to maximize the back yard, but for aesthetic appeal, the customary dimension is 40 feet. This leaves a good planting area, but remember that the utility easement must be able to be accessed, so you had better not plant any trees in it. The side-yard setbacks are fine for planting large trees. Shrubs and lawn can go anywhere.

## Large Lots

These generous lots can be a little more difficult to landscape because it takes more of everything to fill it up, and once planted, the landscaping must be maintained. A good ploy is to cluster the plantings around areas of lawn or decorative rock. The clustering will give the impression of masses of green and will set off the defined open spaces, maximizing the effect.

You can use rock and other features to good effect as well. Homes in the eastern part of the country enjoy more rainfall than in the West, so landscaping must be planted to ensure that there is space to enjoy each plant or tree and avoid overgrowth. In the West, to achieve an overgrown look, you must have copious amounts of irrigation.

# Basic Planting

When a developer builds a home, the landscaping will be minimal (if it is provided at all). Many times developers have a front-yard starter package that looks something like this:

> (2) 24-inch box trees
>
> (3) 15-gallon trees
>
> (8) 5-gallon shrubs

Most nurseries have weekly specials on this type of planting package. For example, a local nursery in Phoenix offers this package at $699 planted and guaranteed (for 90 days).

If you are doing a fixer-upper, you can take advantage of these weekly specials to spruce up your project with a small expenditure. Most nurseries will allow you to substitute and mix and match.

New homes seldom have any planting in the back yard, and it is not uncommon to encounter a newer fixer-upper that has a back yard in which no planting has ever been done. When a newer home becomes a candidate for a fixer-upper, it is because the owners did not have the money to maintain the mortgage let alone the house and yards. It then falls to you to provide a suitable back yard for the resale.

# Irrigation

Watering your plantings is an issue no matter where you live. Even in areas that get a lot of rain, you will have dry times and need to water. In places like Seattle, Washington, there will be little demand for irrigating your landscaping, but for the rest of us, a basic watering system is cost effective because it will consume little of your time and will put the water where it is needed most—on the plant.

A basic irrigation setup, using drip irrigation with a timer, can cost as little as $1,000 installed and can be a strong selling point. People are busy, and hand watering your yard takes a lot of time each week. You must keep your plants watered to protect your investment.

> **CAUTION**
>
> **Warning, Danger Ahead!**
>
> In areas that experience freezing, the landscaping goes dormant for the winter months. You must drain and winterize the irrigation to prevent damage from the freeze-thaw cycles.

# Street Appeal

The most eloquent argument for landscaping in a fixer-upper project is curb appeal. You want people to notice your project and to stop to see it. You can't sell it if they haven't seen it. Good landscaping in the front yard will have them pulling over to write down the number on the sign.

An astute landscaping package can dress up an ordinary house very nicely. It is much more effective than architectural decoration of the building and is much more cost effective. If you have a feature on the house that you want to hide, plant something in front of it. If you want to emphasize some feature, frame it with landscaping. Look at the effect of landscaping on the house that follows. These before and after photos are of my own fixer-upper.

*Before landscaping.*

*After landscaping.*

# Creating the Oasis

With the current trend of cocooning, you may want to consider a more elaborate approach with landscaping on your more ambitious projects. Families today are spending more and more time at home, and their dwellings are starting to reflect this. Additions of media rooms, swimming pools, and other amenities allow people to recreate right in their own houses.

In the old days, formal gardens and mazes were very popular, and today a private and secluded atmosphere is very desirable. I'm not suggesting that you install a pool because it is not cost effective, but if you can transform the back yard into a private oasis, you will have scored a home run with the average buyer.

**This Works** _____

What are needed are lush landscaping and privacy as well as low mainte-nance. Remember the irri-gation system.

# The Need for Privacy

Privacy is a big factor in modern living (see the following graphic). In the western part of the country, fences and walls are accepted as part of a normal subdivision, so most of the houses have a private back yard. In the eastern part of the country, fences are not as common, and privacy can be achieved by planting hedges. With the rainfall in the East, rows of trees and shrubs grow quickly and achieve the same effect as fences and walls.

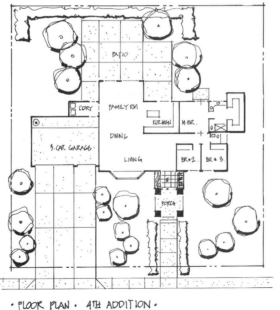

*A landscape plan emphasiz-ing privacy.*

· FLOOR PLAN · 4TH ADDITION ·

Front yards are another matter. Many subdivisions preclude heavy planting in the front so that the homes are visible from the street. This is a safety issue. You can achieve privacy by planting trees and shrubs in front of windows to screen views into the home from the street. This can also block views from the house. Most view lots situate the house so that the views are visible from the back of the house rather than the front, so that is not generally an issue. Judicious planting can achieve a great deal of privacy, and it provides a good selling point.

## The Least You Need to Know

- ◆ Landscaping is an important part of the package: Think of it as "dressing the project."

- ◆ Pay attention to the restrictions so that you do not have to remove plants and trees to allow for utility maintenance.

- ◆ Use your planting for good effect; otherwise, it's just money down the drain.

- ◆ Emphasize privacy and a sense of comfort so that the people who occupy the building have a sense of being in a special place.

# Chapter 21

# Demolition and Modification

## In This Chapter

- ◆ Demolition as a fine art
- ◆ Being selective about your demolition
- ◆ Should it stay or go?
- ◆ Dressing it up a bit

You have most likely seen on TV a live demonstration of the demolition of a building. It is now considered entertaining to televise major demolition events. The practitioners of this explosive decompression art have even become celebrities of a sort. This is not what we will discuss here. What we will discuss is that to do a major remodel and/or modernization, you must decide what parts of the building can be used and what parts cannot be salvaged. Once this decision is made, you can proceed with the demolition.

## The Art of Demolition

Like any other skill, the process of selective demolition must be learned. The first step in the process begins with putting the existing building on a plan. If you are fortunate, you might be able to find a copy of the original plans. Most cities maintain archives of building permits, and the original plans should be there.

### Reality Check

Housing demolition is a little easier to assess than commercial demolition because there are only so many ways of building a house, and the building itself can be easily inspected to find out what walls are structural and what can be demolished.

### Warning, Danger Ahead!

You must make sure that a structural component starts at the foundation. If you are making a replacement that cannot reuse the original foundation, you must pour a new one and place the structural replacement on that new foundation. Do not attempt to build a structural wall without a proper footing.

Most commercial building owners retain the plans as a permanent part of the building files, and it is rare to buy a commercial building and not have a copy of the plans available to the buyer. Re-creating the plans accurately is a costly and time-consuming job, but if you are to make structural modifications, you must know what you are dealing with.

You can alter and replace structural walls if it is done properly. After you have devised your plan, the first step is to erect a temporary support to replace the wall you are taking out. Once this is in place, the wall can be carefully taken down.

Demolition does not imply smash and pulverize; rather, it involves taking the wall apart one component at a time. First the wall covering, sheetrock or lathe, and plaster is removed, and then the wiring and, or plumbing in the wall is removed and saved or discarded as the case may be. Then the wall structure, generally made of wood 2 × 4s, is carefully dismantled. Once the wall is gone, you are free to construct its permanent replacement.

In the plans that follow, you can clearly see the parts of the original house that are being demolished and the parts that are being retained for the new addition.

*The original house.*

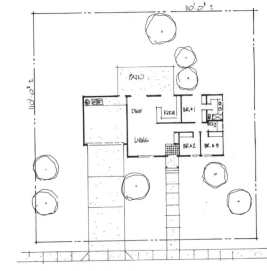

· FLOOR PLAN · EXISTING ·

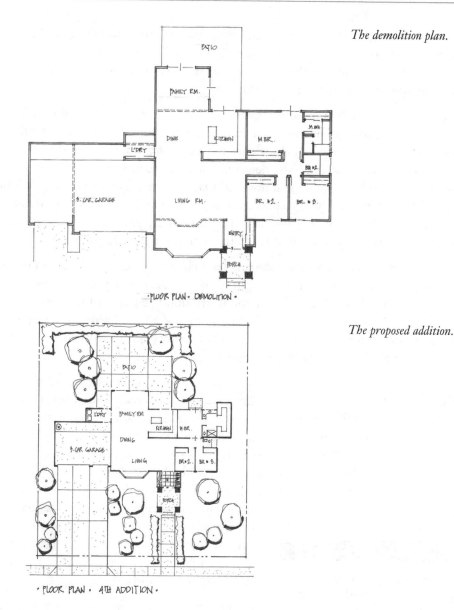

*The demolition plan.*

· FLOOR PLAN · DEMOLITION ·

*The proposed addition.*

· FLOOR PLAN · 4TH ADDITION ·

What is being practiced in these graphics is selective demolition, the topic of the next section.

# Selective Demolition

When you are doing a remodel, you will want to reuse as much of the original structure as you can. This includes all the house's systems from structural to mechanical. If you are dealing with an older period house, you will want to salvage and refit the windows and doors if possible because the original materials will make the finished product more valuable. If the building's electrical system has been modernized, you can salvage and redistribute the circuits.

When you are in the demolition phase, you must carefully remove the wiring. Do not cut it; just remove and bundle it for future reconnection. Using existing circuits for distribution is relatively easy. First check by removing fuses or turning off the circuit breakers one at a time until you determine which circuit you are working with. Once identified, turn it off and tape it down so that someone does not turn it back on prematurely. You are then free to dismantle the wiring and terminate the circuits into new junction boxes for later use. If you position these junction boxes conveniently, they will be available when you get to the wiring stage of the addition.

In my most recent fixer-upper, the one I am currently living in, I wanted to enlarge a hallway to a new room addition. Right in the middle of the proposed walkway was a plumbing wall. It was the collector and distribution center for the water in the house. Removing the wall was easy, but the plumbing was a little harder. We had to jack hammer the concrete to expose the plumbing, which left us with about 4 feet of pipe exposed in all directions from its original location.

### Warning, Danger Ahead!

The aim when relocating pipes under any concrete floor is to not have a soldered joint under the concrete when you put the floor back.

### Reality Check

Today's consumer laws apply to real estate as well, and you must disclose any problems you have encountered in your fixer-upper project. If you say that you made a partial replacement, you might find that it will be a deterrent to a sale.

By removing enough concrete, we were able to carefully bend the pipes enough to redirect them to the new wall. Once this was done, we were able to build a new plumbing wall around the reconfigured pipes. Since there were quite a number of pipes in a small space, we made the new wall an 8-inch wall to accommodate the plumbing and to avoid overcrowding the new installation. Once this was accomplished, we were able to reconnect the pipes with solder joints all above the concrete. This ensured that, if sometime in the future we had any problems, we could comfortably work on the pipes.

In buildings with wood floors over crawl spaces, this will not be a problem, and in second-floor installations, you will be working in the ceiling below. In older houses, you might find that the plumbing is in rough shape. I recommend that if you get into a situation of having to replace some of it, you should replace all of it.

The same is true for the electrical system. If you are dealing with antiquated wiring with brittle plastic or cloth covering, you must replace it. The same goes for the old-fashioned fuse boxes. These need to be replaced with a new service using circuit breakers. Normally, if you find fuse boxes, the wiring will also be in need of replacement.

Sometimes, if you are fortunate, you can use the old wire to pull the new wire, but in most cases, if it was done properly in the first place, the wires will be anchored within the walls. You will have to remove enough wallboard in each room to allow you to pull the new wiring. The same is true for the plumbing, except the plumbing is confined to and concentrated in fewer walls and is accessible under wooden floors.

# What to Save

When you are doing an extensive remodel, what you save depends on where you are going with the remodel. If you are attempting a period house like an old Cape Cod, art deco, or a Victorian, you might want to consider having someone with a cabinet-making background help you strip the house before you start the actual demolition.

Salvaging the original millwork, stair treads, railings, flooring, and wainscotings (the wood trim between partial paneling or paint and the wallpaper in New England style houses) could be valuable when you start the rebuilding process. Likewise, old pedestal sinks and claw-footed bathtubs are fetching a premium these days. Replicas do not have the same cachet when it comes time to sell.

Most people who are willing to buy period homes know enough about the period to appreciate the original touches. The more original millwork and finishes in the home, the higher your sale price will be.

One of the obvious places to look for materials to salvage is under paint and carpeting. Over the years, when homes change hands, people do what is expedient. Refinishing original tongue-in-grove flooring is expensive and time consuming, so many people simply give up and carpet over it. Today, these floors are prized and lovingly cared for. In many of the old eastern houses, the floors were not nailed down; they were *pegged*.

**Trade Terms**

**Pegged** floors were fastened to the joists below with dowels, or round wooden pegs. The holes were hand drilled through the flooring into the joist, the dowels were pounded into the hole, and then the ends were sanded flush with the floor. This type of flooring is hideously expensive to re-create, so restore it wherever you find it. Your finished product will be more valuable.

All you have to do when you are inspecting the house prior to the purchase is pull up one corner of the carpeting in the main rooms to see if you have the original floors underneath. If you do, you are in luck. Similarly, the woodwork has usually been painted over at least twice. Properly removed, stripped, and refinished, it can be reinstalled in its original condition. Old doors and hardware, light fixtures, and windows are also very salvageable. The wiring in the light fixtures can be replaced by modern wiring, the old fixture can be recycled for use, and the windows can be refurbished and refinished.

The same approach on the outside of the house is a good idea. Trim, ornamentation, and light fixtures can be salvaged and reinstalled. Pay special attention to porch railings and ornamental iron fixtures. Many can be successfully copied, but again, if the originals can be reused, you will have authenticity.

If you are not involved in a period house, authenticity is not an issue. You instead will want to be strictly practical. You must examine all parts of the home for materials that can be recycled, but here you are looking to add space and modernize. The kitchen and baths most likely will be a total write off, but the plumbing and wiring should be up to code and expandable. You might find hardwood floors under the carpet since they were popular during certain periods in tract housing.

If you are upgrading a tract with an old asphalt shingle roof and the current one has no significant leaks, leave the old roof on and put the newer roof tiles over the old ones. This will save the cost of demolition and replacing the underlayment. The new tiles will serve as a weather surface, and the results will be a better roof with more insulating value. This does not work with flat roofs, wood shingles, or metal roofs.

| Reality Check |
| --- |
| Stains on ceilings or wallboard will indicate a leak. Floor joists under porches, bathrooms, and kitchens should be examined for water damage. Water damage inside indicates a leak from the roof or the siding. Damage under kitchens and baths indicates a plumbing leak as well as floor and ceiling damage. |

# What to Discard

The important aspect of demolition is discarding what is detracting from the building or what is damaged and unusable. Wherever you find termite damage or dry rot, you will have to completely demolish the damaged parts, treat the remainder against future damage, and replace it with new materials. The most important places to look for this type of damage are around any penetrations in the building shell and along the bottom of the roof joists, especially if there is evidence of leaking.

The electrical service should be examined for sufficiency. Most average houses will require a minimum service of 100 amps. Very large homes will require a 200-amp service. Make sure the service will handle your renovated plan. In houses with basements, you will need to check for water damage on the walls and for general dampness throughout. Check all drains in the floor for signs of rust.

Most basement ceilings are unfinished, so you will be able to get a good look at the mechanical systems and floor joists. Examine the HVAC system or boiler for sufficiency and efficiency. Modern boilers are much smaller than older models and have a larger capacity to heat the expanded house. Modern air conditioning systems, currently available in ratings up to 12*Seer*, are very efficient and will allow the newly renovated home to be cooled more efficiently and, more importantly, less expensively.

**Trade Terms**

A **Seer** rating determines the efficiency and cost of operation of modern HVAC systems. The higher the Seer rating, the better the unit.

# What to Replace

In addition to problem areas that are damaged, you will want to replace the decor items. In homes that are carpeted, replace the carpet and the pad. Old stains can be sucked up into new carpet from old padding. In a major refit and remodel, the following is a basic checklist of items to be completely replaced:

- Carpet, linoleum, vinyl floor coverings, and wallpaper
- Bath fixtures
- Kitchen fixtures and appliances
- Furnace and/or HVAC system
- Hollow-core doors and hardware
- Window coverings (if not, leave them bare)
- Roofing, gutters, and downspouts

Finally, in a remodel, you will want the exterior to call out to prospective buyers as being modern and with it. One of the major differences between older homes and new ones is that the newer ones are copying the very old and are decorating the outsides with architectural features such as cupolas and dormers in the roofs and shutters around the windows. Out West, pop-outs around windows and doorways are used to break up the line of the building. The following graphics are of a typical tract home transformed into an eastern version and a western version.

*As acquired.*

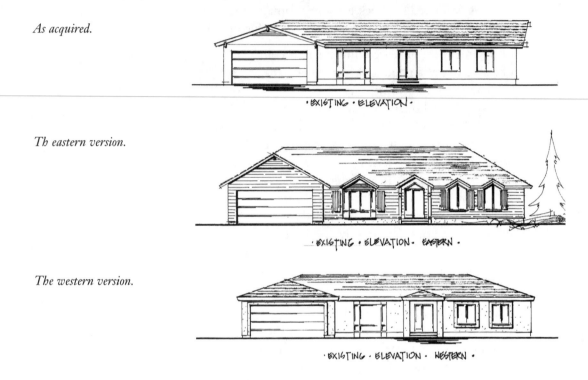

· EXISTING · ELEVATION ·

*Th eastern version.*

· EXISTING · ELEVATION · EASTERN ·

*The western version.*

· EXISTING · ELEVATION · WESTERN ·

One of the best effects that can be added to a house during renovation is texture. This is provided in the East by using trim and shutters and in the West by using stucco, stone, and pop-outs. The roof can also be used as an additional texture change. Western architecture leans toward wood shingles, clay tiles, and concrete roof tile. In the East, you can choose from asphalt shingle, concrete roof tile, slate, and rolled-metal roofing. The blend of different textures is a modern look, and properly done, you can achieve a period look as well. In fact, its distinct pallet of textures can identify period architecture.

The modern roof is also identified by its overhang and underlying trim. The newer houses have a detail (as shown in the following graphics) to distinguish them from the traditional overhang.

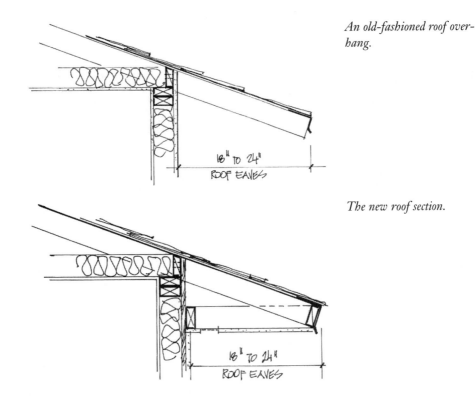

*An old-fashioned roof overhang.*

*The new roof section.*

The different architectural treatments used in various parts of the country are a subtle distinction to most people, and you have been used to it since infancy. If, however, a house stands out from the rest on a given street, the odds are, that the difference is in the styling rather than the substance. Seldom does anyone overbuild a house for the neighborhood, because that investment is very hard to recoup, but often, a transplant from somewhere else will build a house "just like back home." It will always stand out, and it too, will be hard to resell.

## The Least You Need to Know

- Demolish carefully according to plan; otherwise, you will have to replace costly parts that were not in your plan.

- Take care when changing structural elements because one of them may be holding up the roof.

- Replace all damaged materials so that the building will literally be "as good as new."

- Keep the good stuff, it pays. Small trim pieces salvaged at the beginning of the demolition and added back after the renovation will lend an authentic look to the building. They are literally irreplaceable.

# Chapter 22

# Expanding—The Big Bucks

## In This Chapter

- ◆ Transitioning neighborhoods
- ◆ Where to look and what to buy
- ◆ The marketability of trendy

At this point in the game, you should have a grasp of the basic economic factors involved in the fixer-upper process. Rather than take on a simple upgrade, you might want to consider going for the brass ring of the fixer-upper market.

Every area of the country has a neighborhood that is considered fashionable or very desirable. Often these locations are older parts of the city, containing housing that varies from recent to old. In some areas, it might be a neighborhood that used to be summer cottages or winter cabins. As population expands, these formerly remote or once vacation-oriented properties become accessible to the mainstream. The cause of this varies … Most of these places become commutable as highway expansion catches up to growth potential in the area.

The other instance in which this occurs is caused by rising affluence of retirees or people who can commute electronically. They can afford to live well, and they can afford to live wherever they choose. These people are epitomized by the recently emerged "dot.comers." This chapter will deal with the opportunities created by this exodus of the prosperous to the undiscovered lifestyle locations around the country.

# Neighborhoods in Transition

People who live and work in expensive parts of the country, like California or the area in and around New York City, build up tremendous equity in their homes over a period of years. When the time comes to slow down and smell the roses, these people are increasingly heading for the hills, the ocean, the lakes, and the mountains. Normally, the proceeds from the sale of their home in the overcrowded areas they leave are enough to buy their dream house in their destination town and have enough left to purchase a small business. This is happening coast to coast. In the western United States, Nevada, Arizona, Colorado, and Washington are experiencing large migrations from California, and on the East Coast, people are fleeing the big cities and moving to rural settings from Maine to the Carolinas.

The people who go to these places have traditionally been people who are celebrities or who have a real need for privacy and anonymity. It is impossible for these people who are so visible to live any kind of normal life in a traditional setting; therefore, they are constantly searching for somewhere to let their hair down and where their children can have a sense of normalcy. The problem is that, wherever these highly visible types go, the merely affluent follow to rub elbows with them. This creates a trend, an affluence in this market that can be successfully capitalized upon.

Here's the big question: Who is cashing in on this phenomenon? There are really two classes of people who have been riding this wave: the developers and the fixer-uppers. The developers are busy creating lifestyle communities designed and built around golf courses, marinas, ski resorts, and other recreational areas. The fixer-uppers are busy rebuilding the older, established towns that have suddenly become trendy. When a town is discovered, the price of housing can skyrocket 200 to 400 percent in a few short years. Many of these communities, especially the beach communities, were originally built with cottage-like buildings. These structures were at best basic, seldom insulated properly, and very casually thrown together. This fact spells opportunity for the entrepreneur.

These areas seem to always be in transition. The first wave attempts to make these homes year-round dwellings, and the second wave, capitalizing on the increasing popularity of the area, expands them into trendy and spacious houses. There are really two opportunities then for you and your entrepreneurial spirit. If you find such a community in the early acceptance, you can get in on the modernization wave. Just add decor, new baths, and kitchens, and you have a good project. If you see the trend starting to encompass enlarging the smaller year-round homes, and make them fashionable and trendy, you have the opportunity to get on the bandwagon. Locate some of the older unremodeled vacation houses; they are ripe for demolition and renovation. This is where the big bucks are!

### This Works

When you find an area with a pent-up demand, you are in a position to make some real money. You can take a cottage-type dwelling, turn it into a home twice the size, and yield three times the acquisition price. Specific towns where this has happened are Venice, California; Durango, Colorado; Aspen, Colorado; the Hamptons and Fire Island, New York; and the Maine coastal towns. Towns like Sun Valley, Tiburon, Napa, Key West, Mill Valley, Provincetown, Nantucket, Palm Beach, and Vale are competing successfully with Caribbean islands and the more exotic destinations.

By now you know what to look for. In this type of move, you need to concentrate on opportunities that have built-in expansion capability. If there is not enough land, you must go up, adding another story or two. Do not be discouraged; this is not rocket science. Your friendly house designer or architect can show you the way.

The following sketches show an ordinary suburban house with a second-story addition. It involves only selective demolition and addition. You already know how to do that.

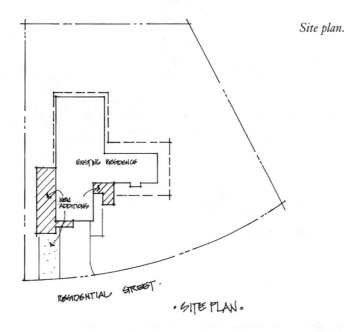

*Site plan.*

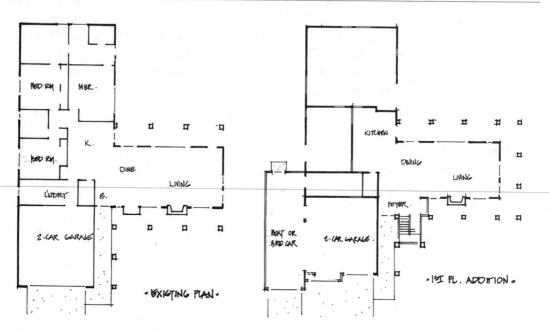

*Existing Floor plan.*

*The first floor addition.*

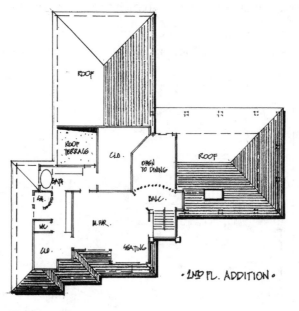

*The second floor addition.*

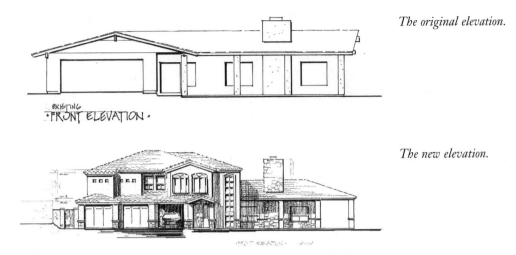

*The original elevation.*

EXISTING
·FRONT ELEVATION·

*The new elevation.*

This trend is also evidenced by a resurgence of inner-city housing. As people become empty nesters and start to have some discretionary income, they are looking toward more recreational possibilities. For the city dweller, moving back to the city with money to spend is a real treat. Big cities offer incredible opportunities for cultural events and diversity of entertainment. Not all these people want to move into new high-rise co-ops and condominiums. This has started and continues to fuel a resurgence of urban housing. These people want brownstones and walk-up flats in fashionable areas of town. What they look for is proximity to theater, restaurants, and shopping. It's your job to find it for them and have it ready when they get there. You will not find this type of opportunity in the suburbs.

Just what does this opportunity mean to your pocketbook? There is no mystery to it. In most of the country, housing sells for $70 to $130 per square foot. In these communities, you will see prices that vary from $200 to $400 per square foot and up. When you buy the small run-down cottage, you will wince at the price, but do not falter. You can make it bigger and better. By applying your fixer-upper expertise and planning the work economically, you can add significant space at a cost of $70 to $100 per square foot. It does not take a rocket scientist to see that if you add space for $100 per square foot and sell it for $200 per square foot or higher, there is money to be made.

# What to Look For

The big question, "What type of project should you shoot for?" has no real answer. Each person will find a type of project that will fit his or her comfort level. The key to the selection of projects of this nature is your comfort zone. A conservative approach will point you to the house that is close to the traditional three-bedroom, two-bath house that can comfortably handle a family. Others will opt for the extreme location and the ultra-trendy retreat. I have no good advice to offer you in this decision; you must go with what you are most comfortable with. I would guess that if you start with a somewhat conservative approach and work your way to the outrageous end of the spectrum, you would be better off.

### Warning, Danger Ahead!

Eventually you will experience a "frustrating" fixer-upper project that when it sells, you will feel you were very lucky to get out from under it. When that happens, veer your course back toward the conservative side. Remember, your defense against having overdone it is to move in and live there until the market catches up with you. If this happens, entertain a lot and entertain people who can afford to buy the house; then sell. Go and sin no more.

## How Do You Discover These Areas?

When going about discovering these types of areas, you look for and pay attention to trends. There is a wealth of information in this area in the form of magazine articles. Go to a good bookstore and raid the magazine section. Look for the following types of publications:

- Architectural (*Architectural Digest*)
- Home design and decor (*Home & Design*)
- Home remodeling (*Today's Homeowner*)
- Vacation (*Vacations*)
- Travel (*Adventure*)
- Island living (*Islands*)
- Fashion (*GQ*)
- Modern health (*Men's Health*)

In the local big-city paper, read the gossip columns and look in the Sunday supplement for vacation places and homes. Articles will tell you where the trendsetters are going. If you are fortunate enough to have some degree of mobility, you could follow them around. Most likely, you can find some area that has been discovered in your own back yard.

## Which Trends to Follow?

A final word about trends: You want to be trendy with your designs and remodeling, but stick to trends that have a built-in usefulness. Do not include things that do not serve a long-term purpose. A great bathroom is far better than a hot tub. Include the location and utilities for the hot tub, but let the buyer add it. It is the same as a swimming pool in its return on investment.

**This Works** _____

If you always go with the practical side of trendy, you won't go wrong. This is true for all fixer-uppers.

# Commercial Trendy

So, with all this to-ing and fro-ing, what's the commercial angle? As with any commercial property, it follows the residential. Without people, you do not need services. The more people there are, the more services are needed. The more trendy and affluent the population is, the more trendy and upscale the services must be.

In these quaint and upcoming towns, the old main street used to be full of homes. These homes can be converted into a myriad of commercial uses at commercial prices commensurate with the surrounding community. Most commercial land sells for three times its residential counterpart. Obviously, larger needs must be served by demolishing groups of these old homes and erecting shopping centers, but these developments serve to supply the necessities only. The niceties and recreation can be served by adapting the old, funky buildings for restaurants and trendy shops.

The idea, when working with these structures, is to go overboard on the gingerbread. You can emphasize the period with more trim on everything—roof, walls, doors, and windows—and by painting in the *candy apple style*.

By overemphasizing the period or creating a period look on a plain house, you will find that the age disappears and the trendy will emerge. The margins on these commercial rebuilds are the same as with the houses. You want to expand the usable square feet and add patios and outdoor amenities in the old back yards.

**Trade Terms** _____

The **candy apple style** uses bright and contrasting paint colors to suggest clean and crisp looks. It has an almost cartoon-like effect. An example would be bright white with a bright yellow trim or chocolate brown with cream-colored trim.

The back yards are also an opportunity to add structures and connect them to the street with landscaped alleys where the old driveways used to be.

## Planning and Marketability

The major difference between the residential fixer-upper and the commercial one in this area is that, in commercial, authenticity is not necessary. It merely needs to look like it is authentic to the period and slightly exaggerated. The insides, due to the nature of commercial buildings, are temporary. The next owner will tear it out and redecorate. You do not need to stretch for super quality, only durability in a commercial setting. You are not building historic preservation, only commercial space. In the photo that follows, you can see some older main street houses that have been converted into trendy commercial businesses.

*Trendy shops.*

When working with the high-dollar fixer-upper, you must learn to think outside the ordinary envelope. You will need a good and "with it" Realtor®, and you might want to consider a partnership in which the Realtor® finds the places for you and sells them. You make your money on the renovation, and your Realtor® makes his or hers on the turnover.

In this economic bracket, these projects are never referred to as fixer-uppers; they are historic renovations. Obviously, there is some tongue-in-cheek aspects to this, but from a marketing point of view, you must learn to say it with a straight face. People who are paying through the nose to be in the right place want all the reassurance you and the Realtor® can produce.

## The Trendy Budget

The budget for this type of project will be a little different than that of an ordinary project. If you are really reaching for the sky, you will want to be known in the community as a person who can produce award-winning projects. This will necessitate some additional expenses not necessarily associated with a run-of-the-mill fixer-upper. First of all, you will want the latest and trendiest design, so you need to find the most in-demand designer. You will likely want to consider the services of the trendiest interior designer as well. You will need to cultivate publicity both locally and in the magazines mentioned earlier in this chapter.

The easiest way to accomplish this is to retain a publicist for each endeavor. This is nothing more than a more elaborate team than usual. It is necessary when you want to soar with the eagles. The other big thing is that you want to see and be seen. You need to mingle with your potential clients as well as those people in the industry who serve these clients. Most of your team will be on the welcome list for parties and so on because buyers want to meet and size up the people who sell them their life's dream. When you get to this stage, you must convince yourself that what you are doing is important and that you do it with a passion. You must really believe this, and it must show that you do.

You cannot afford to be phony about this. You will be dealing with people who are going to pay three times more for something that everyone else takes as ordinary. They will pay it cheerfully if they believe that they are getting their money's worth. You must convince yourself and those around you that the value is there forever.

### This Works

I'm sure your constant question in all this is "Will it work, and how much money can I make?" The answer is simple. Go back to the research material in the previous chapters, survey the rents and finished sales prices, see what the end product can bring, and then calculate your costs. The difference will be the measure of the opportunity. The only one really hanging it out is the first guy to do it. So, if you're nervous, watch and wait. There is no shame in being number two.

## The Least You Need to Know

◆ Become a student of the "with-it" crowd by keeping track of who they are and where they go.

◆ Remember that you will be working in exotic financial territory; do not be faint of heart.

◆ Put together a trendy and savvy team. It's expensive but worth it.

◆ Make yourself a believer in your projects because this type of fixer-upper requires more imagination and money than the run-of-the-mill deal.

# Part 5

# Putting Ideas to Work

If you have never done this before, you might think, "Where do I start?" The chapters in this part will take you through five specific remodeling projects: a typical 1950s-era tract house, two types of Victorians, an urban town house and a small town house, a beachfront cottage, and a conversion from house to commercial building.

As part of this process, we will discus what needs to be done and how to do it. You will start to get the idea after the first few run-throughs. It is not a mysterious process. Simply imagine what you want the finished product to be, and then how to get there becomes pretty straightforward. Moving walls and replacing windows become the details, and a cost item, the plan, and the finished product will dictate the process. Confirm the market before you start, create an affordable plan, and then go to work.

# Chapter 23

# Project Potential and Planning

## In This Chapter

- ◆ Different types of projects
- ◆ Project components
- ◆ What to choose, evaluate the potential for gain

When the time comes for you to seek out a specific project, you need to be able to distinguish between the really old house, the partially upgraded, and the house with no potential left. They can coexist on the same street, and within the contiguous neighborhood. A great area to look in is neighborhoods bordering the affluent areas of your community.

## Ideas That Work

In Chapters 24 through 27, we will review a variety of renovation plans for five different types of housing and some treatments for each of them in an upgrade situation. These chapters will discuss the possibilities for upgrading to increase value and appeal, thereby enhancing the sale of your fixer-upper.

In these chapters, we will discuss how to enhance the properties from the house itself to the outdoors and the miscellaneous buildings that you will find or create on a residential lot. There is no way for me to suggest exactly what you should do with any specific property you acquire for renovation, but I hope to point you toward some appropriate possibilities for some given situations.

Scattered throughout these chapters will be a series of illustrations of how to change older, outmoded houses into newer, more modern ones with as little effort as possible. You will see five total remodels. Although each chapter deals with a specific house, you can refer to the changes made in the other houses that you might care to apply to your specific project. As such, references may be made to illustrations in other chapters, thus avoiding having to print the same illustration several times.

The series of sketches will illustrate five different house remodeling projects:

- A 1950s tract-home expansion (Chapter 24)

- An urban town house circa 1940 modernization (Chapter 25)

- An in-town Victorian modernization (Chapter 25)

- A beach cottage transformation (Chapter 26)

- A house on Main Street altered to a commercial use (Chapter 27)

> **Reality Check**
>
> This book is not intended tell you how to hang a door or install a toilet. For this type of specific instructions, you will need to refer to the myriad of household repair and fix-it books. If you remember, when we searched the Internet, we had more than 33,000 hits on "home remodeling" alone.

The following features will be discussed in the context of the remodeling schemes in these chapters:

- Entries

- Living areas

- Kitchens

- Bathrooms

- Bedrooms

There will also be coverage of the "miscellaneous spaces" you will want to have, such as a baby's room, an exercise room, a home office, or even an au pair's quarters (should you be so fortunate to afford one). And, of course, there will be information about the different types of garages and outbuildings you no doubt will encounter along the way.

# Lots of Choices

As with any fixer-upper, you will be faced with many different choices, the most important of which is just how far to take the remodel. Only you can answer that question. If you are going to fix up a house for your own use, you might want to take it a bit farther than the market might indicate for your own personal enjoyment. Sooner or later, the market will catch up with you.

An example of how these projects are found and can fit into neighborhoods is in the three following pictures of houses side by side on the same street. The first is an as-is original, the second a partially upgraded home, and the final, is a house fully renovated. The difference in price is approximately $175,000 from the first to the last.

*Home 1: An original house.*

*Home 2: The first upgrade.*

*Home 3: A fully renovated.*

There are many different choices involving each room in the house, some of which you might or might not be aware of. I will go through some of these here so that you can have a chance to think them through. Specific designs for each room type are available on the Internet and are detailed in the myriad of books on home improvement.

## Entries

You would think that an entry into a home is a routine thing, but it can vary all over the lot. The following are some ideas you might want to consider, depending on the type and size of house you are contemplating fixing up:

◆ The pulled-out entry covered in Chapter 24 accomplishes two things: It adds space to a house, providing a transition into the home, and it alters the roofline to add interest to the elevation. How large it is depends on the scale of the house and the uses of the entry. Where there is frequent inclement weather, such as a location where you have a winter climate, the addition of a closet and bench area should be strongly considered.

**This Works**

People are often image conscious, and if they think the house is impressive from the street, they might be inclined to overlook a few flaws on the inside of the house.

◆ The *porte co·chere* is an elegant version of this extended entry that is combined with a covered drive at the entrance to the home, usually accessed by a circular driveway. This is the granddaddy of all entries and should be attached only to a very large house. This is an option you can consider when renovating a house on a large lot. To come off well, this feature needs plenty of room and landscaping. If you try to cram it onto a lot that is too shallow, it will look contrived and have just the opposite effect.

When working with larger houses or houses on large lots, achieving a grand effect at the entry may provide enough of an effect to offset some of the negative features of the house.

## Living Areas

Living areas encompass the living room, the family room, the den, the library, and in some instances, the kitchen. Options for these rooms are many and have a distinct cachet when it comes time to sell. The living room is only a living room if the house also contains a family room. These two rooms are considered essential if you want to appeal to the traditional buyer. More modern buyers, especially young families, are looking at the combination room or great room because it serves both purposes and allows the buyer to have an extra bedroom with the same amount of square footage.

You must decide which market you are shooting for when you remodel. If you are looking for a more mature buyer, stick with the living room plus family room, but when appealing to the young family, combine these two rooms into a great room and add an extra bedroom.

## Kitchens

Most American homes center around the kitchen and the TV. It is therefore no accident that the kitchen and family room are designed as an attached set in most homes. There are, however, options for a kitchen area that need to be considered:

- The island kitchen is a room with a central island for food preparation. It is the accepted new version of kitchen design, and one should be incorporated whenever space allows. It is perceived to be the single most important feature in the modern kitchen. This truly is perception rather than reality. Seldom can you pick up a magazine about kitchens without seeing the center island featured prominently.

- The nook provides a table for two in a kitchen for breakfast or for visiting with the cook during meal preparation. It is an old-fashioned amenity but a very pleasant one; it's very popular with the older set.

- The eating counter is important for young families. The cook can dispense food to the kids handily at breakfast or whenever time does not permit a more formal meal. This essential feature for young families can be combined with the central island with relative ease.

**Warning, Danger Ahead!**

The gourmet kitchen is only for the serious cook and should not be attempted in any fixer-upper unless your buyer has ordered it and provided the cash upfront to create it. A gourmet kitchen properly done is obscenely expensive!

◆ The eat-in kitchen combines the dining room with the kitchen and is very common in country homes with limited space. It is also a feature in large houses with room for an expanded kitchen and a formal dining room. It is a customary feature in large period homes.

◆ The gourmet kitchen is a combination of all-of-the-above with professional-grade appliances, marble counters, food-preparation islands, and a generous eat-in area. Approach this one with extreme caution.

## Bathrooms

You would think that bathrooms would be a very straightforward topic, but with new innovations and changing lifestyles, they have become more interesting, varied, useful, and creative. How you decide which style to use is relatively easy; simply look at the market and decide which is most appropriate. You might want to pull some one-upmanship over your competition by choosing a style they do not offer. The choices are as follows:

◆ The traditional bath has a sink, a toilet, and a tub/shower combination.

◆ The larger version comes with two sinks, a separate toilet room, and perhaps a separate shower.

◆ The master bathroom has two sinks and a separate toilet room and shower but is connected to a walk-in closet.

◆ The palatial master bath incorporates a separate shower, a Jacuzzi tub, pedestal sinks, a dressing table, a separate toilet room, a linen closet, and his and hers walk-in closets; it is very common in larger new homes.

◆ The Jack-and-Jill bath connects two bedrooms and is accessible only from the bedrooms.

◆ The second bath and guest bath combination is usually accessible from both a bedroom and the hallway, but it can be locked off from either or both when in use.

◆ The powder room contains only a sink and a toilet.

# Bedrooms

Bedrooms are relatively straightforward and are usually distinguished and labeled according to size and amenities.

- ◆ The master bedroom, even in small houses, is seldom smaller than 12'×14' and always has its own bathroom attached.

- ◆ The second bedroom, while usually small, is seldom smaller than 11'×13'. The closet normally is a single six-footer.

Other variations on this theme will incorporate other features in the master bedroom such as a fireplace, a TV nook, a seating area, huge closets, and palatial baths. The guest rooms or second, third, and fourth bedrooms can be increased in size and, if you want, have their own baths, or they can share a Jack-and-Jill bathroom. Again, your choices about how to modify bedrooms will be dictated by your market.

For example, in senior retirement housing, the two-master-bedroom house is not uncommon, but in a market that caters to families, smaller bedrooms and more of them is the way to go. In the newer houses today, a fourth bedroom has become the standard even for small families because the home office is becoming a fixture in today's economy.

Now that you have acquired some better understanding of components and their impact, you should be prepared to look at a potential fixer-upper with a more critical eye; both for the existing structure and for the potential renovations you might like to make. In the following chapters, you will see urban and suburban Victorian-era homes modernized and expanded, you will see a typical turn of the century to 1950 Main Street home transformed into a business, and you will see a simple beach cottage transformed into an architect's dream house.

 **This Works** _____

In older houses where there is no bath for the master bedroom, you must sacrifice one of the other small bedrooms to add the bath and a large closet. This is a must even for a minimal upgrade.

## The Least You Need to Know

- ◆ A fixer-upper opportunity may exist in the midst of fully modern houses.

- ◆ Decide the target market you are looking for when you remodel; this will make a difference in some of the features you choose to emphasize in the home.

- ◆ The main features of remodeling schemes that can bring the most improvement to your home are entries, living areas, kitchens, bathrooms, and bedrooms.

# Chapter **24**

# The Three-Bedroom Tract

## In This Chapter

- ◆ What you start with
- ◆ The first impression
- ◆ Living and family rooms
- ◆ Kitchen and dining rooms
- ◆ Bedrooms and baths

Probably the most common home in America is the three bedroom ranch with two baths, a two car garage and a private lot. There are millions of them; starting in the late 1940s with Levittown, NY, they have spread throughout the country. They range from 1,200-1,300 square feet for the starter home to approximately 2,500 square feet for the middle class family home. They can be found still in original condition and slightly modified in communities across the country. Unless they are in a blighted neighborhood, almost all of them represent some good fixer-upper potential.

The upgrade potential represented by these houses lies in the lots and the features offered in new homes. The older lots will be larger than those being built upon today, and therefore represent expansion potential, and the new homes of today have led the buyers to look for great rooms and four bedrooms. You therefore have both the room and the expansion need built right into the older houses.

# The Raw Material

Before you start, review the plot plan and the required setbacks to make sure you have the room to accomplish all the additions you want to do. If there is enough room, proceed.

What you see in the following two graphics is a generic, suburban, three-bedroom tract house circa 1950. Most of these homes from the 1950s era contained three bedrooms, one maybe two baths, and a one or sometimes two-car carport. They varied in size from 1,500 to 1,800 square feet and usually sat on a ¼-acre lot.

*A generic 1950s tract house—plan view.*

*Tract home elevation.*

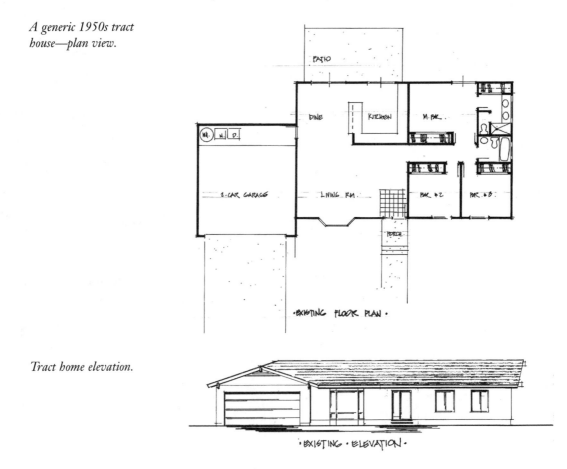

Living areas, as well as bedrooms and baths, can be expanded or more rooms added. These expansions also give you the opportunity to turn a relatively simple and dull-looking structure into one that has some architectural interest with contrasting textures.

The addition of floor space also provides the opportunity to change the exterior in a way that makes the house more interesting.

The particular house we have chosen is a 1,440-square-foot ranch with a two-car garage. The laundry facility is in the garage, and the dining room is a nook off the kitchen. Our plan for this house is to create a more attractive house from the street and expand it to be a more gracious and livable house. We will do the following:

◆ Alter the entry

◆ Expand the kitchen

◆ Add a laundry room

◆ Add a family room and install a rear deck and patio

◆ Modernize the master suite

◆ Create a three-car garage

The above renovation will make this house competitive with the new ones in the marketplace, and if purchased properly, and if renovated shrewdly, should make you a nice profit.

**This Works**

The big plus for tract houses is the lot size. There is and was room to expand. For example, 1,500-square-foot house on a 10,000-square-foot lot affords you an opportunity to enlarge the house almost without limits.

# The Entry

If you watch television or go to the movies, I'm sure you have seen the scenario in which someone answers the doorbell to admit a person into the home. This location at the front door is the entry to the house or foyer. In the movies, to have room to shoot the movie, these entries must be large enough to contain the players and the camera crew. Most of us do not live in a home that spacious.

Older, two-story houses have spacious foyers because the entrance to the house had to accommodate the entry, the stairway, a way into the living room, and a way into the rear of the home. Contrast that with the 1950s-style tract house in which the entry is a 4-foot-by-4-foot piece of tile at the front door, and the rest is the living room.

Transforming a small entry that is part of the living room to something that adds to the house in a way that suggests both space and elegance is not that difficult. In the limited space of the tract-house living room, there is little you can do inside, so the best way to get the effect is to pull the entry outside.

Adding an entryway to the front door can accomplish two things, depending on how you handle it. It can become a separate entry, retaining the original front door that enables people who live in inclement weather to come in out of the weather and get rid of boots, umbrellas, and coats before entering the house, or it can do this while letting people enter the home at the same time.

The weather entry is fine to a point, but it detracts from the welcoming aspects of the new entry. I recommend making it as wide as possible to create a closet for coats on one side of the old front door and a bench seat with storage under it on the other side of the door. By removing the old door entirely, we effectively connect the entry to the living space inside. This creates both an area for discarding the weather gear as well as a spacious entry into the home. You can greet guests and help them out of their coats while at the same time welcoming them into your home.

**This Works**

A weather entry at the front of a house is called a foyer. When the weather entry is at the rear of the house off the kitchen, it is called the mudroom.

A finishing touch is to install a weather surface like tile to the new floor so that it can be easily cleaned. A nice throw rug will finish it off and protect the living room carpeting.

*The plan view reflecting entry addition.*

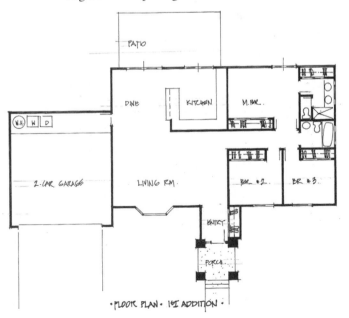

· FLOOR PLAN · 1ST ADDITION ·

# The Living Areas

Next we will add a family room at the rear and, at the same time, expand the kitchen. This transformation will be accomplished by blowing out the back of the dining area wall and cannibalizing the old two-car garage. Radically altering the garage will necessitate the addition of a new garage. At the same time, I suggest that we replace the old living room window with a large bay window to dress up the front of the house and bring in more light.

The results will be a new three-car garage (a necessity for growing families), a new laundry room off the kitchen and garage, a new family room projecting into the back yard, and a separate dining room delineating the new family room and the expanded living room. Remember, by moving the entry to outside the original house, we have added the old entry space to the living room. Another big bonus is that the new family room and the kitchen now are connected to the outdoor patio area with sliding glass doors, effectively making these areas more usable in good weather.

*The second addition.*

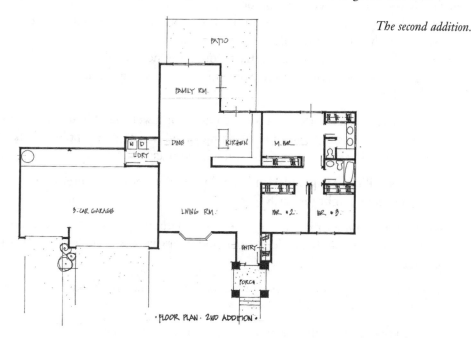

The sequence of work should be to first pour the footings for the addition and then frame and close in the addition, connecting the roofs to render the project weather tight. Then the wall section connecting the two can be demolished and the connection made. Removing some wall to accommodate the addition at the rear of the house is relatively simple. The area to be removed must be braced and a header installed to

**This Works**

To create a successful addition, it must appear that there has been no alteration. The finished product should look as if the house were designed and built that way.

transfer the roof load from the old section of wall to be removed to the footings on either side of the new opening. This header will transfer the load to the foundation and will allow the bearing wall to remain structurally sound. This type of header exists at every opening in the house. It is used to span doors, windows, and garage doors. Once this is accomplished, the wall section can be demolished and the new addition connected. The last step is to marry the floor, wall, and ceiling finishes so that it will appear that the addition is the same as the old section of the house.

# Kitchen and Dining

By moving the dine-in kitchen wall and cannibalizing the old garage, we have created a new family room connected to an outdoor patio, and we have added room for a more formal dining area between the family room and the living room. This change will allow the kitchen to be expanded to a more practical size. The effect is to make the entire living space from the new entry through the new family room and kitchen area a large and spacious living center. Some nice features that can be added to a kitchen are as follows:

◆ A center island can be used as a work counter, or a wet island housing the sink and dishwasher. It might also be a cooking island housing a chopping block, and a stove top and oven combination with a hood over it.

◆ Luminous ceilings are popular and vital in the older houses where there is a lowered ceiling height (under 8 feet).

◆ Skylights are another nice touch to get some natural light into areas with low ceilings, and they can be made to open adding a very desirable feature of natural ventilation.

◆ Ceiling fans and exhausts help remove the built-up heat in the kitchen accumulated from people, lights, and cooking.

◆ Pot shelves over the cabinets allow people to add color as well as store less used but potentially decorative items.

◆ Bay windows over the sink for plants, or a bay window in the eating nook can add space as well as a graciousness to the kitchen area.

Any or all of these features will take up some space, but they have a great impact on the livability and marketability of the house.

# Bedrooms and Baths

Most of the bedrooms in the 1950s era were small, and the master bedroom, if it had a master bath at all, was marred by it being small. The master bedroom closets were also small, generally two six-foot closets. The modern master suite should encompass not necessarily a palatial bath but one that comfortably fits two people at a time (by having two sinks and a generous counter) and also incorporates a walk-in closet or two. This is accomplished here by changing the corner of the house to expand the master bedroom. The additional space is devoted to the bath and closets. By relieving the cramped condition, the bedroom now takes on a grander look and more practical comfort.

Structurally, this is a variation on the header-created change off the kitchen at the other end of the house. Sequentially, we will start with the footings and the construction of two new load-bearing corner walls. Once this is accomplished, a new roof truss is connected to the old corner, now connected by two headers meeting at the corner.

This new connection is then picked up by the new truss and tied back to the ridge of the roof. The resulting change in the corner also provides a more interesting roofline from both the front and rear of the house. This sounds simple, but you must have a structural engineer design this change and lay out the sequence of the work. Any proficient carpenter can make the header change at the other end of the house, but when you are picking up loads from two different walls, it must be done correctly.

*The third addition.*

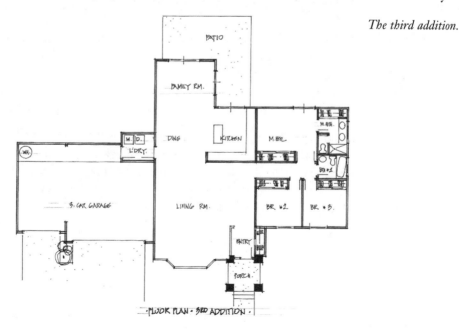

*The finished addition.*

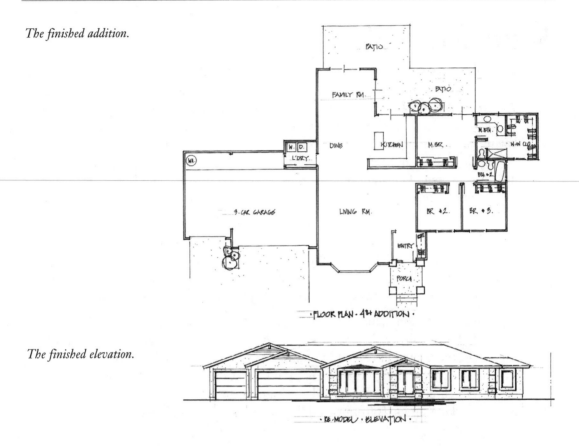

*The finished elevation.*

Having made the changes to the floor plan, you can consider what level of change is required in the kitchen and bath areas as far as fixtures and appliances are concerned. While you are concentrating on the interior and the expansion, do not neglect the trim details and the landscaping. This dressing up will put the finishing touches on your fixer-upper and make it easier to sell.

A future renovation could encompass the addition of a fourth bedroom, a third bath, and/or a recombination of these spaces. It could easily include a guest bath, three bedrooms, and a den or office. Two sketches of possible future projects follow. Rather than overdoing your fixer-upper, leave something on the table for the buyer. You might even use the sketch of the future expansion as a selling point.

The final part of your conversion, in addition to making the home a more gracious place to live also added created a separate laundry room, a three-car garage, a spacious master bedroom, and a very large family room/patio living area. Is this it? Not really, you can see by the following sketches, that there is still some room to improve the house.

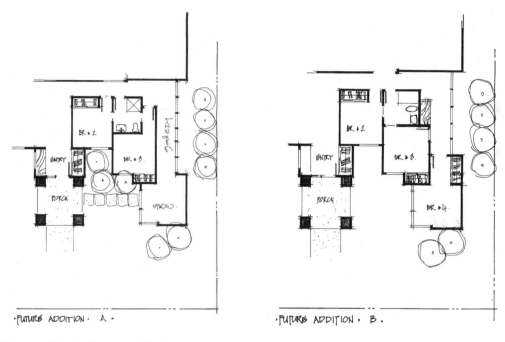

·FUTURE ADDITION · A ·

*Future add-on bedrooms and bath.*

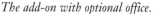
·FUTURE ADDITION · B ·

*The add-on with optional office.*

The configuration of these two sketches, confirms that the buyer can still add on more useful rooms. The only limit to the potential of this house is the coverage (the amount of square footage allowed on the lot) allowed and the economics of the market it sits in.

## The Least You Need to Know

- The generic ranch tract on a ¼-acre lot is a good bet for renovation anywhere in the country.

- Check out the site for setbacks before you start so that you are clear about the expansion potential. Beware of easements encroaching into your planned expansion.

- Try to improve the interior and exterior at the same time; this is a good way to fast track the work without having workmen stumbling over each other.

- Do not overimprove the house for the neighborhood, always make your plan with a competitive exit strategy.

- Leave a little something for the buyer to do, that way the buyer will feel that they are getting a good deal.

# Chapter 25

# Two Victorians

## In This Chapter

- Background on brownstones
- Finding the project and cleaning it up
- Enhancing the main and second floors
- Keeping the character

From the time our settlements became large enough to be cities, Americans have been building various versions of the two-story walk-up for residences. In the early days, one of the most common of this type of building was a multitenant building with flats on each floor. Later versions were two- and three-story homes. The taller buildings were exclusively flats. These buildings became known as tenements.

Most urban single-family houses today are conversions of two-story flats and the later single-family houses known as brownstones. Because of the period in which these dwellings were built, they were also known as Victorians. Their style of exterior was reminiscent of the single-family version, but there the similarity ended.

In this chapter, you will see the approach to a very old and dated urban structure, and the simpler suburban Victorian. In the city, expansion can only go up and out back, whereas in the suburbs, you have a decent sized lot to work with, and can expand in almost all directions.

# A Bit of History

The term "brownstone" comes from the stone quarried for the exterior of the residential buildings, and it seems to be applied equally to houses constructed of brick and stone. The evolution of the city home, unless built in recent years, has been a staged conversion over the years from multitenant walk-up to single-family house to modern single-family house.

When these houses were originally constructed, they came complete with an outhouse and often no electricity. Over the years, they have been rebuilt from the ground up, and many have only the exterior walls in common with the original structure. If you go looking for an urban project, you are likely to find some variation of this type of dwelling built anywhere from the early 1800s to the mid-1900s (see the following photograph of a restored Victorian).

*A restored Victorian without landscaping.*

# Selecting the Project

The reason for looking at a project like this is to challenge us to create a modern house with little space and few amenities. Too often, these buildings are just razed and replaced by multistory apartment buildings. There are many neighborhoods in the city that can benefit from creative renovation rather than demolition.

For our project here (see the original photograph), I have selected a generic two-story common to Chicago in the late 1800s that has been partially converted as a single-family house. Although this project is both doable and most likely feasible, your prospects of actually finding a situation like this would be slim unless you lived or worked in the city. An intimate knowledge of the neighborhoods would be mandatory. Urban neighborhoods are more complex, and a fixer-upper in an urban neighborhood in transition will be less easily sold. The best hope of success in this type of environment occurs when the project is handled by someone local.

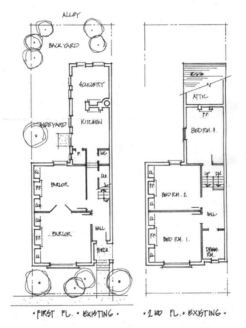

*The project's original configuration.*

Let's look at what we have here. In its original form, the house was heated by fireplaces. The kitchen had an open-hearth stove and oven, and there was one water closet on the main floor.

Off the kitchen was a washroom, an additional food-preparation area, and storage room called a *scullery*. The living area of the house had two rooms: one for guests and the other used as a family room. Upstairs are three bedrooms, all with their own fireplace, and one dressing room. The house was constructed of stone or brick with post-and-beam interior

**Trade Terms** _____

A scullery was a catchall room devoted to mudroom, pantry, washroom, and food preparation, and sometimes, eating.

construction. As you can see, this is a very basic dwelling from the mid-1800s, containing around 880 square feet on each floor.

## Cleaning It Up

As a first pass, to make the project into a more modern dwelling, we are going to assume that we need to redo all the wiring and add a modern plumbing system. Our goal is to keep and emphasize the original features that are a novelty/luxury and replace areas that are no longer part of our concept of a house.

Accordingly, we will retain the fireplaces in the living room, dining room, and kitchen downstairs. The one in the kitchen will be converted to an in-house barbecue grill with a connecting oven. All the units will be gas fired. The kitchen will be converted into a family room, and the scullery converted into a modern kitchen. The original water closet will be enlarged to be a standard guest powder room with a sink and a toilet. The pantry will be left as is for the time being.

Upstairs, we will sacrifice bedroom two to create a more modern bedroom/bath situation. If you look closely, we have two master suites complete with walk-in closets and bathrooms. With the limited space, neither room is overly large, but both boast a working fireplace (gas fired, of course).

*The first pass.*

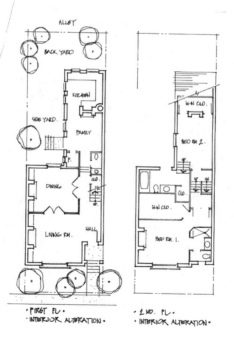

The result is a modest but chic urban town house with some unusual amenities. The biggest plus would be to emphasize the exterior walls inside. The original dwelling was, of course, filled with lathe and plaster walls. On the exterior brick or stone walls, we remove the plaster and sand blast the brick and stone to provide a very striking and rustic touch to the interior. The rest of the interior walls are demolished and replaced by modern stud and sheetrock walls. The original wood floors are restored downstairs and on the staircase, and the upstairs is completely carpeted. The resulting house is a spacious, 1,760-square-foot two-bedroom house with decent amenities and a decent-size yard.

## Making It More Livable

What could we do at this point that would make it grander and more livable? The answer is to open it all up and expand the kitchen. If you look at the final plan, we have completely urbanized the building with controlled patio space and limited and controlled planting. The space to the left of the kitchen is expanded to the lot line and used as a huge informal dining area, connected to two newly created patios.

The patios are planted so that the green is visible from all the rooms inside, making the overall feel of the house one of light and green. The wall between the living and dining rooms is removed as are the walls separating this area from the family room, opening up all the living space. A grander staircase is installed to connect the living/dining area to the family room.

The home is now completely open to the kitchen with lots of light and green from the patio areas. The addition adjacent to the kitchen is only 132 square feet, but by removing all the walls inside and pulling the plantings close to the window spaces, we have created a more spacious and flexible downstairs. The upstairs is as good as we can make it and still have all the modern amenities, so we will leave that alone. All that is left is some attic space that can be used for storage or perhaps converted to a children's room in the future.

**This Works**

By adding windows with planting outside, inside the wall of the yard, we have added defined space, enhancing, through the window, the visual and perceived size of the room.

*The ultimate add-on.*

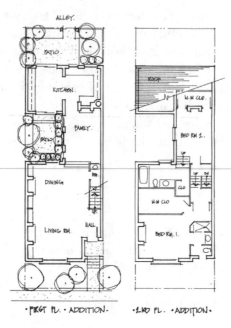

·FIRST FL.·ADDITION·      ·2ND FL.·ADDITION·

# Small-Town Victorian

In almost every small town in America, Main Street used to be filled with period architecture. Today, most of these homes have been demolished to make way for commercial businesses. On the side streets, not too far from Main or Central in many rural towns, you can still find some nice Victorian homes on rather large lots. In college towns and in towns that seek to remain small in spite of the rush to the suburbs, city councils are seeking to preserve all forms of period architecture. One common house type that is found coast to coast is the Victorian. They range in size from 1,500 to 3,000 square feet. If you can find one that is structurally sound, you have a great fixer-upper opportunity.

This style home is so popular that people are building them from scratch these days. These homes, because of their style and graceful designs, have become associated with gracious living. Their rather formal demeanor and interior details make them great candidates for a serious upgrade. You must, however, make sure the neighborhood can support the sale price of your fixer-upper. In many areas, these opportunities have disappeared because savvy buyers have already taken all the good ones. Look farther afield; it's worth it.

*The western version, restored.*

If you are fortunate enough to be working with an old Victorian two-story house, the foyer will not be an issue as far as space is concerned, but the old-style foyer was seldom treated as part of the living space. In most instances, it was walled off as a separate entity. Modern-style houses built in the late 1980s and 1990s treat the entry space as a part of the living/dining complex.

The traditional Victorian plan treated the entry as a separate entity, and it was really well received. Entries and corridors are necessary, but they take away from living space and the general openness of a house. If the corridors can be accomplished without walling them off, the effect is to create larger living areas. The walkway becomes, in effect, just an extension of the living room instead of a narrow, defined space.

Modern design has lifted the ceilings to create more cubic footage in the house, and if you have more space above, you need more room below to give the rooms a sense of proportion. This spacious design was a feature characteristic of the Victorian house.

## Reality Check

If you look at a house and think it looks somewhat elegant and slightly old fashioned, it's most likely to be a Victorian or a take-off on a Victorian. Most of them were two stories, but some of the modern versions are a single story. For our exercise, we have located an older, modest two-story with two bedrooms downstairs and two upstairs. In all respects, it is a nice, modest little house. Our object is to expand it to become a more gracious and livable house.

*The first floor as is.*

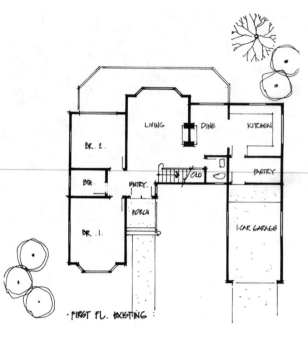

*The second floor as is.*

# Enhancing It

The steps we will take involve the enhancement of the interior and exterior and the addition of another car to the garage.

The exterior addition will be reflected in expanded porches and the garage addition. The addition of a wrap-around porch will provide access from the living areas to more space that can be utilized year round. The new expanded porch roof provides another texture to the exterior. By adding a second car garage to the left of the existing garage, we are taking advantage of the blank space between the garage and the porch entry. By using the two garages as the first floor and removing the roof from the existing garage, we are able to create a second story over the combined garages. This also gives a nicer and more compact look to the building as a whole.

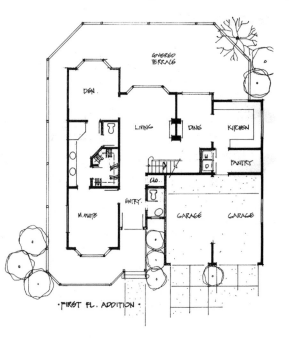

*The expanded ground floor.*

On the main floor, we have decided to cannibalize the bedrooms and bath to create a gracious master suite, extending the rear of the house out to add a den that will be connected to an expanded living room by double French doors. By enclosing the front porch, we expand the entry to be more gracious. To the right of the entry, we add a closet and seat for guest convenience. This leaves a nice space between the house entrance and the new garage wall for some intense landscaping. Smaller spaces are easier to fill and maintain with green.

*The new second floor.*

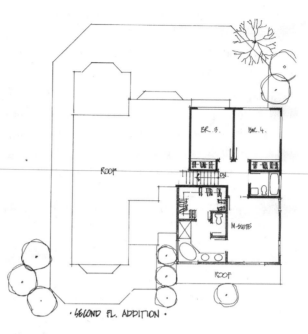

· SECOND FL. ADDITION ·

The second floor, with the space added over the garages, allows us to do many different things. In our scenario, we have chosen to make it into a second master bedroom complex. It might just as easily have been used to create a library, a playroom, or two more bedrooms with a bath. The configuration we have chosen is most likely useful if there is a live-in situation like a parent, an au pair, or a long-term guest. Large families would find the addition of more bedrooms and a playroom to be a bigger benefit.

## Taking It Up a Notch

The Victorian style is so much fun to work with that I believe it lends itself to some real expansion. Many of the early homes had large lots with detached garages, and that adds to the possibilities for expansion.

**This Works**

Since the new floor is being added, it will be designed to hold the load intended for it. The roof and additional walls should be no problem for the original foundation.

A detached garage on a spacious lot cries out for the addition of a garage apartment or an au pair setup. The steps are simple: Remove the roof, put in a second floor, and add on a new roof. The structure should be able to handle the second floor with ease as long as the original foundations are consistent with the current building code. If not, you can add some column footings to handle the vertical load without disturbing the perimeter footings. The only difference will be the structural design for the second floor. Most often, the access to the second floor apartment is by a new staircase on the side of the existing garage structure. This can be accomplished in a compact manner by putting in a landing and bringing the stair to the front of the building. This allows a covered entry to the apartment. You can also have a walkway along the front off the second floor to split the space into two spacious bedrooms. Frequently, older garages were built to be 24' × 24', totaling 576 square feet—enough space for a great one-bedroom apartment or two spacious bedrooms with bath.

# Maintaining the Character

The most important part of working with period architecture is to stay in character. It's okay to replace windows and doors or to make them larger as long as you maintain the same type of window and the trim that goes with it. Attention to detail is important in the grounds as well. Most of these houses boasted great gardens with seasonal plantings and lots of color. This is a great sales tool. Buyers love colorful landscaping, and it will show off your house to perfection.

**This Works**

Character in a Victorian is almost always defined by the trim details, and the grace of the exterior design. Its many angles, porches, overhangs, finishes, and trims are like dressing the house. If you remove all this, what you have left is a modern two-story house.

*The real thing.*

## The Least You Need to Know

♦ Period architecture can be profitable, as it reminds people of a simpler time. Capitalize on the wave of nostalgia sweeping the country.

♦ The key to restoration is all in the details. Salvage the trim when you start, restore it and put it back, and you can claim that it is original.

♦ Victorians lend themselves to gracious living, and project an image of family and better times.

♦ Pick your neighborhoods carefully, and if you can create synergy with their neighbors, you can cash in on the ambiance of the neighborhood. The house will sell itself.

# 26

# The Beach Cottage

## In This Chapter

- ◆ How nearby water affects your fixer-upper
- ◆ The three project phases
- ◆ Choosing what you will renovate

Themed developments—on a golf course, in the mountains, at the seashore, or on a lake—are projects with a totally different set of economics. In the United States, we who are in the business have been following a rule of thumb for years that dictates that the cost of the land should be approximately 20 percent of the total cost or, in market terms, the sale price of a residential product. Simply put, if you pay $20,000 for a building lot, the finished house should sell for about $100,000.

Most residential property here seems to fall into this type of category. The logic of anyone buying a lot for $1 million and then having to build and sell a home for $5 million completely escapes me. In this chapter, we will examine upgrading the typical beach cottage found around almost every lake in this country. We will go through the refit in three different steps, showing you how you can afford, over time, to transform this simple seasonal dwelling into a year-round comfortable family home.

# The Economics of Water

In 1986, I happened to be in Daytona Beach, Florida and was meeting with someone who lived in a home on the beach. After the meeting, he was showing me around, and I asked him what the small lot next to his home was worth. He said that he had offered $1 million for it and was turned down.

High-priced housing like this will most likely fly in Malibu, California, where one is knee deep in movie stars with plenty of dough, but for the rest of us, there must be a better solution. Unfortunately, there is limited shoreline in this country, and all of it is spoken for. What is left that's affordable for the rest of us is lakefront property.

> ### Reality Check
>
> This Daytona Beach lot was approximately 5,000 square feet. For your information, that's $200 per square foot. Granted, this was oceanfront property, but the price was still impressive.

Fortunately, there are many lakes in this country, and in most places, the price of land is not beyond the realm of possibility. A feasible approach is to find an old beach cottage and convert it over a period of years to a year-round house. Most beachfront communities were not planned developments in the same sense that we know developments today. They usually started in the mid-1800s as a get away for city dwellers. These communities eventually grew along lakefronts within a commutable distance from the city.

In the early days before modern roads, the husband came out on weekends, and the wife and kids spent the summer at the beach or in the mountains. As roads improved, the husbands came out more often, and as the modern freeway system was constructed, people started to give some thought to making a year-round house at the beach. We started to see some of the oldest cottages torn down and replaced by year-round dwellings. Eventually, the values of the old cottages increased to the point where renovation and fixer-uppers became a choice rather than doing a total teardown.

 **This Works**

For a time I lived in western New York in a small community on Lake Erie. The beach community in which I rented was approximately 200 houses, 30 of which were year-round dwellings and the rest summer cottages. Since then, more than half of these have been converted into year-round homes. This situation is common to communities spread all along the lake, and I imagine it's pretty common in any state that has lakes. I remember most of these cottages very well, and without exception, they represent a real conversion opportunity. There are two ways to look at this: first as a potential house to live in, converting it over time as you have the money, or second as a full-blown conversion for resale.

# Project Outline

If you look at the following graphic of the typical beach cottage, it is small—30' × 44', or 1,320 square feet. The building is uninsulated, has board siding, has a corrugated tin roof, and boasts no covered parking. It sits on a ¼-acre lot on the beachfront. You can enter the house from the kitchen that faces the road, or you can walk around to the beachfront and enter from the front porch. There are three bedrooms, a kitchen, a pantry, one bathroom, a combination living and dining area, and a porch facing the beach. The floors are unfinished tongue-in-groove planking.

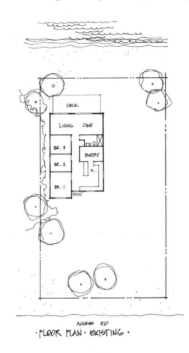

*A typical beach cottage.*

If you can find an appropriate building in a potentially profitable location but your funds are currently limited, you might want to look at a project like this one as a 10- to 15-year investment. We will attack this project in three stages as if you were to buy it and live there, expanding it as the need arises.

If you find a mid-size or large city where development is causing the suburbs to grow, you might want to look further out for a lakefront fixer-upper project. If you are going to live in it for a number of years, financing is readily available for up to 97 percent of the cost. By using the purchase agreement carefully to have a contingent sale, you can draw your plans and secure the financing for the first phase before even purchasing the cottage. Most banks will loan enough to convert such a cottage into a modest year-round house. You can buy it and use the loan proceeds for the conversion.

If you wanted to, you could purchase and go to the final stage in one step; just verify your market before you take the plunge.

## Phase One

If you noted that the house sits to one side on the lot, you will realize that our selection of this layout is deliberate. If you intend to do a live-in fixer-upper, especially if you are going to do it over time as this example suggests, then in your search for a suitable house to renovate, you should apply the following criteria as a minimum:

- The house when renovated should be livable for your family.

- There should be expansion room on the site, preferably on one side.

- There should be a number of year-round dwellings in the area.

- The commute time to the city should be reasonable for the area. In Michigan, one hour is reasonable, but in California, two hours is not uncommon.

- The basic structure should be sound, without termites or dry rot.

- The house should have a concrete foundation.

- The beachfront should be free of erosion.

The fact that there is room on one side of the cottage allows us to plan for a future expansion when the time is right. Many of these cottages had this layout to accommodate spillover parking on the weekends. The planning for the fixer-upper project will include plans for the ultimate conversion you can see in the final elevation graphic, but the phasing will accommodate a more cautious approach.

Our first step is to remove the siding and insulate the building thoroughly. At the same time, we will replace the windows with dual- or triple-pane units for their insulation value. When we are finished, we will replace the old siding with a more permanent, maintenance-free material. In locations where there is winter weather, I recommend a colored, prefinished,

**This Works**

Research during phase one is not all that hard to find. The structure can be inspected by a certified home inspector and a good termite inspector. Information on the beach can be had from the Corps of Engineers, and general history of the area can usually be found at the local library.

vinyl siding. The attic will be insulated with blown-in insulation and the roofing removed and replaced with a more durable year-round roofing material. In snow country, rolled metal roofing serves well, but asphalt shingles are more cost effective.

If you look at the following phase one refit graphic, we have been conservative with our first move, sacrificing the middle bedroom for another bathroom. This bathroom can be set up in several different ways. Currently it is a Jack-and-Jill-type bath accessible from both bedrooms; this is only one solution, and it is shown only to give you a look at another type of bathroom design.

**Warning, Danger Ahead!**

You must resist the temptation to use a fancier and heavier material on the roof. You want to avoid adding to the weight of the finished roof on the original structure.

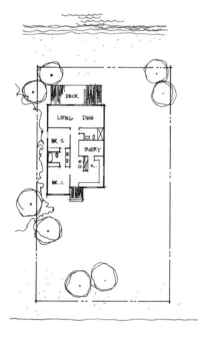

*The phase one refit.*

I would have the bath dedicated only to bedroom one and designate that room as the master bedroom (as shown in the finished addition graphic in the section "The Final Phase"). The bath across the hall can serve the second bedroom and guests.

The final touch for this phase would be to add a more formal covered porch at the rear, incorporating a spacious entry to accommodate people entering the house in inclement weather.

Other possible upgrades, depending on the condition of the house, are as follows:

- ◆ Complete interior painting

- ◆ New floors or carpeting

- ◆ A new HVAC system with the air handler installed in the attic space

- ◆ Adding a carport or garage in a location that anticipates phase three as shown in the final phase graphic

## Phase Two

The first pass at the conversion has resulted in a home that is livable year round, retaining the basic characteristics of the original structure. This second phase will keep these changes and make one more modest alteration. We will expand the kitchen to accommodate a potential future family situation, cannibalizing the pantry in the process. This might not seem like a big change, but a full-blown kitchen conversion can be a big expenditure. We have also dedicated the second bath exclusively for bedroom one only. This sets the stage for the third and final phase—the addition of another 1,248 square feet.

*The phase two refit.*

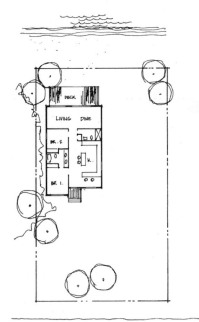

# The Final Phase

In this phase, we will do some selective demolition of the right-hand exterior wall and the kitchen entry wall and porch, installing extensive headers to replace the exterior load-bearing walls. The perimeter footing system will be expanded and reinforced to carry the additional roof load, and the foundation for the coming addition will be poured.

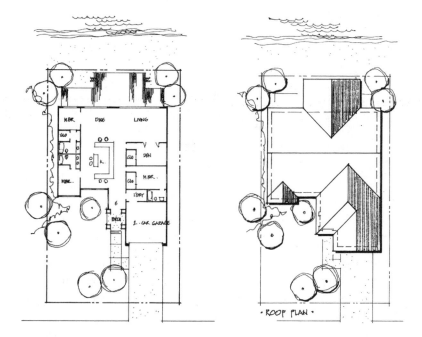

*The finished addition.*                              *Plan view of the final roof.*

If you refer to the finished addition graphic, you can see that we have modified and extended the old kitchen entry to accommodate an extended entry and corridor into a new hallway between the kitchen, which is now open, and a new bedroom and den or fourth bedroom. A new living room has been added and the dining area expanded. Bedroom two has been expanded to the beach wall, and a private bath has been added to that bedroom.

A more appropriate alternative choice would be to have the bath serve only bedroom one, reserving the original bath for the second bedroom and guests. The result is a rather elegant setup with three master bedroom/bath combinations in varying sizes and a den.

The two-car garage has been added at the entry with a full laundry. The deck has been extended to include the entire beachfront of the house. The result is a great 2,568-square-foot home complete with garage and lakefront amenities. You will note that we have taken advantage of the full side yard potential for the addition rather than adding a second story. This attempts to have the house remain in character with the beachfront development while creating a new year-round home.

# Renovation Techniques

If you follow along with the techniques in this three-phase program, you will see that we removed the siding rather than the interior wallboard to add insulation. This serves a twofold purpose. It allows access to the wall framing to insulate and change wiring around, and it allows us to weatherproof the exterior under the new siding.

Many older cottages were never weatherproofed to keep moisture out of the house. The correct method then is to create a layer of insulation within the exterior framing, put a layer of 4' × 8' siding on the house, and then add another layer of rigid insulation, a vapor barrier, and the new siding. This sandwich effect will yield the maximum allowable insulation factor to the old wall. If you installed the new insulation from the inside, you could not have accomplished the complete package, and you would have been left with no moisture barrier and the old siding.

The single-story approach also was very economical in that we did not have to get under the old section of the house to shore up the footings for an additional roof and floor load. The new space was constructed at the same elevation and required only selective wall demolition rather than extensive underpinning. It is also important when reroofing the house to not increase the weight on the footings. The new roofing material should be kept as close as possible in weight to the one it replaces. This will ensure that there is no excessive loading on the existing footings.

Also, please take note of the final roof plan. In an effort to avoid having two roofs come together in the middle of the completed structure, forming a potential leak problem with a gutter, our addition was constructed as one big hip roof to alter the cottage's roofline and provide a more elegant and complex silhouette.

If a beach cottage is a good experience for you, you should also look at other lifestyle communities for the same reason. Areas around mountain communities have summer cabins with fixer-upper potential. In fact, all vacation-type cottages in any area will share the same characteristics. As people start to retire or change careers in mid-life, these areas become very attractive places to live. This family situation is becoming much more common in this era of corporate downsizing. Once you have the idea, you can capitalize on it over and over again.

## The Least You Need to Know

◆ Waterfront property was and is always a good investment, and there are many communities that contain upgrade potential.

◆ The turnaround time for your investment will depend on the commute time to the nearest job center. Try to stay within one hour's time of a significant job base.

◆ Do not over-improve the house. This is a good rule for all fixer-uppers.

◆ Verify your market. Every project must have a market to build to, and this scenario is no exception.

◆ Strongly consider it as a live-in fixer-upper, and that will cut you some slack on the turnaround time. You will also enjoy the location as much as anyone.

# 27

# From House to Commercial

## In This Chapter

- ◆ The goal of the project
- ◆ Selective demolition
- ◆ The new backbone
- ◆ Adding the required infrastructure

There are many charming older towns in this country, and the people who live there want them to stay that way. In the manner of life, though, people tend to flock to charming older towns to live. This creates a need for services that is ever increasing. Supermarkets and discount stores are built on the periphery, but most city councils have decided that the old main street part of town is not a candidate for demolition.

This brings us to our project scenario for this chapter, converting an older in-town house to a commercial use. If the structure you want to work on is a designated or potentially designated historic building, you will have a whole extra set of hoops to jump through. For the sake of this illustration, we are not dealing with historic preservation in this section.

The example used for this chapter is based on an actual conversion that occurred in my old hometown in California. I have taken the liberty of doing it my way, so the actual design of the conversion is slightly different than the building it is modeled after. The real project evolved over time and therefore did not have the luxury of complete planning and execution from the start. Our project assumes that the building is being acquired for the express purpose of remodeling the entire site in one shot.

# The Approach

Our approach is to use the purchase agreement to allow us to accomplish all the front-end work before we actually make the purchase. The chore list is extensive and looks something like this:

- ◆ Draft and execute the purchase agreement.

- ◆ Create the plans and specs.

- ◆ Apply for and get the required permits.

- ◆ Apply for and get the required operating licenses, liquor permits, and/or variances.

- ◆ Bid out the project and the equipment.

- ◆ Arrange construction, equipment, and permanent financing.

- ◆ Consummate the purchase.

**This Works** _____

By doing your research and planning ahead of purchasing, you have established the feasibility of the project before making any significant investment. This is always a good idea, no matter what the project.

This allows us to make sure our project is both feasible and affordable before leaping into the purchase. For specific reference to the purchase agreement, refer to Chapter 18.

# The Project

This project involves converting an in-town house and single-car garage into a restaurant with indoor and outdoor seating. We are not allowed to appreciably add to or change the character of the original buildings. We are allowed to make architectural enhancements to keep the building in character.

The elements that contribute to character are siding, fenestration, trim, lighting, landscaping, paint, and roofing materials. In addition, since we are looking at commercial, we need to attempt to use some of the original yard space for parking if possible. In this example, that was not possible, and we are relying on the existing on-street parking capacity. The finished product must look like it belongs to the area, consistent with its surroundings.

The original building is faintly Victorian in character, and we will add only some additional "gingerbread" to emphasize the exterior. The permitting process is twofold, involving a partial teardown of the interior and an extensive remodeling of both the house and the garage. The original building is a house with 680 square feet per floor and attic and a detached single-car garage at the rear of the yard, connected to the street by a driveway.

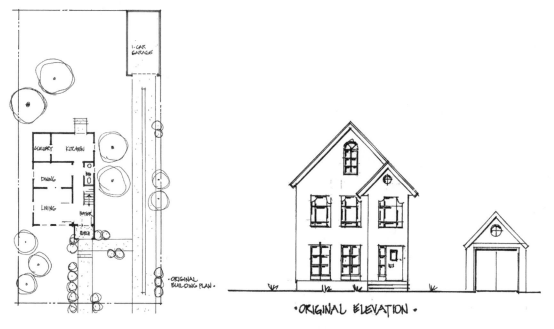

*The original building plan.*                    *The original elevations.*

# Tearing It Out

The demolition is easier on the interior with this type of project because we are not as concerned with authenticity as we are with utility. We can therefore demolish completely, opening up some of the walls, floors, and ceilings that remain to accommodate new insulation, power and gas distribution, fire sprinklers, lighting, and ventilation. To transform the buildings into a restaurant, we need to add a fire sprinkler system, new HVAC, and power and lighting in both buildings, and we need to add restroom and kitchen facilities large enough to service the customer base.

**This Works** —————

The prevailing zoning *code* for parking to accommodate retail buildings is five cars per 1,000 square feet. For restaurants, this is higher, as you also need to add additional parking based upon capacity.

The fortunate part of the town's ordinance regarding this particular type of renovation is that we do not have to accommodate parking for the customers on site. Normal commercial space requires parking to code. This is quite common with towns that want to preserve these buildings. If we had to accommodate the parking, we would have had to buy two more old houses and tear them down to provide land to accommodate the number of cars required by the zoning ordinance. In this particular zoning district, the town has permitted on-street parking.

## Gutting the Insides

The interior demolition, in addition to removing walls, ceilings, and flooring, will also include the removal of the original electrical service. For this transformation, we will need a new and larger electrical service, and we will also need to run in a new gas main from the street. Essentially this building is going to be gutted, and expanded toward the street by adding an enclosed porch to the front of the house on the first floor only. This required demolition, additional structural support, and addition. The graphic that follows is the demolition plan.

*The demolition plan.*

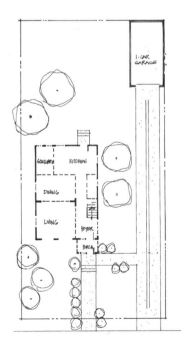

## The Front of the House

We will also demolish the front wall of the house to accommodate an expansion and addition of a seating area for the restaurant. This demolition will entail the addition of a new structural component to carry the existing second floor, attic, and roof area. To accomplish this, we will add some new footings with tubular steel columns to support a *gluelam* beam.

**Trade Terms**

A *gluelam* is a wooden beam fabricated by gluing together smaller pieces of wood to form a larger beam. This process is called glue laminating. The resulting whole is much stronger than the sum of its parts. It takes up less room than a steel beam of the same carrying capacity, is less susceptible to fire damage, and can be decorated with wood stain or paint. By using this type of structural component, we can maximize our headroom in the restaurant seating area.

The newly opened wall will be the transition into the dining-room expansion. The addition in the front of the main building will be both interior and exterior, replacing the old exterior with a similar look that offers larger windows and a new porch. The roof over this will be an extension of the new porch roof, in keeping with the original architecture. In addition, the exterior of the building will be refitted with new architectural trim and a new roof and gutter system.

## The Garage

The building at the rear of the yard will also be transformed into restaurant seating with a movable wall that allows it to flow into the newly created patio dining area or to be closed off during inclement weather. The two structures, the original house and the newly expanded garage structure, will be connected by a new breezeway to give both service personnel and customers easy access to restrooms and seating during inclement weather.

# Utilities and Services Considerations

Since we are changing the use of the building and adding a very large kitchen, we have several needs that the old house did not have. They are as follows:

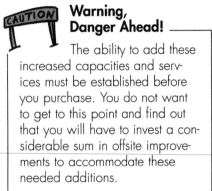

**Warning, Danger Ahead!**

The ability to add these increased capacities and services must be established before you purchase. You do not want to get to this point and find out that you will have to invest a considerable sum in offsite improvements to accommodate these needed additions.

- Increased power supply and distribution
- The need for gas for cooking
- Fire protection
- Building safety considerations due to vastly increased occupancy
- Increased restroom needs
- Increased waste capacity and grease traps
- A power supply to the site, patio areas, and the expanded garage structure

# The Transformation

Once the demolition inside of the house and garage is accomplished, we are free to add the required infrastructure. The actual sequence of the work looks something like this:

- Create the design and obtain permits.
- Complete the purchase.
- Do the demolition.
- Install new electrical service and distribute it to the main house, patio, and garage.
- Increase the size of the sewer connection, add the required grease traps, and rough in the new restrooms.
- Install gas service to the new kitchen area.
- Install a complete fire sprinkler system.
- Pour concrete footings for the new building areas and the main house, kitchen, and garage expansion.
- Pour new concrete floors in the kitchen, bath, and garage.
- Frame in the two additions, the new dining room and porch at the main house, and the extension to the garage.

At this point, we have a completed building shell and can start on the interior decor. The insides, while designed to look the period, will be modern and functional with materials selected for durability and ease of maintenance.

# The Main House

The ground floor of the main house is then expanded to accommodate a new dining area, restrooms, entry, and kitchen. The entry is installed outside (as we did on the tract home renovation) to keep as much usable space as possible in the old main house. Prior to installing anything in the main house and garage, both structures need to be insulated with state-of-the-art insulation. In areas where space and access are tight, the insulation is blown in. In normal wall and attic areas, rolled insulation is utilized. In the main house with the raised floor, the underside of the main floor is blanketed with new insulation.

# The Second Floor and Attic

The second floor has been gutted, retaining only the restroom and separating walls, and the attic has been completely cleaned out. The restroom is modernized, and the balance of the second floor space is partitioned for use as an office and employee locker and changing room. The attic space is converted into storage for paper goods and occasional and seasonal furniture.

In keeping with the period architecture, the walls are finished in wainscoting and wallpaper, both washable. New period lighting is installed throughout. As a concession to the period decor, the dining room areas are floored with wood. The wood floor is not traditional wood flooring but the new easy-care synthetic. The kitchen and bath areas are tiled over concrete for easy maintenance.

# The Garage

Since the garage was originally a single-stall unit, we are pouring a new perimeter to double the size. One side of the roof is then extended to cover the additional space, giving the new building a slightly lopsided shed look. The exterior wall near the outside patio dining area is constructed as a movable wall to allow al fresco dining in good weather.

When the building renovations are complete, the new restaurant will have indoor seating in the main building and garage, connected by a breezeway, and outdoor seating on the rear patio and front porch.

> **Reality Check**
>
> On a project of this type where the work must be done in sequence, the availability of storage and room to work is vital. Planning the work also requires some logistics. Always keep that in mind when planning any project.

*The garage conversion.*

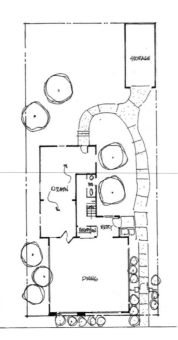

## The Site and Patio

The site is the last to be finished as the area was required for storage and work room while the other work is accomplished. Once the building is complete, we start at the back of the site and install lighting distribution and irrigation lines. Then the concrete patios and walkways are poured, the decorative lighting and fencing is installed, and the landscaping is completed.

If you look at the completed plans that follow, you can see the original house and garage in concept, but the structure is now completely different. By maintaining the period look, we have retained the original feeling of the residential character of the neighborhood and converted it to a completely new use.

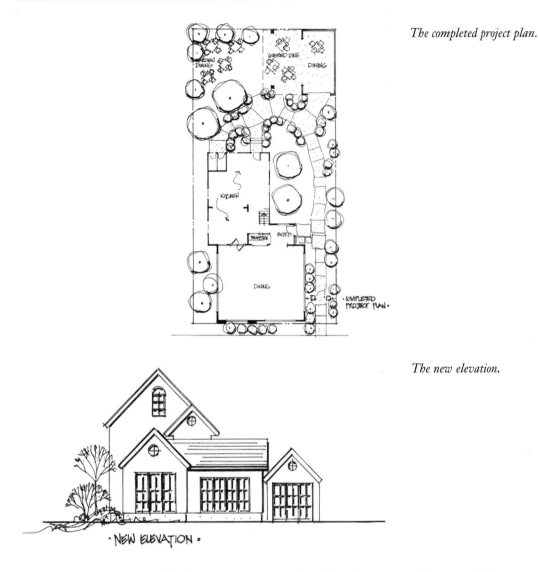

*The completed project plan.*

*The new elevation.*

Not everyone can afford to take on something like this in one fell swoop. The original restaurant that we used as a model for this project transformed the site in three or four phases because that's what the owner could afford. The first phase dealt only with the main house without any additions and the rear patio area. The second phase converted the garage and connected the buildings with a breezeway. The third and final phase was the addition to the main building and a re-landscaping of the entire site.

## The Least You Need to Know

◆ Remember to use the contingency section of the purchase agreement for your free-look period, and do not neglect any potential off-sites.

◆ Make your plans carefully before you buy the house; this should be consistent with any fixer-upper project.

◆ Determine if you can do what you need to do to have a feasible project. Make the plans as complete as you can during the feasibility period.

◆ Value engineer all the improvements, as usual. Get the biggest bang for your buck.

◆ Get all your required permits before you buy, that way there will be no doubt that you can do the conversion.

◆ Phase the project carefully if needed, remember your need for storage and working room.

# Chapter 28

# Miscellaneous Spaces

## In This Chapter

- ◆ Rooms that you *will* use
- ◆ Exercise and work at home
- ◆ A place for baby and the au pair
- ◆ Different kinds of outbuildings

Whenever you become involved with older housing, you're likely to run into the unexpected or someone else's custom designs. Many homes have been added onto over the years, and some (if not most) of these add-ons are customized to the occupant's needs at the time. What usually drives the addition of space in a home is need: an extra bedroom for an unexpected child, a workroom, a hobby area, or a music room. Whatever the reason, the room was added for convenience. Few if any add-ons were designed by an architect or house designer. They were sketched by the owner and may or may not have been built with the benefit of a building permit. What are you apt to find, and what should you do with it? This chapter will explore the types of spaces you are likely to find, and suggest some uses for them that can have a more universal appeal when you go to sell the project.

# Keepers

Rooms with a practical bent are always good to find and should be enhanced and preserved if possible. They were built to serve a need, and most of those needs revolved around the weather, the family, or the owner's occupation or hobbies. Some common "keepers" are described in the sections that follow.

## The Mudroom

The mudroom is one of the most useful rooms found in country homes. It is always found in areas with frequent inclement weather and is almost always off the kitchen or rear entry into the house. It is generally spacious, containing a bench and a set of coat hooks. Sometimes you will find this type of entry in the front of the house, and when you do, it will generally be a little fancier and will contain a closet rather than coat hooks. This is a useful room, and since the weather has not likely changed, you should retain this use, just fixing it up to be as presentable as possible. If it is too cramped, it should be expanded.

## The Laundry Room

The laundry room is another example of space that is useful and should be considered as a retained space. Old-fashioned laundry rooms tend to be large because they contained the old-fashioned equipment; washer, wash tub, scrubbing board, mangle, and indoor drying racks. Today's efficient washers and dryers do not require much space, so the extra room can be converted into a variety of uses.

> **Reality Check**
>
> I have never seen a house with too much storage. Nature abhors a vacuum, so any available storage space will be filled to capacity.

Since most laundry rooms are off the kitchen, the extra space can be converted into a pantry or used as part of the kitchen itself. There is always a need for a half bath or powder room on the first level, and don't forget the trendy wine cellar. The current rage is for a limited wine collection, so there is no need for an elaborate setup, just enough for a wine cooler and a couple of cases.

## The Library

In older homes, you are likely to find an extra room that is not a family room or a living room. This used to be the library, a traditional male retreat. Today we call this room a den, but it's the same thing. It's a natural to be converted into the home office that's so popular today. This can be done by retaining the characteristics of the library (bookcases and so on) and just adding connections for the family computer and related equipment. The fashion today is to convert a closet with bi-fold doors and put the computer and other unsightly equipment behind doors when not in use. This will give your fixer-upper project a touch of elegance and practicality at the same time.

## The Atrium or Solarium

A very old-fashioned room is the atrium or solarium, sometimes known as the morning room. This room usually faces east because that was best for the plants often found inside. Today's homes do not tend to include this type of room, and as beautiful as it might be when properly done, it does not fit modern lifestyles. I would recommend that you incorporate this room into the living area. If that would create too much space, convert it into a game room with a pool table or something like that. This will appeal to families with children. A recreation room is a seldom seen luxury today.

> **Reality Check**
>
> Today's families need more for the kids to do at home, so any recreational space will be very popular. Media centers are popular and when combined with an at-home office, can become a focal point for the family.

# Modern Rooms

There are other rooms you will run across that are in fact today's type of room. They are not necessarily large, but they fit well with the lifestyle of the times. They include the following:

- ◆ The exercise room
- ◆ The workroom
- ◆ The office

While these rooms are self-explanatory, a few comments are in order.

> **This Works**
>
> A mirrored wall in an exercise room will make the room look twice as big. This type of room has great appeal to buyers because everyone harbors an ambition to stay in shape.

## The Exercise Room

The exercise room is likely to be sizable because most include space for at least one large piece of equipment as well as floor space for general exercise and weight training. A great touch for this type of room is good carpeting with very little padding and one full wall of mirrors. If the full wall is too much, then just mirror the closet doors. The firm carpet allows people to exercise without losing their balance; the mirrors allow people to admire the muscles they are building or deplore the flab they are striving to eliminate.

## The Workroom

A workroom is not generally found in the main house, but sometimes there is a hobby-driven homeowner who likes to work indoors. This will not have universal appeal. This room should be converted or promoted to be an extra bedroom, an office, a recreation room, or an exercise room. Most often, if there is a workroom in the house, it will be found in the basement. If it is in the basement, just refinish the walls to look as neutral as possible and leave it to the buyer's imagination. Basement spaces are very subjective. Let the buyer make up his or her own mind about the probable uses.

## The Office

The modern home today will have provisions for a home office. It is the single-most-sought-after extra feature in the new home market. If your fixer-upper has one, enhance it as far as possible. It is a great selling feature. The added flexibility of today's wireless capabilities will make this an easier chore, as the need for extensive wiring is eliminated. The only crucial wiring that you must have is telephone and cable hookups near the power in the room.

# The Baby's Nook

A room you will not see very often is a baby's nook. It is traditionally a small bedroom off the master bedroom, and it will contain its own closet. This has incredible appeal for people who want to raise large families and who have the money to buy large houses. You will not find this room in a small house, and I have never seen one in a house with less than 4,000 square feet.

If you have the space in a fixer-upper, should you create such a room? If the house is large enough and you have more than five bedrooms, I'd suggest that creating a baby's nook would be a great way to reach out to the large family market. We had one in one of our houses, and even though we were not looking to raise many kids, I found that the room was great as a reading room.

# The Au Pair's Quarters

This type of accommodation is generally reserved for the very large house or estate-class home. Live-in baby sitters or nannies are rare among the general population but are common in affluent neighborhoods. If you are doing an estate remodel or a large-lot remodel, you should consider creating a separate living space for this purpose. Sometimes people like to incorporate the au pair space next to the nursery, and sometimes they like it separate.

If I were incorporating it into a large house, I'd put it next to another bedroom. The au pair quarters should contain a sitting room, a bedroom, and a private bathroom. It is in effect a mini-suite. When a live-in nanny is no longer required, the suite can be used for an aging parent or as a luxurious guest suite.

> **Trade Terms**
>
> **Au pair** is French for nanny. For people with a certain economic standing, the word "au pair" has more cachet. It is also a great sales tool because almost everyone is a secret snob, and if a person does not know what you are talking about, he or she will not admit it.

# Outbuildings

Another class of buildings that you are likely to encounter in your fixer-upper career is outbuildings. They might range from chicken coops to 10-car garages and everything in between. The most common type of detached building is the garage. No matter what you find, the most desirable garage is the three-car garage. It is becoming standard on houses over 2,400 square feet. I once looked at a house to buy that had garage space in four separate outbuildings for over 30 cars. I could think of no practical use for this in my lifestyle except demolition. Since the price of the house reflected the cost of the garages, I passed.

> **Reality Check**
>
> Outbuildings aren't becoming popular because people are buying more cars; it is most common for the third-car garage to be used for storage. In the western part of the country where homes are built on a concrete slab, the third garage has replaced the eastern basement or attic.

# Carports

Houses built during the late 1940s and 1950s commonly had carports rather than garages. At the very least, enclose them on all sides and add a double door. Carports today are passé. Garages are in. You might find that you are working with a patio home or a condo where there are *CC&Rs* regarding carports. Make sure you are able to enclose it because the sale will be a much easier one. If you are not allowed to do so, consider giving that house a miss and finding another to tackle.

*The carport.*

## Freestanding Garages

Freestanding garages are quite common in the East as part of older houses. Generally they are found at the rear of the house and are frequently a one-car garage. Most common full-size garages are 24' × 10', but you will encounter many variations on that theme.

> **⚠ CAUTION**
>
> **Warning, Danger Ahead!** _____
>
> I had a partner once who built a two-car garage that was 18' × 18', and I could not talk him out of it. He insisted that he only drove small European cars and did not need a larger unit. Needless to say, when it came time to sell the house, he ran into a lot of trouble. He finally unloaded it at a big loss. The buyer tore it down and replaced it with a standard 24' × 24' garage.

# Single Garages

Today, the single garage is a liability. If you cannot expand it to at least a two-car garage, give the project a miss. You can get away with a garage that is 20' × 20', but that is the absolute minimum. This size garage is associated with inexpensive housing or starter homes.

*A standard two-car garage.*

# The Basic Two-Car Garage

The standard garage today is 24' × 24' and has a raised portion of the floor in front of the cars. If the garage is attached to the house, this raised portion is at the same level as the house and is required by code.

# The Modern Three-Car Garage

This is deceiving because it comes in a variety of shapes and sizes. The standard approach in a middle-priced house will have the three-car garage built with a double door and one single door. More upscale versions will have three single doors. The additional door costs about $400 more to build, but I would spend the money. It gives the house that added bit of class.

*The standard three-car garage.*

*The upscale three-car garage.*

## The RV Garage

Something you are not going to see too often is the RV garage, although it is becoming more popular among the more affluent retired set. A full-blown RV garage at its fullest has a 14-foot door, is 12 feet wide, and is 70 feet long. This structure will house any RV on the road today. Obviously it is a costly item, and you would not normally include it in a fixer-upper renovation, but you might find a home that you want to remodel that has one. What should you do with it? In general, it is quite difficult to work with. Since it is taller than the other garages, the elevation does not lend itself to conversion easily. I have no ready answers. Some possible solutions include recreational rooms and/or exercise rooms. The garage door can be removed and conventional siding added.

**Reality Check**

Unless you have a great imagination or the site lends itself to a unique and marketable solution, I'd give the RV garage a miss.

*Three examples of an RV garage.*

## The Garage Apartment

The ultimate add-on for a freestanding garage is the garage apartment. On a large-lot situation, the solution is ideal. It can be used for the hired help, overflow guests, undesirable in-laws, or as a rental unit. A description of the conversion was covered in Chapter 25.

## Extras

This category is a catchall because some spaces defy logic and call for some creativity. If the space is large, you might create a mother-in-law apartment, an elaborate workroom or hobby shop, or a recreation room complete with a home theater and pool table. Both are popular but generally unaffordable items. There are no specific guidelines on what to do with weird or unusable space. Sometimes it's best to demolish it and plant some bushes, but if it is inside the dwelling, you must do something with it.

I looked at a house once that was built into a hill, and under the house was 1,200 square feet of space without any floor that was 12-foot or better tall. This is a lot of unused cubic footage to have in a house. The owner who built the house had left it unfinished. The access was very poor because the home was built into a hill, and the access was on the downhill side and in the back yard.

Several years later, I met the couple that bought the house. They told me that they converted the space into a great mother-in-law setup for one of their parents, adding a staircase at the back of the house to connect the main dwelling to the newly created apartment. This was a major and expensive addition because the cost was equivalent to or greater than building a house from scratch.

> **Warning, Danger Ahead!**
>
> The results of the conversion of what is essentially basement space would be usable only for the same purpose or as a luxurious guest accommodation. This fixer-upper created a house that would appeal primarily to someone who needed a similar setup. Think twice before creating a single-purpose addition of that magnitude.

## The Least You Need to Know

- Little extras can be interesting, and often they do not cost much. A little imagination applied to the odd nook or cranny can create great charm.

- Try to mainstream the extra room, by converting it into something that has universal appeal such as an extra bedroom or an office.

- If you keep in mind the trendy uses when you are deciding what rooms to create and/or preserve, you can't go wrong.

- If you are working with large houses, you can go for the snob appeal; it has an appeal all its own.

- Look at all spaces with a practical eye and do something useful rather than frivolous. In the final analysis, people have to have what they need rather than what they want.

# Part 6

## Wrapping It Up

This final part deals with you and what you will do with your newfound expertise. If you work hard you can make a good living, but beyond that you must learn to take some risks. Taking calculated risks is the heart of real estate investment and development. If you become a fixer-upper, you will join the ranks of the developers.

It can be profitable, but more importantly it can be a great living and can provide you with a secure future. Once you have proven that you know how to find and do a fixer-upper to your satisfaction, you will be faced with the choice of making your living that way or just using your new-found skills to augment your existing income. Properly planned and executed, a career in fixer-uppers can make you independently wealthy.

# Chapter 29

# Selling at a Profit

## In This Chapter

- Looking at the market
- Different types of residential homes
- What about commercial?
- More about pricing

Selling anything starts before you buy it or create it. The old adage that you make your money when you buy is very true, but to collect it you have to do some work and dispose of the product. Houses and commercial buildings are similar to any other product when it comes to selling. First and always, there is the market.

In this chapter, we will explore the product and the endgame. You will be forced to determine where you want to end up before you launch, that way you will avoid any nasty surprises when the time comes to sell.

## The Market

The market for real estate is huge, and there are thousands of niches that break it down. Most people see the real estate market as simply residential or commercial, but in reality, these two segments are further divided into some general classes. For residential, we can look logically at the following categories of housing:

- Single-family detached

- Single-family attached

- Mobile and modular homes

For commercial property, broad categories are as follows:

- Multifamily rental

- Office

- Retail

- Industrial

- Recreational

- Institutional

> **Reality Check**
>
> When considering what type of property to tackle, remember to choose something you can feel comfortable with rather than something you think might be more profitable. You need to relate to your project, and its end uses must make sense to you.

Are these categories really the marketplace? I do not think you could effectively evaluate your property's potential with just these categories. To fully understand what you will need to look at, we need to dissect each broad segment of the market as it might pertain to your project—whether it is residential or commercial. If we take each segment and break it down to the neighborhood, we will be able to compare your property to others with comparable features very accurately.

# Residential

As you must have observed, the residential market in any standard metropolitan statistical area (SMSA) stretches from the inner city to the surrounding farm country. Obviously, these properties are not directly comparable even within the same city. To take a more realistic approach, we will keep differentiating them.

The first category, single-family detached, can be further broken down into:

- New homes

- Resale homes

This is true of every category of homes or commercial buildings, so let's keep going. Your fixer-upper will not be in the new-home category, even though it might be competing with new homes in the marketplace, so let's look at the resale part of this market. It can be further broken down as follows:

♦ Urban

♦ Suburban

♦ Rural

This gets us to a clearly defined choice of submarkets. So far with this breakdown, we are looking at a single-family, detached, resale house in any of the three submarket locations. If you have chosen one of these submarkets, say the suburban market, we can further break down the homes again as follows:

♦ Age

♦ Size

♦ Amenities

♦ Location

Now you are looking at your property to fit into a more clearly defined submarket that can be defined by the following criteria:

♦ **Single-family detached.** This is self-explanatory.

♦ **Resale.** Used homes only.

♦ **Age.** Broken down in increments of 10 years: 1980s, 1990s, and so on.

♦ **Size.** Under 1,000 square feet, 1,000 to 1,500 square feet, 1,500 to 2,000 square feet, and so on.

♦ **Amenities.** The number of bedrooms, number of baths, living room, family room, great room, dining room, den, and so on.

♦ **Location.** Neighborhood areas by east side, north side, and so on or more specifically by subdivision and/or neighborhood.

Using the new computerized MLS system, you should be able to get a fairly exact picture of where your project house fits into this specific segment of the market.

## New vs. Used

Even though you are clearly dealing with used or resale property, the fact that you are renovating it removes it completely from the time period it was originally constructed in. If you are fixing up a 1950s house, is it fair to compare the results to other 1950s houses only? The answer is no. Most Realtors® representing buyers will try to argue that you can only make a comparison to other houses of that vintage.

| Reality Check |
| --- |
| Pricing is, in the end, completely subjective. It is an art more than a business decision, as different price points will attract different types of buyers. In the end, your knowledge of the market, together with advice from a savvy Realtor®, will determine your pricing. I tend to go with my gut feeling. |

I believe that the correct approach is to compare homes of the original vintage and new homes with the same features and then take an average weight on the pricing depending on the extent of the renovation. For example, if you have done a complete modernization and expansion, you should use a 90 percent-of-the-new-home price comparison. If you have only lipsticked the old house, then perhaps a 120 percent-of-the-older-home comparison is in order. Use your common sense and promote your price reasoning.

## Single-Family Attached

For the sake of diversity, we need to clearly define some categories for the attached markets as well. We will use the new and used categories as a given and look at some potential attached subtypes of housing:

♦ Common-wall houses (town houses, flats, co-ops)

♦ Zero-lot-line patio homes (included in this category because one wall is connected to the neighbor by sharing the lot line)

We can then further break down the submarket you will be addressing by the same criteria used in the detached home analysis: age, size, amenities, and location. Again, a search of the MLS will give you a great picture of your market.

## Mobile and Modular Homes

This segment of the market is divided into two classes of property: the mobile and the modular. Mobile homes are constructed to a different code and have been largely discontinued. They were designed to be movable throughout their economic lifetime. The modular home is designed to be a permanent part of the land and is constructed according to the same building code (UBC—Uniform Building Code, which governs construction methods countrywide) as site-built homes.

By further breaking down these markets using the same categories as with the other types of the single-family homes, you can get a better handle on the particular submarket you wish to deal in.

> **This Works** _____
>
> Taking the time to dissect the marketplace is known as "finding your niche." If you know a lot about the type of home and the locale you are working in, you are more likely to hit the nail on the head when planning and executing your fixer-upper project.

# Commercial

Much the same breakdown as used in residential property also applies to commercial properties. There will be a few different distinctions as follows:

- ◆ **Multifamily rental.** High-rise, low-rise.
- ◆ **Office.** Urban high-rise, mid-rise, garden, strip.
- ◆ **Retail.** Regional mall, community, neighborhood, strip, freestanding single use.
- ◆ **Industrial.** Heavy, light, rail-served, nonrail-served, multitenant, single tenant.

Some of the most obvious recreational buildings are as follows:

- ◆ Theaters
- ◆ Theme parks
- ◆ Marinas
- ◆ Golf courses

Institutional buildings are not a normal class of fixer-upper unless you are in the industry and are building a portfolio of similar properties. The most obvious types are as follows:

> **Warning, Danger Ahead!** _____
>
> When considering taking a building of one type and transforming it into something else, remember innovation can be very profitable, or very costly.

- ◆ Hospitals
- ◆ Nursing homes
- ◆ Assisted-living centers
- ◆ Sanatoriums and treatment centers

These buildings were designed as single purpose structures and can only be adapted to uses that share the same characteristics. In most cases these characteristics would include room sizes and utility distribution. Because of the nature of these buildings, the uses might be interchangeable. An old decommissioned hospital might make an ideal nursing home or assisted care facility.

# Pricing the Product

Once you have located your place in the scheme of things, you will have to come up with a price for your finished product. The largest obstacle to making your goal is a buyer like yourself who will want to get the best buy he or she can. I know everyone wants the best possible deal he or she can get, but the people I'm speaking about are people like you who have taken the time to inform themselves, have read this book and others like it, and understand the nuts and bolts of renovated properties. If you have done your job properly, they will be willing to grant you a fair profit. If you have cut some corners, they will try to negotiate you down. For these people, leaving a little on the table that they can do themselves is a good ploy, like the further addition to the bedroom area planned for the tract home in Chapter 24. This may entice them into considering a further upgrade with its attendant potential for profit.

> **Reality Check**
>
> Don't try to make your whole pile on one deal. Leave some on the table for the next guy. You might find yourself with repeat business.

## Constructing the Price

When you are pricing your fixer-upper project, you need to consider several different aspects of the picture. Items that must be factored into the sales price are as follows:

- Acquisition cost

- Renovation cost

- The interest on the money (yours and the borrowed funds)

- Any direct labor contributed by you, together with your overhead for these chores, mileage, and so on

- The costs associated with the sale: advertising, promotion, brochures, and sales commissions

- Your entrepreneurial profit

This is a good way to look at a residential project, and it can be validated by a careful market comparison, but this will not work for a commercial property. A commercial property will be sold on the value of the leases. The net income before debt service (NIBDS) will be capped at an appropriate rate commensurate with the perceived risk and the market for comparable properties.

How close you can get to this number will depend on the quality of your tenants and the condition of the building. There are some specific steps you can take to get ahead of the curve:

- Show the history of the building.
- Present it properly.
- Document your numbers.
- Compare your building to the market.
- Select the selling team and remain proactive.

The thing to keep in mind when creating a presentation package is to answer all potential objections before they are voiced. If you remember what you were looking for and at when you purchased, you should have a good idea what your potential buyers are going to be looking for.

## Constructing the Legend

Housing is pretty straight forward, due to the method of marketing. The remodeled house will be listed with the local MLS service through a Realtor®, and the most you can do to help out is to make sure the sales agent has all the materials needed, and that the house is show-ready. Builders do this with model homes, and you will also need to put your best foot forward by eliminating clutter and dressing the rooms to best advantage.

Housing generally shows better when furnished, so if possible, furnish your renovated house with rented furniture if you are not living there. If you are, remove all the extra clutter and put it in storage. Your Realtor® should be a very reliable guide in this matter.

With commercial buildings, the building's history is composed of the condition it was in when you purchased it. You should have photos, your original tenant-information spreadsheet, and your initial building-condition reports. What does this show a prospective buyer? First of all, it shows him that you are a knowledgeable buyer in your own right. It puts him on notice that you know how to buy a building and, by implication, how to sell one. This, coupled with the next two components of the package, will prove it to the buyer.

# Presentation

The next component is your game plan. If you did it right, you have two versions: your initial one and your current one. Show the buyer both plans. First, it bolsters your position, and second, it may be a big help to the buyer. The buyer may be a novice buyer who could greatly benefit from your input. Not all buyers are proactive ones. You might find one who wants to buy a great building and just clip his or her coupons. Aggressive buyers will not want your building anyway. They, like you before, will be looking for a building that is sound but has unrealized potential. If you have done your job right, your building will not qualify for that type of buyer. Your buyer will be a fatter cat who does not want to work too hard. This represents the bulk of the buyers out there today. They are too busy to spend the time to make the extra money.

**This Works**

Your numbers should include future income potential based upon your leases and the trend in the market. You might not be able to sell based on the future, but these numbers will make it easier for you to defend your cap rate on your current figures.

## Authenticate Your Numbers

To be irrefutable, your numbers should be projected from today through the next five years. You have these records, so use them. Since they represent fact and projections based on solid leases, no one can tear them apart. If the buyer sees how the building has progressed under your ownership, he or she can see that it can be sustained by simply following your game plan. You have nothing to lose by sharing it with the buyer.

The best way for your package to work is for it to be self-supporting. The numbers are the key, and their support is the lease documents themselves. Your package should contain the following numbers:

- The historical cash flow year by year, or better still quarter by quarter, or best yet month by month

- An equally detailed expense history, broken down the same way

- Your initial tenant-information spreadsheet

- Your current tenant-information spreadsheet

♦ A side-by-side comparison of these two with a column showing the percentage increase in revenue

## Compare Your Building to the Market

You must, when doing a market comparison, use an apples-for-apples approach. The reality is that a garden office building with a heavily landscaped campus and a very modern, state-of-the-art, mid-rise building with a five-story parking garage do not provide a true comparison, even if their per-square-foot rents are similar. They have completely different appeals, but there is no reason why they cannot have the same rents. They appeal to a different type of tenant.

The important point I am making here is that for an individual or a small investor, the garden office building is an easier building to keep competitive with the market. The size of the structure lends itself better to modernization, and its amenity (the landscaped common area) is easier to upgrade and maintain than seven stories of steel and concrete. Is it a better building? I cannot answer that question. For me, as a small investor, it is a better deal, but for a large REIT, the mid-rise building is a better deal. When you purchase and when you sell, you should know who you are competing with. These two buildings can stay competitive on rents and NIBDS, but in reality, they will never be competitors. They appeal to a different clientele. Showing your building against both garden buildings and mid-rises will give a buyer some perspective, but the most valid price comparison will be against other garden buildings.

## The Sales Package

The sales package consists of eyewash rather than substance. I do not mean that it is devoid of fact; rather, it is designed to attract someone to the project rather than bury him or her in detail. In residential real estate, a simple pictorial brochure of the house with the distinctive features prominently displayed is very effective. For the commercial building, you need a summary of the numbers and a sample floor plan. The numbers summary is a current income and expense pro forma without any detail on the tenants' leases. You never release any pertinent data relative to tenants or income until the buyer has made an offer and the deal is in escrow, and then only after the buyer has signed a nondisclosure agreement do you show him or her the actual leases and numbers.

> **Reality Check**
>
> A commercial buyer typically is only interested in the bottom line and the leases, because the building merely serves to keep the rain off the tenants. Any problems with the building can be fixed, so the leases become the primary indicator of value for the building.

## Select the Selling Team and Remain Proactive

Unless you are a real estate broker, you will be working with a third-party sales agent. This is a good idea anyway because it maintains a separation between buyer and seller. Face-to-face negotiations sometimes precipitate hasty decisions. A little time and distance generally make the negotiations easier on both parties. Your buyer may want the detail of the renovation, and if he or she is a serious buyer, you should provide it, pictures of the process included if you have them. The buyer will be able to appreciate the hard work that has gone into the finished product and will be more amenable to your price and profit.

## The Least You Need to Know

- Identify your specific competition, not only for the building type that you are contemplating, but for the buyers and/or tenants you need to complete the project.

- Plan and build your fixer-upper to your chosen submarket. It is easier to compete in a focused, unsatisfied strata of the market than across the whole spectrum of the marketplace. Aim at the ignored tenant market.

- Proudly display the results of your hard work; by effective advertising and promotion.

- Price your product comprehensively and have a well-thought-out sales and promotion pitch.

- Have as many answers as possible ready for questions and/or potential objections to your sales approach.

# Chapter 30

# The Daily Grind vs. Building a Portfolio

## In This Chapter

- ◆ The live-in renovation
- ◆ Timing the renovate-and-move option
- ◆ Renovation as a career
- ◆ Flip it or rent it?
- ◆ Reviewing your tax options
- ◆ The big payoff

Now that we have covered what to do and how to do it, you need to examine your goals for doing it at all. You should have at least one of the following reasons to become involved in the fixer-upper process:

- ◆ To have a nicer home by renovation of an older but promising property
- ◆ To make some extra money
- ◆ To launch a new career as a fixer-upper/developer
- ◆ To build your net worth for the future

If you have any or all of these reasons, you are a definite candidate for the fixer-upper business. Let's examine the impact of these choices on you and your wallet. If you find a house that you like and decide to move in and renovate, be aware that it is very disruptive to your life and daily routine. If you are intending to keep the house for some time, you have the luxury of doing one bit at a time, but if not, you are faced with a totally disruptive lifestyle during the renovation. This chapter will delve into the implications of your various choices for pursuing a fixer-upper, or a career as a developer/fixer-upper. It will also give you a look at the possibility of becoming wealthy.

# Living Through It

As I write this chapter, my wife and I are hanging pictures after a 10-week renovation of our home. We added over 600 square feet to the house; replaced all the floor tile, bath fixtures, and ceiling fans; and painted the entire house. For a period of four weeks, the only habitable rooms were the master bedroom and my office (which I renovated the year prior). The following subcontractors were hired:

- Architect
- Masons
- Concrete contractors
- Carpenters
- Electricians
- Carpet layers
- Tile setters
- Painters
- Plumbers
- Sheet rockers
- Drapery hangers
- Cabinetmakers
- Landscapers

Here are some tips I can pass along that will be important to your interpersonal relations during a process like this:

- Keep the habitable areas as clean as possible.
- Go out to dinner a lot.
- Supervise everything.
- Take frequent breaks from the routine.
- Go to bed early; the workmen show up at the crack of dawn.
- Communicate frequently and accurately.
- Remember to breathe.

Sounds like fun, doesn't it?

Because of the constant disruption, I do not recommend that you spend a lifetime living in your fixer-upper projects, but you might want to do one or two that way to get started. If you are living in it and have a two-year timeframe, you can take a much more relaxed approach and, if you are qualified, do much more of the work yourself. This will increase your profits and be gentler on the nerves. It is also a great way to build up some serious cash equity for future use.

| Reality Check |
| --- |
| If you are renovating your primary residence, you can sell it after two years of occupancy and pocket the proceeds tax free. You can do this again and again for life. It sounds like a good deal and it is, but take my word for it, you will earn your money. |

# Renovation and Moving

If you take on the renovate-and-move scenario, you will be changing addresses frequently. There are timing issues to address to finesse the entire idea. You should line up your new project well before you sell your current one, and using the purchase contract to control the front-end timing, you should do your planning and financing before you actually buy the building. On the sale side, you need to have the renovations complete and the property ready to sell by the eighteenth month. This will give you a comfortable six months to market the property.

By starting the purchasing process for the new project in the eighteenth month, you should achieve the perfect timing. You can control the date of closing on your sale to ensure that it is two years and a day, and if you are really clever, you might pull off a simultaneous closing on both properties. You can then move out and into your next property on the same day. There are obvious disadvantages to this process, and I'd like you to be aware of some possibilities:

- ◆ You change addresses frequently.

- ◆ Your family life is constantly disrupted.

- ◆ Your children will change schools a lot unless you stay in the same general area.

- ◆ You will have many of your belongings in storage for some time.

- ◆ Your cars will never be in the garage because it is always the only place to store materials.

- ◆ Parties and get-togethers are very difficult in a house that is torn apart. Your social life can be a casualty of this process.

I'm sure you can think of other reasons to be cautious about this approach, so do not take this process on lightly.

# The Business of Renovation

If you have accomplished one or two fixer-upper projects and are feeling comfortable with the process, you might want to consider the business of renovation as a career. It has many advantages, not the least of which is a good income and the blessings of being self-employed. If you make this decision, you will most likely arrange to do more than one project at a time, and you will need to develop a team of good tradesmen to help you with the process. A good ploy is to have two projects going at the same time and live in another, doing only one room at a time. This way, in addition to your normal income from the fixer-uppers, you can occasionally sell your own home and move up in the world tax free.

As a career, all your income from this business will be taxable as ordinary income, but at the same time, you will garner many of the tax advantages of the self-employed. Talk to a good accountant before you start. Set up your company so that you maximize your income and minimize your taxes. You will find that many of your day-to-day expenses incurred as an employed person can be legitimately expensed against your new business, thereby lowering your taxable income without lowering your standard of living.

This truly is why there are so many self-employed people. You can literally make less and keep more of what you make. Check it out.

# Renovate and Build Your Portfolio

There are many different approaches to this business, but the one that is really impressive is the one in which you sell occasionally to keep the required cash flow but retain some of your projects for investment purposes. How does this work? Let's set up a scenario for the purpose of analyzing the possibilities. We will make the following assumptions:

♦ You have completed one live-in renovation project and have made $100,000 profit tax free.

♦ You will use the $100,000 to set up the business.

♦ You will tackle two projects at a time, and these will be in the $100,000-to-$300,000 price range.

To analyze this, we will need to make some reasonable assumptions about the market. You will be working in an older, established neighborhood that is experiencing a renaissance. The old homes are selling for $120,000 on large lots, and the upper limit of the market is around $350,000. This is not a far-out scenario, and you can find locations like this if you look.

The renovation budget might look something like the following project spreadsheet.

## Project Spreadsheet

| Item | Cost | Notes |
|---|---|---|
| Acquisition price | $120,000 | 1,750 square feet 3/2/2car ($68 per square foot) |
| Landscape | $5,000 | Minor planting and cleanup |
| Painting | $5,000 | Inside and out |
| Add rooms | $36,000 | 600 square feet @ $60 per square foot |
| New carpet | $3,150 | 210 yards @ $15 per yard |
| Appliances and fixtures | $10,000 | Kitchen and baths |
| Loan fees | $1,000 | 80% loan, 1% of 100K |
| Interest | $4,500 | 9% for six months |
| Misc. overhead | $5,000 | |
| Total costs | ($189,650) | |
| Proposed sale price | $265,000 | After commission and marketing costs |
| Gross profit | $75,350 | Sale less cost |

If you assume for the sake of this scenario that both your projects during this particular year were approximately the same in size and profitability, then we have a year in which you have made approximately $150,000 if you sell both houses. If we assume you are a prudent and parsimonious person and have a desire to build a portfolio for your future, you could sell one and keep one to rent out. If you can live on the $75,000 that is left, you can accomplish this goal. In the following mortgage analysis, let's look at the impact of keeping the one house.

**This Works**

The difference between selling and keeping is that the one you retain continues to make money for you as long as you keep it. It's like a double play, more bang for the buck. You sacrifice potential immediate gain for a solid future of appreciation and growth of your net worth.

## Mortgage Analysis

| Item | Values | Notes |
| --- | --- | --- |
| Appraised value | $265,000 | At completion |
| Mortgage value | $198,750 | As an investment property, let's assume 75% of value |
| Your cost | $189,650 | Look carefully |
| New financing | | $190,000 for 30 years @ 7% .0799 K |
| Monthly mortgage | $1,265 | Above at APR .0799 |

To keep this property and let someone else increase your equity, you need to rent this house out for a net of $1,265 monthly. Anything else is gravy. In a neighborhood where homes are valued at the prices listed in the table, it is not at all unreasonable to assume that this is possible.

## Flipping It or Renting It Out

If we look at the scenario of selling one and keeping one, we can see that you have accomplished the following during your first year of operation:

♦ Made an income of $75,000

♦ Made a capital gain of $75,000 in the rental home

♦ Recovered your working capital from both homes

♦ Made a start on your long-term goal of financial security

**This Works**

The scenario of sell one and keep one will astound you after a few years. You will literally wake up some morning to realize that you have accumulated some serious net worth, which, by the way can be sold anytime if you need more capital.

Let's take this a step further and assume you are able to keep doing this every year over a 10-year period. What then have you accomplished? You have supported yourself for 10 years and accumulated 10 rental properties. Not too bad!

If you make the following assumptions …

♦ There has been no increase in the value of these homes over the 10 years.

♦ The tenants have repaid none of your principal.

Then the following is your new net worth.

## Net Worth Calculations

| Item | Value |
|---|---|
| Ten houses worth $265,000 each | $2,650,000 |
| Less mortgage debt of 10 × $190,000 | ($1,900,000) |
| Net value | $750,000 |

So if the assumptions are correct, you have accumulated $750,000 in net worth over the period. However, when you factor in a conservative appreciation, noncompounded, increase in value of 5 percent per year on the houses and the amortization of the original debt, the values look like this:

## Increased Valuation Calculation

| House # | Original Value | 5% Per Year | Mortgage Balance | Net Value After Mortgage Balance |
|---|---|---|---|---|
| 1 | $265,000 | $132,500 | ($163,020) | $234,480 |
| 2 | $265,000 | $119,250 | ($166,630) | $217,622 |
| 3 | $265,000 | $106,000 | ($170,050) | $200,953 |
| 4 | $265,000 | $92,750 | ($173,090) | $184,664 |
| 5 | $265,000 | $79,500 | ($176,130) | $168,375 |
| 6 | $265,000 | $66,250 | ($178,790) | $152,466 |
| 7 | $265,000 | $53,000 | ($181,450) | $136,557 |

## Increased Valuation Calculation (continued)

| House # | Original Value | 5% Per Year | Mortgage Balance | Net Value After Mortgage Balance |
|---|---|---|---|---|
| 8 | $265,000 | $39,750 | ($183,730) | $121,028 |
| 9 | $265,000 | $26,500 | ($186,010) | $105,499 |
| 10 | $265,000 | $13,250 | ($188,100) | $90,160 |
| Total Net value | | | | $1,611,804 |
| Total increase | | $728,750 | ($1,767,000) | |

I bet you're impressed.

## Tax Impacts

If you take a long, hard look at this potential scenario, you can easily see that there is considerable merit to considering this approach. Obviously, you can adjust your goals to suit your resources and needs. Keeping every other one may not meet your annual income needs, but at least consider retaining some of your projects. The big bonus when you decide to cash it in is that 100 percent of the profit is taxed at capital-gains rates of 20 percent. In the interim, while you have been accumulating these assets and renting them out, you have also been able to depreciate them.

Rental property is depreciable over an average lifespan of 30 years. It's less for some residential properties and more for some commercial properties, but for estimating purposes, if you use a 30-year depreciation schedule, you are safe. The depreciation is based on your cost, so each house in this example cost you $189,000 approximately.

> **Reality Check**
>
> This is not magic, it merely reflects the results of hard work, taking calculated risks, and making good decisions. It's no crime to get rich you know.

When divided by the 30-year average, that means your write-off for tax purposes is approximately $6,300 per year. The impact of this on your income is shown in the table that follows. For the purposes of this illustration, I have assumed that all your $75,000 of income starts out as taxable in the first year.

### Depreciation Calculations

| Income Years 1-10 | # Houses | Depreciation | New Taxable |
| --- | --- | --- | --- |
| $75,000 | 1 | $6,300 | $68,700 |
| Same | 2 | $12,600 | $62,400 |
| Same | 3 | $18,900 | $56,100 |
| Same | 4 | $25,200 | $49,800 |
| Same | 5 | $31,500 | $43,500 |
| Same | 6 | $37,800 | $37,200 |
| Same | 7 | $44,100 | $30,900 |
| Same | 8 | $50,400 | $24,600 |
| Same | 9 | $56,700 | $18,300 |
| Same | 10 | $63,000 | $12,000 |

As you can readily see from the depreciation calculations, while your fortune has been growing, being paid for by your tenants, your taxable income has been shrinking each year and your income has been stable. The net result of this is that you are retaining more of your own money for your use each year.

When you look at the whole picture, it is very favorable. The depreciation you are using to lower your taxable income each year is not *avoiding* the taxes; it merely *defers* these taxes until you sell the depreciating property.

## Should You Pay the Tax?

Silly question, you say. Not at all. You do not have to pay the taxes unless you want to. How is this possible?

Our tax code allows for you to exchange investment property "like for like." If you decide it is time to take your profit on some of these houses, you can arrange for a tax-free "exchange" of these properties and continue depreciating the new asset. Houses are residential rental property and can be exchanged upon the advise of your tax accountant for other residential rental property.

Millions of dollars of income property change hand each year by virtue of the 1031 tax-free exchange statutes in the federal tax code. It is quite legal and is as available to you as it is to me or any other investor. The mechanism is to set up the exchange before you sell, using a facilitator. The facilitator helps you find another property and handles the details of the closings to make sure the exchange is accomplished according to the IRS rules for tax-free exchanges. So, once you go down this path, you are faced with enviable choices: to keep, to sell, or to exchange your properties at your pleasure. If you sell and take the cash, the taxes are reasonable and affordable. You can decide to keep accumulating and exchanging until you dump the whole mess into the laps of your heirs.

**Warning, Danger Ahead!**

At the time of sale of each specific property, the depreciation you have taken can be "recaptured" and added to your profit for tax purposes. This only occurs if you have taken any "accelerated" depreciation. Straight line depreciation is never recaptured, and it is not all bad because your profit is still taxed at the lowest capital-gains rate of 20 percent.

**Warning, Danger Ahead!**

I am not offering you any tax advice here; I'm merely alerting you to the opportunity offered as part of the IRS tax code relating to investment property. Do not make any decisions without advice from your attorney and taxman. The term "like for like" is an IRS-determined definition. You must consult your attorney and accountant for a ruling on each property exchange.

**This Works**

The increase in value of commercial properties will vary, not necessarily keeping pace with inflation of the market in general but with the increase in net income of your tenant leases. These will then be capitalized at the then-prevailing rate to calculate your value at the time of sale.

# Commercial Impacts

The scenario described for the residential fixer-upper works as well for commercial real estate. The only exception is that your tax-free profits are limited only to your own residence. So, if you want some periodic tax-free money and keep your work confined to commercial buildings, you might have to move periodically yourself. All your commercial profits and "sell and/or keep" options apply in the same manner for commercial as they do for residential. You can do the calculations for income and appreciation in the same manner as well as the calculation of the effects of depreciation on your income.

# The Final Bonus

If you don't want to sell the properties and you don't want to pay taxes, there is again another little bonus in store for you. Using the 10-house scenario that increased in value, you will recall that the houses' value increased such that your net value is $1,611,802 plus the outstanding mortgage amount of $1,767,000 for a total gross value of $3,378.802.

This increase in value now has a mortgage value of between 75 and 80 percent of the new value. The resulting increase in value will allow you to remortgage these properties and produce, at 75 percent of value, a new total mortgage amount on the same 10 properties of $2,534,101. After you retire, the existing mortgages totaling $1,767,000 the new financing will put $1,611,802 tax-free cash in your pocket.

What can you do with that amount of cash? Perhaps you might buy some more real estate. Maybe not, it's up to you. It's now your money. May your choices all be this hard to make.

## The Least You Need to Know

◆ Fixing up and selling your home can result in a tax-free profit.

◆ You can make a business of the process, by renovating and selling your personal residence every two years.

◆ Keeping some of your projects can be indecently profitable in the long run, and can provide not only income, but also a dramatic increase in your net worth.

◆ You can defer paying taxes until you're ready to cash out.

◆ You can cash out without selling by simply refinancing to get your cash out.

# Glossary

**100 percent location**   The best location in town. Today that would equate to the most vehicle traffic, and the best access, such as a major freeway exit.

**absolute net**   Income with no expense deductions.

**absorption**   The rate at which available space is leased.

**acceleration**   To call a note early; to force a premature payoff.

**accessibility**   The ability of a person or vehicle to gain access to a property or building.

**acknowledgment**   A document attesting to the fact that the tenant has taken possession, is occupying the premises, and is paying rent.

**agency**   The legal representation of another party. It does not imply the ability to "bind" them to a transaction.

**agent**   One who represents another.

**agreement**   A written contract between parties involving real property.

**all-inclusive deed of trust (AIDT)**   A recorder lien wrapping an existing first deed of trust.

**ALTA survey**   A survey that includes the results of a physical inspection of the property.

**ALTA title insurance**   Insurance against any and all documented or undocumented flaws in the title to a property.

**amateur**   One who is learning the trade and is inexperienced.

**Americans with Disabilities Act (ADA)**   Ensures access to all buildings for all handicapped people.

**amortization**   The prepayment of principal over time, creating level payments.

**anchor tenant**   A tenant with sufficient net worth to enable financing for a project.

**apartments**   Multiple-dwelling units for rent.

**appraisal**   A formal document that gives an "expert's" opinion of value.

**arbitration**   The binding settlement of disputes between parties by a third party selected by the parties in dispute.

**architect**   A licensed designer of buildings.

**arterial road**   A major road or highway emanating from the city center.

**article**   A section in a legal contract.

**assessment**   A special lien for a specific improvement benefiting two or more properties.

**assessment districts**   An area, usually contiguous; multiple properties included in a special assessment.

**asset**   Something with a positive worth definable in currency.

**attorney**   A licensed lawyer approved to practice law.

**bank**   A public depository and lending institution.

**bankable**   A loan commitment that can be borrowed against and easily financed.

**bean counter**   An accountant (who has great attention to detail).

**bench appraisal**   An estimate of value informally given by an appraiser.

**beneficial title**   As good as ownership rights to real property.

**bid**   A binding commitment to build for a specific price.

**boilerplate**   Required clauses in a contract.

**bonds**   Publicly sold financial instruments generally guaranteed by a municipality.

**boundary survey**   A map showing the boundaries, direction, and geographic orientation of a parcel of land.

**box store**   A large discount store.

**break-even**   Where income equals expenses.

**bridge loan**   A loan to tide one over until another can be funded.

**broker**   A licensed real estate agent who can employ other agents.

**building department**   A city function to evaluate and approve proposed building projects within a community.

**build-to-suit**   A project designed and built for one tenant.

**buy-sell agreement**   A contract between the interim and permanent lenders and the borrower to pay off the interim loan.

**buyer**   An entity purchasing a piece of real property.

**call the loan**   Accelerating a loan's due date.

**CAM charges**   Costs of CAM (see *common area maintenance*) that are passed on to the tenants.

**campus**   A collection of buildings in a park-like setting.

**cap rate**   Abbreviation for capitalization rate.

**capital**   Cash, money, and funds available for investment.

**capitalization rate**   The process of valuing an income stream by assessing a numerical factor to the probability of risk.

**carry-back financing**   Financing given by a seller to a buyer.

**carry-back loan**   A loan made by the seller to the buyer to finance part of the purchase price of real estate.

**cash**   Money, gelt, spendable dinero. The absolute required commodity in any real estate deal.

**cash flow**   Income less expenses.

**cash on cash**   Net income (NIBDS) divided by total project cost.

**category**   A use designation for a piece of real property; a zoning definition.

**ceiling height**   The height of the ceiling above the finished floor (FF).

**chain store**   One of a series of repetitive stores under one ownership; also known as, in large form, "credit tenant."

**city**   A large municipality.

**city council**   The governing body of a city, always elected.

**"class A" building**   A high-rise of good-quality construction; an "institutional" building.

**clause**   An article in a contract dealing with a specific subject.

**co-housing**   Housing that shares common features or amenities.

**collateral**   Land or other saleable assets pledged against the timely repayment of a debt.

**commercial**   Nonresidential or residential on a large scale.

**commercial real estate**   Real estate that is not single-family oriented; the practice of development of investment property.

**commitment**   A contract to lend money.

**common area maintenance (CAM)**   Common expenses prorated to the tenants of a building.

**compaction**   The degree of compression of soil, expressed in terms of its bearing capacity or as a percentage of ideal requirements.

**complex**   Two or more buildings in one development.

**condominium**   Common ownership of central facilities that benefit all owners.

**construction**   The building of structures or other improvements to the land.

**contingency**   An event that will preclude consummation of a contract.

**continuing guarantee**   A guarantee that survives a closing event.

**contract**   A legal, binding agreement between two or more parties.

**contractor**   One who is licensed to construct buildings and make other improvements to the land.

**contribution**   A donation toward the whole (an offering).

**convertible**   A construction loan that may be converted to a permanent or "miniperm" loan.

**co-op**   Residential units in a high-rise building that are individually owned and do not include the land. The land is held by the co-op association.

**core**   The original center of a city.

**corporation**   A form of company ownership in which the stockholders' liability is limited to the loss of their investment.

**corridor**   Land accessed by a traffic arterial; a linear description of a zone.

**costs**   The amount of money required to do something.

**County Board of Supervisors**   The elected governing body of a county.

**coverage**   The amount of building allowed on a given site area, generally defined as square feet per acre.

**credit tenant**   One with a "bankable" financial statement, meaning easily financed.

**criteria**   A list of requirements for an event or item.

**critical path schedule**   A sequence of events, the execution of which depends on the successful completion of a prior event.

**cross-collateralization**   Assets liened as a result of a loan on other assets.

**debt coverage**   The amount of NIBDS over the amount of a loan payment, expressed as a percentage of total income (as in "a 50 percent loan to value").

**debt coverage ratio**   The total net income before debt service (NIBDS) divided by the amount of the debt payment.

**debt service**   The mortgage payment.

**deed of trust**   A recorded lien on real property, generally a mortgage.

**default**   When one party fails to live up to the terms of a contract.

**deflation**   When money increases in value.

**demised**   The legal definition of a premises.

**demographics**   The statistical sampling of a population; information pertaining to a specific population.

**department store**   A chain store selling a varied selection of goods.

**depreciation**   The systematic accounting of building obsolescence through time.

**depreciation allowance**   The legal amount allowed for annual depreciation.

**depreciation schedule**   The unequal depreciation allowance over a period of time.

**depth**   The dimension of a premises measured from the front door to the rear windows.

**design**   The creation of a building's configuration.

**design build**   A construction contract in which a contractor agrees to deliver a finished building within a certain price range, without the benefit of final plans and specs.

**design review**   The municipality's review of a project's proposed design.

**developable**   The ability to build on a piece of land.

**developer**   One who creates commercial real estate for a living (the principal; the owner).

**developer's risk**   The period of time during which the developer's cash is at risk.

**development**  The production of income-producing real estate.

**dirt**  Land, project, subject parcel, and site.

**disclosure**  The process of revealing all the pros and cons involved in a project.

**discount store**  A store that sells a large volume of goods at less than the manufacturer's suggested retail cost (a.k.a. a "box store").

**distressed**  A property whose value has decreased due to loss of tenants, economic obsolescence, or both.

**DOE**  The U.S. Department of Energy.

**down payment**  Cash invested to buy something with a balance due; a percentage of the price.

**downsizing**  The reduction of a workforce or leased premises.

**draw**  The tenant that attracts people to a shopping center.

**due date**  The date on which a loan must be fully repaid.

**due diligence**  The process of discovery of all the pertinent facts about a piece of real property.

**early call**  An acceleration of a loan's due date, usually for cause.

**earnest money**  Money given as a deposit against the purchase price for real property.

**easements**  Portions of real property reserved for use by the public or third parties, generally restricted so that no buildings can be erected thereon.

**elevation**  Height above sea level. A graphic depiction of a building's facade above ground.

**encumbered property**  Property with liens recorded against the title.

**end game**  Exit strategy; the time to divest and reinvest.

**endangered species**  A life form designated by the government as threatened with extinction and protected by law.

**engineer**  A licensed designer of structural components.

**entitlement**  A legal use (benefit) that goes with the land.

**entrepreneur**  One who seeks to profit through innovation and risk.

**environmental**  Dealing with the physical environment on and surrounding any given property. Pertaining to the physical world.

**environmental impact report (EIR)**   Also known as an environmental impact statement, an EIR is a report on all the potential ramifications involved in a specific development on a specific piece of real estate.

**equity**   The value evidenced by ownership.

**errors and omissions insurance**   A policy designed to protect architects' and engineers' clients from malpractice or error.

**escrow**   A real estate sales and purchasing facilitator.

**escrow instructions**   Executed instructions to the escrow agent from both buyer and seller in a real property transaction.

**Estoppel Certificate**   A document stating that the tenant is in possession and paying rent, that the lease is in force, and that the landlord is not in default.

**exchange**   The process of trading one piece of real property for another to avoid immediate taxation of profits.

**exclusive**   The right to represent a property without worry about another agent's preemption of the listing position/commission.

**executed**   A document that has been signed.

**executory**   A document ready for execution.

**exhibits**   Documents attached to a contract detailing specific issues.

**exit strategy**   How and when to dispose of an investment.

**expansion**   To increase the number of or size of anything is to expand it.

**expenses**   Costs of operation of a project.

**expert**   A person paid to do a specific chore and acknowledged as competent and highly experienced in the field.

**fat**   Budgetary surplus, contingency monies.

**fauna**   Animals, species, critters.

**feasibility**   The likelihood of successful execution of a planned action.

**feasibility study**   The process of evaluating a deal.

**fee**   The land or a payment for services rendered.

**fee simple absolute**   The unequivocal, unencumbered ownership of land.

**fee title**   The land; clean ownership rights to land.

**fees**   Money charged for services rendered.

**fiduciary**   An enforceable, legal obligation undertaken by an agent or partner to another person or entity.

**fire department**   A government agency charged with fire prevention and eradication.

**first deed of trust**   A recorded, primary lien on real property, second only to the local taxes assessed.

**flipping**   The practice of reselling land before having purchased it.

**floor**   One story.

**floor plan**   The layout of tenant improvements in a specific location.

**floor plate**   The layout of a building floor prior to tenant improvements.

**flora**   Plants, vegetation, naturally occurring growth.

**force majeure**   Acts of God or natural disasters.

**Fortune 500**   A designation by *Fortune* magazine of the 500 largest companies in the United States.

**free look**   The time period in a real property contract during which the buyer's deposit is fully refundable.

**free-trade zone**   A legal tax-free zone for import, export, and manufacturing of goods.

**gap loan**   The loan that covers the gap between equity and permanent financing; usually a land loan or a seller carry-back loan.

**general partner**   A partner who is "jointly and severally" liable for all debts of a partnership.

**general plan**   A map showing the distribution of zoning categories in a designated area such as a township, city, or county.

**general provisions**   Boilerplate clauses in a legal document.

**geotechnical**   Pertaining to geology, seismology, and soil condition.

**going dark**   A tenant's closing of a store but continuing to pay rent.

**graphic**   A visual representation.

**gross leasable area (GLA)**   The maximum square footage available for lease in any given building.

**gross lease**   A lease that includes all costs of operation.

**gross potential income (GPI)**   Total income before deductions or offsets.

**guarantee**   A promise to pay if another does not.

**guest**   An invited party, a nontenant, an invitee.

**hard costs**   Construction costs.

**hazardous materials**   Materials defined by the government as hazardous to human beings and animals.

**hazardous waste**   Waste decreed by the government to be hazardous to human and animal health and well-being.

**health department**   A government agency charged with protecting the health of citizens.

**high-rise building**   A building with more than seven floors.

**highway department**   A government agency in charge of roads and transportation.

**holding over**   The month-to-month extension of a tenant's occupancy after a lease expires.

**home**   A dwelling for one family; synonymous with the term "house."

**hotel**   A mid-rise to high-rise transient lodging facility.

**house**   A home, a dwelling for a single family.

**HVAC**   An acronym for heating, ventilation, and air conditioning.

**improvement bonds**   Bonds sold to the public to pay for improvements to real estate.

**improvements**   Construction, additions to land.

**industrial building**   Single and multitenant manufacturing or warehouse buildings.

**inflation**   When money becomes worth less.

**institution**   A financial entity, usually a bank, savings bank, life insurance company, or trust.

**interest**   Rent paid on capital or money borrowed.

**interim loan**   Temporary or construction financing.

**investment**   Capital devoted to equity or ownership of real property.

**investment grade**   A property worthy of investment for the long term.

**investor**   One who risks capital in a venture.

**joint and several**   All parties are liable for the total amount of all unsecured obligations.

**joint venture**   A project undertaken by two or more entities.

**KISS**   Keep it simple, stupid!

**land**   Real property, a.k.a. the fee, the site, the plot, or the dirt.

**land lease**   A contract for the use of land without the transfer of ownership; it conveys a beneficial ownership.

**landlord**   The owner, the lessor.

**landscaping**   Plantings added to a piece of real property.

**late fees**   Fees charged when rent or mortgages are paid later than contracted for.

**lawyer**   A licensed practitioner of the legal profession, an attorney.

**leasable**   Able to be leased (rented) for money.

**lease**   A written contract enabling the use of an item or premises for money.

**leasehold interest**   Is the legal right to occupy or possess real property; Not ownership rights but an enforceable and transferable beneficial interest.

**legal notice**   Notice recognized by the courts as having been duly received by the party being notified.

**lender**   One who lends money for a fee.

**lessee**   An occupant of a building, evidenced by a written or oral agreement.

**lessor**   The owner or landlord.

**leverage**   The principle of increasing one's yield through borrowing money.

**liability**   A legal obligation.

**lien**   A recorded legal obligation; a flaw in the title to a piece of property. A legal notice of an obligation of the landowner.

**like kind**   A piece of real property defined by the IRS as being equivalent to another for tax purposes.

**limited liability company**   A form of ownership with the limitation of liability of a corporation and the tax benefits of a partnership.

**limited partner**   A partner whose risk is limited to the loss of his or her investment.

**limited partnership**   A form of ownership in which the general partner assumes the liabilities and the limited partners can lose only their investment.

**lineal foot**   A linear or lateral measurement.

**liquidity**   The relative speed of converting an asset to cash.

**load factor**   An added burden on the leasehold. A surcharge to pay for inefficiency in design or common areas.

**loan package**   A collection of documents that constitutes a complete loan application: the loan request, collateral description and appraisal, financial statements and projections, and sample documentation.

**location**   The relative position of a parcel of land within a designated zone (city, town, and so on).

**lot line**   The property boundary.

**main body**   The business deal part of the lease.

**majority in interest**   Ownership totaling over 50 percent.

**manufacturing plant**   An industrial building where goods are produced.

**maquilladora plant**   A plant on the U.S./Mexican border employing Mexican labor and U.S. or imported parts.

**market**   The free, legal exchange of money, real property rights, and entitlements between parties.

**master plan**   A plan for the whole project.

**master planned development**   A planned development, usually a large residential community.

**MBA shop**   A company that employed masters of business graduates in the 1980s, generally credited with causing the Great Recession of 1988 to 1991.

**mediation**   The process of negotiating a nonbinding settlement between opposing parties.

**meets and bounds**   A legal description of real property using geographical coordinates.

**member**   A person or entity in a limited liability company.

**mini-storage**   An industrial multitenant storage building.

**modified gross**   A lease that includes only some of the operating expenses.

**modified net**   A lease that includes at least one expense of operation.

**mom-and-pop stores**   Local retail stores with limited credit.

**mortgage**   A recorded loan on real property.

**mortgage payment**   Principal and interest payments calculated to amortize the principal over the term of the loan.

**motel**   A low-rise transient lodging facility.

**multifamily**   A residential building housing more than one family.

**multiple listing service**   A real property information-exchange system used by residential Realtors® for the sharing of information on house listings. To be a member of this system—and all residential Realtors® belong—means that all agree to cooperate and split commissions on all cooperative sales. Most MLS systems today are becoming computerized and therefore are increasingly effective in the home sales business across the country.

**multitenant building**   Buildings designed for occupancy by more than one tenant.

**multi-use complex**   Projects mixing two or more of the following uses: office, retail, and industrial.

**municipality**   An aggregation of population acting as one political entity.

**negative**   Below zero, in the minus column, in debt, or without positive value.

**net income (NI)**   The receipt of money over a designated period of time. Money left over after all bills are paid.

**net lease**   A lease that does not include operating expenses.

**NIBDS**   Net income before debt service is deducted.

**NNN**   Also known as a Triple Net Lease Rent, rent that excludes absolutely all operating expenses.

**nonrecourse**   A loan without personal guarantees.

**note**   A contract for repayment of a loan.

**numbers**   Financial projections, accounting documents, a.k.a. the pro forma.

**obsolescence**   The process of rendering a building economically useless over time.

**occupancy permit**   A legal document entitling occupancy of a building.

**occupant**   A tenant occupying a demised premises.

**office buildings**   Single and multitenant buildings housing office users only.

**offset**   The right to pay expenses and deduct the cost from rent or other monies due.

**OPM**   Other people's money, equity capital, or loans.

**option**   A right to purchase; a beneficial interest (generally transferable).

**ordinance**   A law passed by a community regulating land use.

**over standard**   Improvements other than those offered as standard.

**owner**   An entity that takes title to a piece of real estate.

**parcel**   A piece of land.

**parcel number**  A legal description of property within a county, generally assigned by the tax assessor (the assessor's parcel number [APN]).

**parking space**  A temporary storage location for automobiles.

**pension fund**  A company investing for future income for its members.

**percent**  A portion of a whole divided by the whole.

**percentage**  A portion of less than the whole.

**permanent loan**  A loan for 10 or more years whose payments include principal and interest (in other words, amortized, a take out loan).

**personalty**  Personal property.

**planning and zoning department**  A governmental agency devoted to examination and evaluation of building projects.

**planning commission**  A government body, generally elected, charged with the oversight and approval of building projects.

**point(s)**  One percent of the principal. Money paid to secure a loan, either interim or permanent.

**preleasing**  Executing leases prior to the start of construction of a building.

**preliminary lien notice**  A legal notice that a supplier or contractor is starting work on a property that could result in a lien if unpaid.

**premises**  A specific location within a building or project, designed for and occupied by one tenant.

**principal**  The owner. The balance of a loan.

**private placement**  The limited solicitation of equity capital. The legal securing of investment capital from others without public solicitation.

**pro forma**  Projections of cost and income.

**pro rata**  A percentage share allotment.

**project**  A deal, a development, an investment, a building, or a group of buildings, land, lots, or subdivision. Any specific real property involved in your deal.

**project costs**  Costs involved in the creation of a project.

**property description**  A legal definition of a piece of real property.

**punch list**  A list of unfinished or defective work.

**purchase agreement**  A contract to buy and sell real property.

**quadrant**   A one-quarter portion of any whole that is divided into four parts. Generally divided north to south and east to west.

**range and township**   A form of property description common to the western United States.

**rate of return (ROR)**   An annual or cumulative percent return on monies.

**real estate industry**   Inclusive term denoting all individuals and entities, all property, skills, disciplines, and functions involved in the production of Commercial Real Estate.

**real estate investment trust (REIT)**   An owner of many projects, usually publicly owned.

**Realtor®**   A licensed salesperson or broker engaged in the sale of homes.

**realty**   Real property, generally defined as a house and land.

**recession**   A period of economic downturn.

**recourse**   The ability to enforce repayment of a loan or obligation.

**regional mall**   A very large shopping center usually anchored by three or more department stores.

**remedies**   A negotiated or adjudicated compensation for a default.

**rendering**   A perspective graphic representation of a proposed project.

**rent**   Money paid for the temporary use of someone else's real property.

**restrictions**   A list of uses denied for a particular site.

**retail buildings**   Single or multitenant buildings used for sale of merchandise to the public.

**return**   A positive return on capital or effort (work) expended.

**return on investment (ROI)**   Cash back from an investment, return of capital. Expressed as a percentage of the money invested.

**right of offset**   The ability to offset expenses against monies owed.

**risk**   An estimate of the likelihood of an event taking place; quantifying an investment's potential.

**risk capital**   Money invested in a nonguaranteed venture.

**rollover**   The ability to convert an interim loan to a permanent loan.

**sale**   To dispose of a property.

**saleable**   The marketability of an item.

**schedule**   A timed sequence of events.

**schematic**   A preliminary, rough graphic representation of a project.

**section**   A graphic "slice" through a building or 640 acres.

**Security and Exchange Commission (SEC)**   The federal agency in charge of regulating the securities industry.

**seismic**   Pertaining to the earth's stability.

**seller**   An entity selling a piece of real property.

**service the debt**   Paying the mortgage or note.

**setback**   The distance from the property line in which nothing may be constructed.

**shell**   The outside of a building without tenant improvements.

**shoppers**   People who exchange credit or cash for goods and services.

**sign**   A graphic mode of advertising the occupant of a premises.

**signage**   A coordinated group of signs designed to work closely together.

**Silicon Desert**   The area in Arizona where the computer industry flourishes.

**Silicon Valley**   The area in California where the computer industry was founded (Santa Clara County or San Jose).

**single-family**   A dwelling for one family unit.

**single-tenant building**   A building designed and built for a specific tenant. A building leased to one tenant.

**site**   Subject parcel, a.k.a. the land, the dirt, a location, or the fee.

**site plan**   A graphic depiction of site improvements and buildings on a parcel of land.

**soft costs**   Costs of a project other than land and construction.

**soils analysis**   The examination of soils for bearing capacity and consistency.

**special assessments**   Specific liens for specific benefits to real property.

**specific density**   The relative compaction of soil.

**specifications**   The specific description of an item as to use, dimension, construction, and quality.

**specs**   See *specifications*.

**speculation**   The risking of capital for potential inordinate gain due to possible increased demand for a commodity.

**speculator**   One who buys and resells unimproved land for a profit.

**square foot**   A one foot by one foot area. 1'×1' = 1 square foot.

**standard metropolitan statistical area (SMSA)**   Usually a core city and surrounding suburbs lumped together for statistical study. Also known as an MSA or metropolitan statistical area.

**standard survey**   A survey showing the physical boundary of a parcel of land with any recorded easements shown.

**stipulations**   A list of items to be done prior to improving or entitling a piece of real property.

**stockholder**   One who owns stock in a corporation.

**strip commercial**   A retail building that's small and usually without an anchor tenant.

**structural**   Pertaining to the building's support skeleton.

**structure**   A building or constructed edifice; the skeletal support for a building.

**subcontractor**   A contractor employed by another contractor or supplier rather than by the owner.

**subdivision**   The process of breaking up raw land into five or more separate and saleable parcels.

**subject site**   The land, the current project referred to; also known as "subject parcel."

**subletting**   The tenant executes a lease to a subtenant while remaining on the original lease. (This generally requires the landlord's consent.)

**subordinated**   The status of a lien, junior in position to another lien (as in lien x is subordinate to lien y).

**subordinated land lease**   A land lease that is junior to financing in the event of default. The loan can foreclose out the land lease.

**suburban**   Outside the core city, usually located in adjacent towns.

**supplier**   One who supplies materials to a project.

**supply and demand**   A prime determination of price; the greater the demand, the higher the price (and vice versa).

**survey**   The act of gathering data for the graphic legal description of a piece of land.

**syndication**   The raising of capital pools by public solicitation.

**take-out loan**   A permanent loan designed to pay off the interim or construction loan.

**tax write off**   The depreciation allowance.

**taxes**   The government's pound of flesh.

**tenant**   An entity occupying any premises.

**tenant broker**   One who represents the interest of the tenant rather than the interest of the landlord.

**tenant improvement (TI)**   Items constructed within a demised premises for the exclusive use of the tenant, such as walls, windows, doors, carpet, ceiling, air condition and heating distribution, outlets, phone jacks, computer wiring, etc.

**terms**   The conditions of a transaction.

**title**   Ownership rights to real property or a document outlining the condition of a property's legal encumbrances.

**title insurance**   Insurance issued to protect the buyer or lender in the event of flaws to the ownership of real property.

**title report**   A written report regarding liens and claims recorded and not recorded on real property.

**topo**   Abbreviation for a topographic map.

**topographic map**   A graphic description of the grades (contours and elevation) of a piece of land.

**topography**   The shape of land (ups and downs, contours).

**total costs**   The all-inclusive number. Nothing excluded. Includes land and hard and soft costs.

**township**   A map section used to locate land.

**trade zone**   A legally created tax-free zone used to promote international trade.

**traffic**   People or vehicles passing a given point.

**traffic count**   The number of vehicles or people passing a specific point in an average 24-hour period.

**traffic study**   A report dealing with the extent and effects of vehicular activity within a given area.

**triparty agreement**   A contract or buy-sell agreement between the construction and permanent lenders and the borrower.

**unsubordinated land lease**   A land lease that has a higher lien priority than the loan.

**urban renewal**   A government-mandated land acquisition to promote the redevelopment of blighted areas of a city.

**urban sprawl**   The result of controlled low-rise development. New buildings spread out rather than up.

**usable**   The designation of space that can actually be occupied solely by the tenant.

**use permit**   A document that allows a specific activity on a particular site.

**useful life**   The government's appraisal of the length of economic service of any given building.

**utilities**   Water, gas, electric, cable, sewer, and telephone services.

**value engineering**   The practice of reviewing the cost benefit ratio on all proposed new improvements or amenities.

**vehicle**   Automobile or motorized conveyance.

**vet**   The process of evaluating a site or project.

**WAG**   Wild-ass guess.

**warehouse**   An industrial building where goods are stored.

**width**   The dimension of a building or a premises from side to side along the street frontage.

**wrap loans**   A loan that is in second position, but that assumes the responsibility to repay the first loan, under the existing terms.

**zero-lot line**   The ability to build right up to the property boundary.

**zoning**   The process of categorizing uses for real property.

# Agreement Between Owner/General Contractor and Subcontractor

This Agreement is made as of (*Insert date*) between *contractor's name* (Contractor) and *contractor's name, address, phone, fax, and e-mail* (Subcontractor).

**The Project**: (*Insert project name*)

**The Owner**: (*Insert owner's name*)

**The Architect**: (*Insert architect's name, address, phone, fax, and e-mail*)

**The Contractor and Subcontractor hereby agree as set forth herein below:**

The Contract Documents for this Contract consist of this Agreement, Exhibit A attached hereto, the Drawings, the Specifications Exhibit B, and Exhibits C, D, and E. These form the Contract and are as fully a part of the Contract as if attached to this Agreement or repeated herein.

The Work to be performed under this Contract shall be coordinated with all other subcontractors and shall be performed in a timely manner to prevent delays or conflicts. Time is of the essence of this Contract. The estimated start date is (*Insert date*). The start date will be determined by a Notice To Proceed from the Owner that work may commence. Without a Notice To Proceed from the Owner prior to (*Insert date*), this contract is null and void.

The Contractor shall pay the Subcontractor in current funds for the performance of the Work, subject to additions and deductions authorized in writing by the Owner in advance, the Contract Sum of (*amount spelled out*) and 00/00 Dollars ($XXX,000.00) plus per-unit tenant improvements more particularly described in Exhibit B attached hereto.

Applications for monthly progress payments shall be submitted to *Contractor's name, address, phone, fax, and e-mail* for approval by the Owner on or before the 20th day of each month. Payments will be made for approved work by the first of the following month. The Contractor shall use the Owners Standard Application For Payment, attached hereto as Exhibit C, for all monthly progress payments. All applications for payment shall be accompanied by unconditional waivers of lien from all suppliers or subcontractors in full for a cumulative total of all prior progress payments.

Final payment, constituting the entire unpaid balance of the contract Sum, shall be due when the Work described in this Contract is fully completed and performed in accordance with the Contract Documents and is satisfactory to the Owner. Walk-through repair requests shall be completed within two (2) working days upon notice from the Contractor. Subcontractor must submit notarized, final, unconditional lien releases from Subcontractor and all material suppliers for all payments received to date plus the full amount of the final progress payment at the time of final payment.

Customer punch-list work requests shall be completed within five (5) working days upon receipt of notice of repair order. Subcontractor shall further assign an individual qualified in making such repairs to work directly with the Contractor and the Owner. Said individual shall be (*Insert name*), contacted by calling (*Insert number and mobile number*).

Contractor:                               Subcontractor:
Date:

By _____          By _____
    (*Insert name & title*)                      (*Insert name & title*)

On a separate page put: Exhibit A, the legal description

On a separate page put: Exhibit B

**Description of the Work**   The Subcontractor shall perform all the (*Insert description*) work outlined in the Plans and specifications listed below, the requirements of the Town/City of (*Insert name*), and in the Subcontract Proposal attached as Exhibit E.

**The Contract Documents**   The documents that are applicable to this Contract, except for Addenda and Modifications issued after execution of this Contract, are attached hereto and enumerated as follows:

List all plans and specifications, soils tests, and surveys

   All of the above are modified by revisions required by the Town of (*Insert name*) and dated (*Insert contract date*), a copy of which, approved for construction by the Town of (*Insert name*) is attached hereto and made a part hereof. Subcontractor certifies that it has visited the site and observed the actual conditions, read and acknowledged all of the above, and bid the project accordingly. In the event of any conflicts between the subcontractor proposal and the above plans and specifications, the plans and specifications shall govern.

**The Contract Price:**   $xxx,000.00

**Please initial attachments**:

## Initials

| | | |
|---|---|---|
| Exhibit A | Property Description | |
| Exhibit B | Plans and Specifications | |
| | Description of the Work | |
| Exhibit C | Progress Payment Request | |
| Exhibit D | Project Schedule | |
| Exhibit E | Subcontractor Proposal | |

Attachments: Listed above. **Please Initial.**

## General Conditions

**Insurance**  Prior to starting work, the Subcontractor shall obtain the required insurance from a responsible insurer and shall furnish satisfactory evidence to the Contractor that the Subcontractor has complied with the requirements of this Article. The Subcontractor shall provide proof of liability insurance in a minimum amount of $1,000,000.00 and proof of disability coverage for all employees in the form of workmen's compensation.

**Assignment**  The Subcontractor shall not assign this Contract without the written consent of the Contractor. The Subcontractor shall not assign any amounts due or to become due under this Contract without written notice to the Contractor.

**Lien Releases**  The Subcontractor shall pay for all materials, equipment, and labor used in, or in connection with, the performance of this Contract through the period covered by previous payments received from the Owner and shall furnish satisfactory evidence, with each subsequent progress payment request, to verify compliance with the above requirement. A final release of lien shall be required of the Subcontractor and any major suppliers for final payment. The Subcontractor shall give all notices and comply with all laws, ordinances, rules, regulations, and orders of any public authority bearing on the performance of the Work under this Contract.

**Compliance**  The Subcontractor shall secure and pay for all permits required and not procured by the Contractor and all governmental fees, licenses, and inspections necessary for the proper execution and completion of the Contractor's Work. The Subcontractor shall comply with federal, state, and local tax laws, social security acts, unemployment compensation acts, and worker's or workmen's compensation acts insofar as applicable to the performance of this Contract. In carrying out his Work, the Contractor shall take necessary precautions to protect properly the finished Work of other contractors from damage caused by his operations.

**Safety**  The Subcontractor shall take reasonable safety precautions with respect to his Work and shall comply with all safety measures initiated by the Contractor and with all applicable laws, ordinances, rules, regulations, and orders of any public authority for the safety of persons or property in accordance with the requirements of the Contract Document. The Contractor shall report within 24 hours to the Owner any injury to any of the Subcontractor's employees at the site. The Subcontractor shall, at all times, keep the premises free from accumulation of waste materials or rubbish arising out of the operations of this Contract. Unless otherwise provided, the Contractor shall not be held responsible for unclean conditions caused by other contractors. The Subcontractor warrants to the Contractor and the Owner that all materials and equipment furnished shall be new unless otherwise specified and that all Work under this Contract shall be of good quality, free from faults and defects, and in conformance with the contract Documents. All Work not conforming to these requirements, including substitutions not properly approved and authorized, may be considered defective. The warranty provided in this paragraph shall be in addition to and not in limitation to any other warranty or remedy required by law or by the Contract Document.

**Change Orders**   The Subcontractor may be ordered in writing by the Contractor, without invalidating this Contract, to make changes in the Work within the general scope of this Contract consisting of additions, deletions, or other revisions, the Contract Sum and Contract Time being adjusted accordingly. The Subcontractor, prior to the commencement of any changed or revised Work, shall submit promptly to the Owner written copies of any claim for adjustment to the contract Sum and Contract Time for such revised Work in a manner consistent with the Contract Documents. All changes carried out by the Subcontractor shall be supported by a written claim approved and signed by the Contractor. The Owner shall not give instructions or orders directly to employees or workmen of the Subcontractor except to persons designated as authorized representatives of the Contractor.

**Claims**   To the fullest extent permitted by law, the Subcontractor shall indemnify and hold harmless the Owner, the Contractor, and all of their agents and employees from, and against, all claims, damages, losses, and expenses, including but not limited to attorney's fees, arising out of or resulting from the performance of the Sub-contractor's Work under this Contract, provided that any such claim, damage, loss, or expense is attributable to bodily injury, sickness, disease, or death, or to injury to or destruction of tangible property (other than the Work itself), including the loss of use resulting therefrom, to the extent caused in whole or in part by any negligent act or omission of the Subcontractor, anyone directly or indirectly employed by him, or anyone for whose acts he may be liable, regardless of whether it is caused in part by a party indemnified hereunder. Such obligation shall be construed to negate, or abridge, or otherwise reduce any other right or obligation of indemnity that would otherwise exist as to any party or person described in this paragraph. In any and all claims against the Owner, the Contractor, or any of their agents or employees by any employee of the Subcontractor, anyone directly or indirectly employed by him, or anyone for whose acts he may be liable, the indemnification obligation under this paragraph shall not be limited in any way by any limitation on the amount or type of damages, compensation, or benefits payable by or for the Subcontractor under Worker's or Workmen's Compensation acts, disability benefit acts, or other employee benefit acts. If the Contractor does not pay the Subcontractor through no fault of the Subcontractor, within seven days from the time payment should be made as provided in this agreement, the Subcontractor may, without prejudice to any other remedy he may have, upon seven additional work days' written notice to the contractor, stop his

Work until payment of the amount owing has been received. The Contract Sum shall, by appropriate adjustment, be increased by the amount of the Subcontractor's reasonable costs of shutdown, delay, and startup.

**Schedules**   The Subcontractor shall cooperate with the Contractor in scheduling and performing his Work to avoid conflict or interference with the work of others. The Subcontractor shall promptly submit shop drawings and samples required to perform his Work efficiently, expeditiously, and in a manner that will not cause delay in the progress of the Work of the Contractor. As part of this contract, the Contractor has provided the Subcontractor a copy of the estimated progress schedule (attached hereto as Exhibit D) of the Contractor's entire Work that the Contractor has prepared, together with such additional scheduling details as will enable the Subcontractor to plan and perform his Work properly. The Subcontractor shall be notified promptly of any subsequent changes in the progress schedule and the additional scheduling details. The Contractor shall provide suitable areas for storage of the Subcontractor's materials and equipment during the course of the Work. All stored material shall be the responsibility of the Subcontractor until incorporated into the building and accepted by the Owner.

**Layout**   Subcontractor shall be solely responsible for the proper location and/or elevation and placement of Subcontractor's work. Contractor shall survey the offsets for the building corners and shall establish a benchmark elevation for the building project, which will be maintained throughout the duration of the building project. Subcontractor shall establish location and/or elevation for all Subcontractor's work using those reference points. Subcontractor may elect to have the Contractor establish these locations and/or elevations and in so doing agrees to repay Contractor's costs for the establishment of the location and/or elevation of Subcontractor's work.

**Damages**   The Contractor shall make no demand for liquidated damages for delay in any sum in excess of such amount as may be specifically named in this Contract, and liquidated damages shall be assessed against this Subcontractor only for his negligent acts and his failure to act in accordance with the terms of this Agreement and in no case for delays or causes arising outside the scope of this Contract or for which other contractors or the Owner are responsible. If the Subcontractor defaults or neglects to carry out the Work in accordance with this Agreement and fails within three (3) working days after receipt of written notice from the Contractor to commence and continue correction of such default or neglect with diligence and promptness, the Contractor may, after three (3) days following receipt by the Subcontractor of an additional written notice and without prejudice to any other remedy he may have, make good such deficiencies and deduct the cost thereof from the payments then or thereafter due the Subcontractor.

**Arbitration**  All claims, disputes, and other matters in question arising out of, or relating to, this Contract or the breach thereof shall be decided by arbitration. If the Contract Documents do not provide for arbitration or fail to specify the manner and procedure for arbitration, it shall be conducted in accordance with the Construction Industry Arbitration Rules of the American Arbitration Association then obtaining unless the parties mutually agree otherwise. The award rendered by the arbitrators shall be final, and judgment may be entered upon it in accordance with applicable law in any court having jurisdiction thereof. This Article shall not be deemed a limitation of any rights or remedies that the Contractor may have under any Federal or State Mechanics' Lien laws or under any applicable labor and material payment bonds, unless such rights or remedies are expressly waived by him.

**Work Stoppage**  If Work is stopped for a period of thirty days through no fault of the Subcontractor because the Owner has not made payments thereon as provided in this Agreement, then the Subcontractor may, without prejudice to any other remedy he may have, upon seven (7) additional days' written notice to the Contractor, terminate this Contract and recover from the Contractor payment for all Work executed and for any proven loss resulting from the stoppage of the Work, including reasonable overhead, profit, and damages. If the Subcontractor persistently or repeatedly fails or neglects to carry out the Work in accordance with the Contract Documents or otherwise to perform in accordance with this Agreement and fails within three (3) days after receipt of written notice to commence and continue correction of such default or neglect with diligence and promptness, the Contractor may, after three (3) days following receipt by the Subcontractor of an additional written notice and without prejudice to any other remedy he may have, terminate the Contract and finish the Work by whatever method he may deem expedient. If the unpaid balance of the Contract Sum exceeds the expense of finishing the Work, such excess shall be paid to the Subcontractor, but if such expense exceeds the unpaid balance, the Subcontractor shall pay the difference to the Contractor.

Owner/Contractor:                              Subcontractor:

Date:

By _____        By _____
   *(Insert name & title)*                          *(Insert name & title)*

# Agreement of Purchase and Sale and Joint Escrow Instructions

THIS AGREEMENT, made this ___ day of_____, by and between _____ (hereinafter called "Seller") and [insert buyer's name] (hereinafter called "Buyer").

## WITNESSETH;

WHEREAS, Buyer has offered to purchase from Seller that certain real property, hereinafter more particularly described, which is located in the County of_____, State of _____, (hereinafter referred to as the "Property"), for a purchase price equal to

_____ for approximately ____ acres, subject to a complete and accurate survey to determine the precise number of acres contained in the property and adjustment of the purchase price as provided in Paragraph 3 hereof; and

WHEREAS, Seller is willing to sell the property on the terms and conditions contained herein; and

WHEREAS, the parties desire not only to enter into a formal detailed agreement of purchase and sale but also to establish an escrow through which the purchase and sale contemplated herein will be consummated.

NOW, THEREFORE, in consideration of the terms of this Agreement, the parties hereto agree as follows:

1. **DESIGNATION OF ESCROW HOLDER.** Buyer and Seller designate _____ the escrow holder (hereinafter referred to as the "escrow holder"). This Agreement shall constitute Escrow Instructions for the sale of the Property, and a copy hereof shall be deposited with escrow holder for this purpose. Should escrow holder require the execution of its standard form printed Escrow Instructions, the parties agree to execute same, provided, however, that such instructions shall be construed as applying only to escrow holder's employment and that if there are conflicts between the terms of this Agreement and the terms of the printed Escrow Instructions, the terms of this Agreement shall control.

2. **AGREEMENT TO SELL.** Seller hereby agrees to sell, and Buyer hereby agrees to buy from Seller, the property located at _____ and described in Tax Assessor's Parcel #_____, which is attached hereto as Exhibit A and is incorporated herein by reference that shall subsequently be replaced by a complete and accurate survey as soon as the same is available.

3. **PURCHASE PRICE.** Buyer agrees to purchase the property for the sum equal to the product of the number of square feet times $_____ (this sum is hereinafter called the "purchase price"). The precise number of acres shall be determined by the survey and shall not include any existing or now known dedications or easements that cannot directly be utilized by the proposed development under _____ Ordinances. The purchase price shall be payable in the following manner:

    (a) Cash in the amount of _____ ($_____) shall be deposited with escrow holder in an account bearing a minimum of $5^{1/4}\%$ interest to Buyer upon the execution of this Agreement and the designation by escrow holder of the "effective date." This payment shall constitute consideration for this contract. This payment shall be refundable except as noted hereinafter. This payment shall become nonrefundable and shall be released to Seller upon Buyer's completing to his satisfaction all items of work outlined in Paragraphs 4, 6, 7, and 10. If the Buyer for any reason except as noted in Paragraphs 4 and 5 does not release the above payments, this Agreement becomes null and void with no further obligation or liability by either party. Escrow agent shall not release any funds to Seller until Seller has delivered the executed deed as outlined in Paragraph 8 herein.

(b) The balance of the purchase price, approximately _____ ($____) shall be deposited in escrow on or before the date of closing and together with the original deposit of _____ ($____) shall constitute 100% of the purchase price pursuant to Paragraph 3 herein.

Seller agrees to execute all governmental documents consistent with the application to _____ County and the _____City Council for the permits necessary to _____ within a five (5) day period from presentation by Buyer.

4. **TITLE OBLIGATIONS.** Within fifteen (15) days from the effective date of this Agreement, Seller shall cause to be delivered to the Buyer, at Seller's sole cost and expense, a current title commitment for an ALTA owner's extended policy of title insurance to be issued by escrow holder, showing the status of title of the Property and all exceptions, including easements, restrictions, rights-of-way, covenants, reservations, and other conditions, if any, affecting the Property that would appear in an owner's extended policy of title insurance, if issued, and committing to issue such policy of title insurance to Buyer in the full amount of the purchase price for the Property. Accompanying such title commitment, Seller shall also cause to be furnished to Buyer legible copies of all documents affecting the Property referred to in such title commitment. Provided Seller has timely provided Buyer with the preliminary title report (and copies of the exceptions), Buyer shall notify Seller of any objections that Buyer may have to the status of title within thirty (30) days from the date Buyer receives such title report. If Buyer fails to give such notice of dissatisfactions as to any exception or other matter within such thirty (30) day period, such exception(s) shall be deemed approved by Buyer. If Buyer disapproves of condition of title, the earnest money deposit shall be returned to Buyer, the Agreement shall terminate, and neither party shall have any liability or obligation to the other. Time is of the essence in this agreement. Should Seller not deliver title commitment within the timeframe specified, then all dates in this agreement are automatically extended by the amount of the delay of Seller's submittal.

Seller shall convey marketable title to the property to Buyer by grant deed in fee simple absolute, subject to no exceptions other than those specifically set forth in this Agreement and those approved in writing by Buyer. Any exceptions to title approved in writing by Buyer in the aggregate are referred to herein as "permitted exceptions," and they shall not constitute a breach of Seller's duty to convey marketable title or of Seller's implied covenants of title arising from said deed. Buyer shall be provided, at Seller's cost, at close of escrow a policy of title insurance written by escrow holder on a American Land Title Association (ALTA) Title Insurance Policy Standard Form with liability in the amount of the purchase price (hereinafter referred to as "title policy"). Such title policy shall show no exceptions other than the permitted exceptions, the usual printed exceptions, and/or conditions and stipulations of the ALTA Standard Form policy.

5. **RIGHT OF CANCELLATION.**

   (a) Anything to the contrary notwithstanding in this Agreement, including but not limited to Paragraphs 3(1) and 4 hereof, Buyer may, for any reason, cancel this Agreement and the escrow provided for herein at any time within the first thirty (30) days following receipt by Buyer of the preliminary title report to be furnished by Seller. Such cancellation shall be effected by Buyer providing Seller and the escrow holder with written notice of election to terminate prior to the expiration of such thirty (30) day period, in which even escrow holder shall pay to Buyer the initial _____ ($_____) earnest money deposit, at which time this Agreement shall terminate and be of no further force and effect, and neither party shall have any further obligation or liability to the other. If Buyer does not cancel this Agreement within such thirty (30) day period as provided for herein, the initial _____ ($_____) earnest money deposit shall be released to Seller, upon completion and approval by Buyer of items covered in Paragraphs 4, 6, 7, and 10, including the permit to _____ from the City of _____.

   (b) Anything to the contrary in this Agreement notwithstanding, including but not limited to the provisions of Paragraph 3(a) and (b), Buyer shall have the right to cancel this Agreement for any reason, at any time between the date that the initial _____ ($_____) earnest money deposit is released to Seller and the earlier of (i) the date upon which the City of _____ shall approve a permit to _____ for the Property without stipulations, or upon such conditions and stipulations as may be approved by Buyer, or (ii) ___ (___) days from the effective date of this Agreement. Such cancellation shall be effected by Buyer providing Seller and the escrow holder with written notice of election to terminate prior to the expiration of such ___ (___) day period.

6. **RIGHT OF INSPECTION.** Buyer shall have ___ (___) days from the effective date of this Agreement, at Buyer's sole cost, to effect a feasibility study on the subject property for Buyer's intended use. Buyer and Buyer's engineers, employees, and representatives have the right to enter the Property for the purpose of making the necessary investigations, including

but not limited to surveying, soils tests, location of utilities, storm drainage, and any other tests Buyer deems necessary. If Buyer shall enter the subject property during the term of this Agreement for any reason whatsoever, Buyer hereby agrees to indemnify and hold Seller harmless from and against any and all claims, liabilities, causes of action, and damages that Seller may have filed against it or may suffer or incur, arising out of or attributable to the entry upon the subject property and the acts thereon of Buyer or its agents, employees, and representatives. Such indemnification shall extend to the costs of litigation incurred by Seller, if any, and to the reasonable attorney's fees that may be expended by Seller in connection therewith.

7. **SURVEY.** During the first thirty (30) days after the effective date of this Agreement, Seller shall furnish an ALTA survey acceptable to escrow holder and Buyer. The contents of the survey and map shall be deemed approved by Buyer unless disapproved by Buyer in writing conveyed to Seller within ten (10) days of the receipt of the survey.

8. **PLACING DEED IN ESCROW.** On the _____ day after the effective date of this Agreement or Buyer's approval of the Title commitment and prior to escrow holder releasing to Seller, Seller shall execute and deliver to escrow holder the duly executed and acknowledged deed conveying the property to Buyer. Buyer then, subject to having received within ___ (___) days of the effective date of this Agreement approval from the City of _____ a permit to _____ the project with stipulations by City acceptable to Buyer, shall instruct escrow holder to release to Seller the _____ ($_____) earnest money deposit. Said deposit shall be nonrefundable and deemed earned by Seller subject to Paragraphs 3, 4, 5, 7, and 23 herein.

9. **PLACING PURCHASE PRICE IN ESCROW.** Prior to the close of escrow, Buyer shall deliver or cause to be delivered to escrow holder, as set forth in Paragraph 3(b) above, cash and all other documents in the amount of the balance of the purchase price, inclusive of all deposits plus those closing costs to be paid by Buyer.

10. **CONDITIONS PRECEDENT.** The following conditions are conditions precedent to Buyer's obligation to consummate its purchase of the property:

    (a) Seller shall have performed each and every, all and singular, its obligations and promises contained in this Agreement.

    (b) Bonds and assessments. Buyer understands that there are not outstanding assessments against the property. Seller shall deliver title to Buyer free of all liens and encumbrances at the close of escrow.

(c) Buyer at Buyer's expense shall obtain rezoning, variances, use permits, engineering approvals, and other development approvals, including building permits from the City of _____ and other appropriate regulatory agencies. Buyer agrees to exercise all due diligence to pursue the above approvals and hereby agrees, subject to Paragraphs 4 and 7 herein, to make application to the City within _____ (__) days of the effective date of this Agreement.

(d) Buyer shall give written notice to Seller, through escrow agent, thirty (30) days prior to closing of escrow to vacate the property.

If any of the above conditions precedent shall fail to occur, Buyer's obligation under this Agreement shall terminate by Buyer's giving written notice thereof to Seller and the escrow holder. Thereupon, Seller shall instruct the escrow holder to return all payments to Buyer, unless forfeited as provided for hereinabove, and both Buyer and Seller agree to execute such documents, releases, and/or instructions as may be necessary to reflect fully the termination of Buyer's obligations hereunder.

The Conditions of Closing are exclusively for the benefit of Buyer, and Buyer may, in writing (at his option), at any time waive any such condition. In the event that Buyer fails to notify Seller in writing prior to the end of such investigation period that all such Conditions of Closing have occurred or been waived, then this Agreement shall immediately terminate, neither party shall have any further obligation or liability hereunder, and Buyer's deposit of _____ shall be immediately returned to Buyer.

11. **CLOSING OF ESCROW.** Escrow holder shall *not* close escrow until it holds the following items in its file:

(a) The monies, documents, and instruments specified in Paragraphs 3, 4, 7, 8, and 9 hereof.

(b) The title policy ensuring that Buyer holds title to the property as of the time of closing escrow and showing the following additional matters:

   (1) The permitted exceptions

   (2) The usual printed exceptions and/or conditions and stipulations of the title policy

(c) A duplicate original of this Agreement executed by Seller and Buyer.

   This escrow shall close within fifteen (15) days of receipt of building permits for Buyer's contemplated project.

(d) Notwithstanding anything to the contrary above, Buyer has the right at Buyer's discretion to extend the escrow two times for a period of _____ (\_) days each upon payment by Buyer to Seller to escrow of _____ (\$_____) for each _____ (\_) day extension. Said funds shall be paid into escrow and released to Seller at Buyer's option and shall be subject to Paragraph 23 as additional earnest monies.

12. **CLOSING COSTS AND PRORATION OF EXPENSES.** Escrow holder shall pay immediately upon closing the required documentary transfer tax and recording fees on the conveyance charging the same to Buyer. Seller shall pay the title insurance premium for the title policy as set forth in Paragraph 4 above. Property taxes shall be prorated as of the date of closing on the basis of the latest available information. The amount of any bond(s) or assessment(s) that is a lien against the property shall be paid in full by Seller as of the date of closing. Seller and Buyer shall share equally in paying the escrow fees of escrow holder. Other charges shall be allocated in the manner customary in _____ County.

13. **EXISTING INFORMATION.** Seller shall provide Buyer with all existing information in Seller's possession, including but not limited to Engineering, Civil and Geology, Land Plans, Architecture, Appraisals, Market Studies, and potential leases within 48 hours from opening of escrow. If Buyer fails to complete this purchase, all items delivered hereunder shall be immediately returned to Seller.

14. All of Seller's representations stated in this Agreement and in any addendum attached hereto shall be true and correct as of the date of execution of this Agreement, and Seller shall notify Buyer immediately in writing if at any time prior to Close of Escrow, Seller believes that it would not be able to make any one or more of the representations provided herein. All of Seller's representations shall be true and correct as of the date of Close of Escrow and shall survive Close of Escrow. Seller hereby represents as follows:

    A. Seller is the owner of and has full right, power, and authority to sell, convey, and transfer the Property to Buyer as provided in this Agreement and to carry out Seller's obligations under this Agreement and shall convey to Buyer at Close of Escrow marketable fee title to the Property, free and clear of all liens, assessments, covenants, conditions, restrictions, easements, encroachments, leases, rights of third parties, encumbrances, exceptions, and other title defects.

B. Until Close of Escrow, Seller shall maintain the Property in its present condition and shall not enter into any lease of the Property or any contracts or agreements pertaining to the Property without first obtaining the prior written consent of Buyer.

C. Seller has not received any notice and has no knowledge of:

   (1) Any requirement by any governmental authority requiring that any expenditures be made in connection with the Property.

   (2) The widening of the streets adjacent to the Property.

   (3) Any proceeding to change the zoning applicable to assessments upon all or any part of the Property. To the best of Seller's knowledge, the Property is in full compliance with all applicable building codes, environmental zoning, subdivision, and land-use laws and any other applicable local, state, and federal laws and regulations.

D. To the best of Seller's knowledge, the Property does not contain and no activity upon the Property has produced any hazardous or toxic waste, deposit, or contamination that violates any federal, state, local, or other governmental law, regulation, or order that requires reporting to any governmental authority. See Paragraph 15.

E. To the best of Seller's knowledge, there exists no management, maintenance, operating, service, or any other contract of similar nature, commitments, agreements, or obligations of any kind affecting the Property that would be binding upon Buyer after close of escrow except those enumerated in the title report and approved by Buyer as permitted exceptions.

F. To the best of Seller's knowledge, there are no existing actions, suits, or proceedings pending or threatened against or involving the Property.

G. To the best of Seller's knowledge, Seller has not filed or been the subject of any filing of a petition under the federal bankruptcy code, any insolvency laws, or any laws for composition of indebtedness or the reorganization of debtors.

H. To the best of Seller's knowledge, Seller has obtained all licenses, permits, easements, and right of way requested for the normal use and operation of the Property and to ensure vehicular and pedestrian ingress and egress from the Property.

I. To the best of Seller's knowledge, all documents submitted to Buyer for Buyer's review shall be true, correct, complete, and not misleading, and Buyer shall be immediately notified if any documents are altered, amended, modified, terminated, or canceled.

J. At the Close of Escrow, there are no sums due, owing, or unpaid for labor or materials furnished to the Property at the request of Seller that might give rise to a mechanics', material men's, or other liens attaching to the Property.

K. There exists no breach nor any state of facts that with the passage of time, the giving of notice, or both would constitute a default under any contract that relates to the Property and will be assumed by Buyer at the Close of Escrow.

15. **DOCUMENTATION.** Prior to Close of Escrow, Seller shall furnish Buyer any and all documentation required by Internal Revenue Code 1445 ("1445"), including, without limitation, a Certificate of Non-Foreign Status. Seller further agrees that in the event that Seller does not furnish Buyer a Certificate of Non-Foreign Status, Buyer is authorized to withhold and deduct from the Purchase Price any and all amounts required by 1445 and transfer said sum within ten (10) days to the Internal Revenue Service.

16. **HAZARDOUS WASTE.** Seller warrants that, to the best of Seller's knowledge, no toxic materials have been stored on or under the soil, used or disposed of on the Property, nor have toxic materials migrated on or into the subject property, including but not limited to asbestos, heavy metal, petroleum products, solvents, pesticides or herbicides, unless otherwise disclosed in writing to the Buyer. Seller agrees to indemnify, defend, and hold the Buyer harmless from and against any claims, costs, liabilities, causes of action, and fees, including attorney's fees arising from the storage, use, or disposal of existence of any toxic materials on the Property that result in contamination or deterioration of ground water or soil at a level of contamination greater than established by any governmental agency having appropriate jurisdiction. In the event that the soil, subsoil, ground water, or other constituent parts of the Property are determined contaminated as provided above, Buyer shall have the option to either (a) require Seller to clean up and otherwise restore the soil, subsoil, ground water, or other constituent parts of the Property to a condition that would comply with the requirements of any governmental agency or body having any jurisdiction over the property, or (b) terminate this agreement without further liabilities on the part of either party. In the event of such termination, the Deposit shall be returned to the Buyer. Buyer and Seller acknowledge that neither Broker nor their sales people have made any representations regarding the absence of toxic materials on the property and further warrant that neither Broker nor their salespeople are qualified to detect the presence of toxic materials on the property.

17. **COOPERATION.** Seller agrees to fully cooperate with Buyer and to use its best efforts in obtaining all governmental approvals, to execute all necessary applications and related documents in such form as may be required by such governmental authorities, all without cost to Seller.

18. **LIQUIDATED DAMAGES.** IF BUYER FAILS TO COMPLETE SAID PURCHASE AS HEREIN PROVIDED BY REASON OF ANY DEFAULT OF BUYER, SELLER SHALL BE RELEASED FROM HIS OBLIGATIONS TO SELL THE SUBJECT PROPERTY TO BUYER AND MAY PROCEED AGAINST BUYER UPON ANY CLAIMS OR REMEDY WHICH HE MAY HAVE IN LAW OR EQUITY, PROVIDED, HOWEVER, THAT BY PLACING THEIR INITIALS HERE, BUYER(S) (_____) (_____) SELLER(S) (_____) (_____) AGREE THAT IT WOULD BE IMPRACTICAL OR EXTREMELY DIFFICULT TO FIX ACTUAL DAMAGES IN CASE OF BUYER'S FAILURE TO COMPLETE THE PURCHASE DUE TO BUYER'S DEFAULT, THAT THE DEPOSIT(S) ACTUALLY PAID AS LIQUIDATED DAMAGES AND AS AND FOR HIS SOLE AND COMPLETE REMEDY.

19. Buyer shall be allowed to place marketing signs upon the property.

20. **DISTRIBUTION OF TITLE POLICY.** Escrow holder shall distribute to Buyer as immediately as possible after close of escrow the Buyer's policy of title insurance mentioned above.

21. **POSSESSION.** Possession of the property shall be delivered to Buyer at closing. Notwithstanding the foregoing, at any time or times prior to closing, Buyer and its agents and contractors shall have the right to enter upon and inspect the property, testing the physical properties thereof and evaluating the feasibility of development activity thereon as set forth in Paragraph 6 above.

22. **AMENDED ESCROW INSTRUCTIONS.** Amended or additional instructions may be received into escrow at any time until escrow is ready to close. To be effective, such amended or additional instructions must be in writing and signed by both Buyer and Seller. Buyer and Seller agree to execute such other documents and papers consistent with the provisions of this Agreement as may be required by escrow holder to complete escrow.

23. **ENTIRE AGREEMENT.** The terms of this Agreement contain the entire agreement between the parties and supersede any and all previous agreements. No representation, covenant, agreement, or conditions not included herein have been or are relied upon by either of the parties.

24. **WAIVER.** Any condition contained herein for the benefit of either one of the parties may be waived only by the party to be benefited.

25. **REAL ESTATE COMMISSIONS.** Commission shall be the sole obligation of the Seller. Buyer and Seller agree that they are as follows and shall be paid from proceeds of escrow:

Commission Amount: _____

Paid as follows: _____

BUYER DISCLOSES THAT IT IS A LICENSED REAL ESTATE AGENT BUT IS ACTING AS A PRINCIPAL IN THIS TRANSAC-TION AND SHALL NOT BE PAID ANY COMMISSION. (     ) SELLER.

26. **MULTIPLE ORIGINALS.** This Agreement may be executed in one or more counterparts, each of which shall be deemed an original.

27. **TIME IS OF THE ESSENCE.** Time is of the essence in the performance of this Agreement.

28. **BINDING EFFECT.** This Agreement is binding upon the parties hereto and upon their successors and assigns.

29. **NOTICES.** Any notice or written direction required or designed to be given pursuant to this Agreement may be given personally or by United States mail, certified mail, return receipt requested, with postage thereon fully prepaid, addressed to Buyer at:

[*Insert Buyer's name*] _____

[*Insert Buyer's address*] _____

[*Insert Buyer's phone #s*] _____

To Seller at: _____

_____

_____

To Escrow Holder at: _____

_____

_____

Or to such other address as either party may designate from time to time by written notice to the other. The date of service of such notices, certificates, documents, statements, or requests required by this Agreement shall be the date such notices are received as evidenced by the return receipt or the date such notices are refused if such be the case.

30. **ATTORNEY'S FEES**. If either party to this Agreement resorts to legal action to enforce any of the terms or provisions hereof or to recover damages for the breach hereof, the prevailing party shall be entitled to recover reasonable attorneys' fees, court costs, and other expenses incurred from the unsuccessful party.

31. **ASSIGNMENT**. Seller agrees that Buyer may assign its rights under this Agreement to other persons or entities, and it will deliver title to such nominee upon written notice prior to the close of escrow of the identity of the nominee taking title. Seller agrees that this Agreement shall be binding on its heirs, assigns, and successors.

32. **RECORDATION**. If Buyer records this Agreement, Buyer shall simultaneously deliver an executed quitclaim deed to the escrow holder to be recorded by the escrow holder upon termination of this Agreement or default by Buyer.

33. **COVENANT TO SIGN DOCUMENTS**. Within five (5) days of presentation thereof, Buyer and Seller agree to execute such other documents as may be required.

34. This Agreement expires if Seller's written acceptance or response is not received by Buyer on or before _____ at 5:00 P.M.

    BUYER: [*Insert Buyer's name*]

    by _____


    SELLER: [*Insert Seller's name*]

    by _____

    _____


**Effective Date.** This Agreement, fully executed by Seller and Buyer, together with the cash deposit, has been received by escrow holder on the date specified below. Such items, together with the deposits to be received within five (5) days of the effective date, will be held in escrow and handled by escrow holder pursuant to this Agreement by the undersigned escrow agent. Escrow agent accepts this Agreement as its escrow instructions without the necessity of executing its standard printed form of escrow instructions.

Effective Date: _____

Agreed and Accepted by: [*Insert Title Company*]

_____
Escrow Officer

# Index